# The Four Paradigms in Economics

# The Four Paradigms in Economics

## *Theories, Concepts, and Analytical Tools*

Kavous Ardalan

BLOOMSBURY ACADEMIC
NEW YORK • LONDON • OXFORD • NEW DELHI • SYDNEY

BLOOMSBURY ACADEMIC
Bloomsbury Publishing Inc, 1359 Broadway, New York, NY 10018, USA
Bloomsbury Publishing Plc, 50 Bedford Square, London, WC1B 3DP, UK
Bloomsbury Publishing Ireland, 29 Earlsfort Terrace, Dublin 2, D02 AY28, Ireland

BLOOMSBURY, BLOOMSBURY ACADEMIC and the Diana logo are trademarks of Bloomsbury Publishing Plc

First published in the United States of America 2025



A catalog record for this book is available from the Library of Congress

ISBN: HB: 978-1-6669-7784-4
ePDF: 979-8-2162-6331-9
eBook: 978-1-9787-6110-0

Typeset by Deanta Global Publishing Services, Chennai, India

For product safety related questions contact productsafety@bloomsbury.com.

To find out more about our authors and books visit www.bloomsbury.com and sign up for our newsletters.

*To my family.*

# Contents

# Figures

# Introduction

This book is the twelfth book that reflects the change in how I think about the world, and in writing it I hope that it will do the same for others. I began writing my first book[1] a few years after receiving my terminal degree in finance from York University in Toronto, Ontario, Canada. However, its origins date back to my days as a graduate student, when I took a course in "Philosophy and Method" with Professor Gareth Morgan. At that time, I was exposed to ideas which were totally new to me. They occupied my mind, and every day I found them more helpful than the last in explaining what I experienced in my daily, practical, and intellectual life.

I grew up overseas while in high school, and I was raised to appreciate mathematics and science at the expense of other fields of study. In college, I was exposed only to economics while studying for my bachelor of arts. Afterwards, in order to obtain my master's degree and terminal degree in economics, I attended the University of California, Santa Barbara, and received specialized training in economics. My further specialized studies in finance at York University ended in a second terminal degree. As is clear, throughout the years of my education, I was trained to see the world in a special, narrow way.

Among all the courses that I took during my years of training, one course stood out as being different and, in the final analysis, most influential. It was the "Philosophy and Method" course that I took with Professor Gareth Morgan at York University. It was most influential because none of the other courses gave me the vision that this one did. While all the other courses trained me to see the world from the same narrow perspective, this course taught me that the world can be seen from different vantage points, each of which is insightful in its own way. Over the years, the constant application of this idea in my daily, practical, and intellectual life proved quite an eye-opener for me, such that I naturally converted to this new way of thinking about the world. This happened despite the fact that my entire education had almost exclusively trained me to perceive the world in a limited way. Since then, I have been writing based on this new approach, and this latest book represents what has been accumulated since the publication of my first eleven books.[2]

This book crosses two existing lines of literature: social philosophy on the one hand and economics on the other hand. More specifically, its frame of reference is Burrell and Morgan (1979) and Morgan (1983); and applies their ideas and insights to various dimensions of economics. Clearly, a thorough treatment of all the relevant issues referred to in this work is well beyond the scope of a single book. Within such limits, this book aims only to provide an overview, a review, a taxonomy, or a map of the key topics, leaving further discussions of all the relevant issues to the references cited herein. In other words, the aim of this work is not so much to create a new piece of the puzzle as it is to fit the existing pieces of the puzzle together in order to make sense of it. To achieve this aim—and given the specialized and abstract nature of the philosophy of social science—this book first discusses the framework of Burrell and Morgan (1979); within this context, the following chapters bring some of the important dimensions of economics into focus. The choice of what to be included in the book and what to be excluded was a difficult one. On numerous occasions, it was decided to refer to some major topics only briefly. In any case, this book is only an overview; but a comprehensive set of references is provided to avoid some of its shortcomings.

The main theme of the book is that social theory can usefully be conceived in terms of four key paradigms: functionalist, interpretive, radical humanist, and radical structuralist. These four paradigms are founded upon different assumptions about the nature of social science and the nature of society. Each generates theories, concepts, and analytical tools that are different from those of the other paradigms.

These four paradigms are not airtight compartments into which all theories must be squeezed. They are heuristic devices that are created to make sense of the messy reality of any real-life phenomenon. They are merely useful constructs to aid understanding. They are not claimed to be the only constructs to aid understanding. They are not claimed to be the best constructs to aid understanding. They are merely certain constructs, among many different possible constructs, to aid understanding. They provide an analytically clear and compelling map of the terrain. They help in distinguishing the various perspectives that exist with respect to a given phenomenon. Their purpose is to help understand differences, not to make invidious comparisons. There is no one paradigm that can capture the essence of reality. Paradigm diversity provides enhanced understanding. In intellectual as well as natural environments, diversity is a sine qua non of robust good health. There is no singular approach that, in its universality, can apprehend the totality of reality. Since academic models are inevitably the product of a partial viewpoint, they will always be biased; hence, a multiplicity of perspectives is required to represent the complexity and diversity of phenomena and activities. The four paradigms provide a full-circle worldview.

The mainstream in most academic fields of study is based upon the functionalist paradigm, and for the most part, mainstream scholars are not always entirely aware of the tradition to which they belong. An understanding of different paradigms leads to a better understanding of the multifaceted nature of their academic field of study. Although a researcher may decide to conduct research from the point of view of a certain paradigm, an understanding of the nature of other paradigms leads to a better understanding of what one is doing.

These four paradigms are of paramount importance to any scientist, because the process of learning about a favored paradigm is also the process of learning what that paradigm is not. The knowledge of paradigms makes scientists aware of the boundaries within which they approach their subject. Each of the four paradigms implies a different way of social theorizing.

Scientists often approach their subject from a frame of reference based on assumptions that are taken for granted. Since these assumptions are continually affirmed and reinforced, they remain not only unquestioned but also beyond conscious awareness. In this way, most researchers tend to favor the functionalist paradigm.

The partial nature of this view only becomes apparent when the researcher exposes basic assumptions to the challenge of alternative ways of seeing and starts to appreciate these alternatives in their own terms. To do this, one has to explore other paradigms from within, since the concepts in one paradigm cannot easily be interpreted in terms of those of another.

Knowledge of any phenomenon is ultimately a product of the researcher's paradigmatic approach to that multifaceted phenomenon. Viewed from this angle, the pursuit of knowledge is seen as much as an ethical, moral, ideological, and political activity as a technical one. Each paradigm can gain much from the contributions of the other paradigms.

The ancient parable of the six blind scholars and their experience with the elephant illustrates the benefits of paradigm diversity. These six blind scholars did not know what an elephant looked like and had never even heard of one. They decided to obtain a mental picture—that is, knowledge—by touching the animal. The first blind scholar felt the elephant's trunk and argued that the elephant was like a lively snake. The second blind scholar rubbed one of the elephant's enormous legs and likened the animal to a rough column of massive proportions. The third blind scholar took hold of the elephant's tail and insisted that the elephant resembled a large, flexible brush. The fourth blind scholar felt the elephant's sharp tusk and declared it to be like a great spear. The fifth blind scholar examined the elephant's flapping ear and was convinced that the animal was some sort of fan. The sixth blind scholar, who occupied the space between the elephant's front and hind legs, could not touch any parts of the elephant and consequently asserted that there was no such beast as an elephant at all and accused his colleagues of making up fantastic stories about nonexistent things. Each of the six blind scholars held firmly to his understanding of an elephant, and they argued and fought about which story captured the correct understanding of the animal. As a result, their entire community was torn apart, and suspicion and distrust became the order of the day.

This parable contains many valuable lessons. First, reality is probably too complex to be fully grasped by imperfect human beings. Second, although each person might correctly identify one aspect of reality, each may incorrectly attempt to reduce the entire phenomenon to their own partial and narrow experience. Third, maintaining communal peace and harmony might be worth much more than stubbornly clinging to one's understanding of the world. Fourth, it might be wise for each person to return to reality and exchange positions with others to better appreciate the whole of the reality.[3]

This book—like its eleven predecessors—advocates a multi-paradigmatic approach that juxtaposes heterogeneous viewpoints in order to illuminate more comprehensively the phenomenon under consideration. The multi-paradigmatic approach uses a systematic and structured method to explain the phenomenon from the viewpoint of each paradigm and juxtaposes them in order to transcend the limitations of each of the worldviews.

My first book, entitled *On the Role of Paradigms in Finance*, applied the multi-paradigmatic approach to the following phenomena: (1) development of the academic field of finance, (2) mathematical language of the academic field of finance, (3) the mathematical method of the academic field of finance, (4) money, (5) corporate governance, (6) markets, (7) technology, and (8) education.

My second book, entitled *Understanding Globalization: A Multi-Dimensional Approach*, applied, within the context of globalization, the multi-paradigmatic approach to the following phenomena: (1) world order, (2) culture, (3) the state,

(4) information technology, (5) economics, (6) production, (7) development, and (8) Bretton Woods Institutions.

My third book, entitled *Paradigms in Political Economy*, applied the multi-paradigmatic approach to the following phenomena: (1) the state, (2) justice, (3) freedom, (4) democracy, (5) liberal democracy, (6) the media, and (7) the great recession. These applications of the multi-paradigmatic approach show that the multi-paradigmatic approach is very versatile, in the sense that it can be applied to almost any phenomenon; and that the multi-paradigmatic approach can be applied not only to categorical concepts such as the state, justice, freedom, and the media, but also to categorical and sub-categorical concepts such as democracy and liberal democracy, as well as practical categories such as the great recession.

My fourth book, entitled *Case Method and Pluralist Economics: Philosophy, Methodology, and Practice*, applied the multi-paradigmatic approach to education and economics, and noted that both the case method and pluralist economics emanate from the same foundational philosophy which views the world as being socially constructed, and that both advocate pluralism. Therefore, the case method seems to be compatible and congruent with pluralist economics. To this end, the book discussed the philosophical, methodological, and practical aspects of the case method through their comparisons with those of the lecture method, which is commonly known and experienced by most people. The book also discussed pluralist economics through the exposition of the philosophical foundations of the extant economics schools of thought, which is the focal point of the attention and admiration of pluralist economics.

My fifth book, entitled *Global Political Economy: A Multi-Paradigmatic Approach*, applied, in the context of global political economy, the multi-paradigmatic approach to the following phenomena: (1) the driving force of globalization, (2) governance, (3) modernity, (4) finance, (5) regionalization, (6) war, and (7) democracy. These seven applications of the multi-paradigmatic approach continued to show that the multi-paradigmatic approach is very versatile in the sense that it can be applied to almost any phenomenon, both national and international, as well as local and global.

My sixth book, entitled *Equity Home Bias: A Place-Attachment Perspective*, introduced "place attachment" as a new explanation for the "equity home bias" puzzle—the empirical finding that people overinvest in domestic stocks relative to the theoretically optimal investment portfolio. For this purpose, Chapter 1 provided a comprehensive review of the extant literature on the equity home bias puzzle. Chapter 2 provided an overview of the literature on place attachment.

Chapter 3 crossed the two lines of research to present place attachment as a new explanation for the equity home bias puzzle. Chapter 4 considered the future of place attachment and its effect on home bias. At first sight, this book might not seem to have any relationship with the multi-paradigmatic approach. However, it should be noted that: (1) the qualitative methodology, rather than the quantitative methodology of mainstream finance, which is used in this book stems from the teachings of the multi-paradigmatic approach—that is, there are paradigmatically diverse research methodologies, and (2) the review of the literature on place attachment that is provided in Chapter 2 applies a multi-paradigmatic approach—that is, there are paradigmatically diverse views on place attachment.

My seventh book, entitled *Understanding Revolution: A Multi-Paradigmatic Approach*, aimed to show how a multi-paradigmatic approach can be used in order to better understand social revolutions. The book started with the discussion of four broad worldviews, or paradigms. It then discussed several major social phenomena from the viewpoints of the four paradigms: (1) culture, (2) religion, (3) revolution, (4) the Iranian Revolution, (5) ideology, and (6) the ideology of the Iranian Revolution. The intention was to present the benefits and characteristics of the multi-paradigmatic approach. The book also showed how the multi-paradigmatic approach facilitates a better and more comprehensive understanding of the phenomenon under consideration. Finally, it illustrated how the multi-paradigmatic approach substantively improves the analysis and understanding of social revolutions and rectifies many extant controversies. Against this background, the book introduced a comprehensive approach to the understanding of revolution.

My eighth book, entitled *Understanding Feminist Theories and Feminist Economics: A Multi-Paradigmatic Approach*, aimed to provide an understanding of feminist theories and feminist economics through a multi-paradigmatic approach. To this end, Chapter 1 discussed the four paradigms. Chapters 2 through 7, in turn, applied the four-paradigmatic framework to the extant literature on six relevant dimensions of social life: human nature, feminist theories, family, patriarchy, discrimination, and feminist economics. Chapters 8 through 11 then applied the four-paradigmatic framework to four relevant scholarly subjects of research: feminist research, feminist education, economics versus sociology, and men versus women. Chapter 12 concluded by recommending paradigm diversity. In this way, the book showed, among other things, that the four-paradigmatic framework can be used not only as a classificatory device, but also as an analytical tool.

My ninth book, entitled *History: A Multi-Paradigmatic Approach*, aimed to provide an understanding of history. For this purpose, Chapter 1 discussed the four paradigms. Chapters 2 through 5 then applied the four-paradigmatic framework to the extant literature on four relevant dimensions of history: histography, grand narratives, progress, and time. Chapters 6 through 8 went on to apply the four-paradigmatic framework to three historical events: the French Revolution, the American Civil War, and the Iranian Revolution. Chapter 9 concluded by recommending paradigm diversity.

My tenth book, entitled *On the Methodology of Financial Economics: A Multi-Paradigmatic Look at Bias in the Mainstream*, critically discussed the scientific methodology of mainstream financial economics and made suggestions for its improvement. It used a multi-paradigmatic approach as its frame of reference in discussing eleven biases within the scientific methodology of mainstream financial economics: intellectual bias, local bias, fad bias, ideological bias, automaticity bias, confirmation bias, cultural bias, stereotyping bias, under-productivity bias, homogeneity bias, and isolation bias. These biases indicate that the knowledge produced via the scientific methodology of financial economics is biased and therefore partial. Consequently, the book suggested the use of the multi-paradigmatic approach as a way to improve the methodology of mainstream financial economics, as it provides a broader and more balanced understanding of the multifaceted phenomenon under consideration and overcomes such biases.

My eleventh book, entitled *Understanding Identity: A Multi-Paradigmatic Approach*, was about understanding identity through a multi-paradigmatic approach. For this purpose, the book started with a discussion of the four most diverse worldviews or paradigms (i.e., functionalist, interpretive, radical humanist, radical structuralist). Then, it discussed identity and several aspects of it (i.e., human nature, identity, place attachment, nationalism, racism, feminism, discrimination, multiculturalism) from the viewpoints of the four most diverse worldviews or paradigms. The book recommended paradigm diversity.

This book, entitled *The Four Paradigms of Economics: Theories, Concepts, and Analytical Tools*, is about understanding economics through a multi-paradigmatic approach. For this purpose, the book starts with a discussion of the four most diverse worldviews or paradigms. Then, it discusses four fundamental aspects/dimensions of economics from the viewpoints of the four most diverse worldviews or paradigms. With this background, the book looks at the major extant schools of thought in economics (neo-classical economics, new institutional economics, behavioral economics, Austrian economics, post-Keynesian economics, institutional economics, social economics, radical economics, and Marxist economics) from the point of view of the four paradigms and locates them within the four paradigms.

This book is unique because the other books do not have the special characteristics of this book, which are listed as follows:

- It is systematic and methodic: it discusses each of the four fundamental aspects/dimensions of economics from the same four paradigmatic viewpoints. This method of analysis can be applied to any phenomenon, that is, each phenomenon can be viewed from these four perspectives. This method is, indeed, versatile and resilient.
- It is fundamental and applied: it applies four fundamental viewpoints to each of the four fundamental aspects/dimensions of economics.
- It is fair and unbiased: In each chapter, it allocates the same number of pages of the book to each paradigmatic viewpoint.
- It is multi-disciplinary and inter-disciplinary: It is based on philosophy, incorporates sociology and humanities, and goes on to include discussions about economics, culture, politics, and social class structure.
- It is enlightening: In each chapter, it provides four different views with respect to a given phenomenon, and therefore, it provides a broader and a balanced understanding of the phenomenon under consideration.
- It is multi-dimensional and multi-perspectival: It regards and treats any phenomenon as being multi-dimensional, and in addition, it looks at each dimension of the phenomenon from four different paradigmatic perspectives. There are other books written on economics, but they are specialized and have tunnel vision; in contrast, this book regards all disciplines as inseparable, and therefore, discusses them within a multi-paradigmatic approach. Furthermore, other books focus on a particular aspect of economics and their explanations are made from a specific viewpoint. But this book discusses as many aspects of economics as a book's space allows, and, in this way, proposes a comprehensive approach to the understanding of economics. Moreover, the approach used in this book, when learned, can be applied to any other phenomenon.

This book will be useful to everyone in society. As a textbook, it can be used in upper-level undergraduate and master-level courses in a variety of disciplines because it discusses various fundamental aspects/dimensions of social and economic life. Especially, this book will be useful to students in economics, philosophy, political science, social studies, liberal studies, sociology, and humanities. This book can be used as either a main text or a supplementary reading. This book is about fundamental aspects/dimensions of human social life, and therefore, it can be used in any country.

The writing of the chapters of this book involved extensive work over several years. It required peace of mind and extended uninterrupted research time. My deepest expressions of gratitude go to my wife Haleh, my son Arash, and my daughter Camellia for their prolonged patience, unlimited understanding, sustained support, constant cooperation, and individual independence during all these long years. I hold much respect for my late parents (Javad and Afagholmolouk), who instilled in their children (Ghobad, Golnar, Alireza, and Kavous) the grand Ardalan family's values of respect, openness, and love of learning, among others. I sincerely appreciate the heartfelt support of my in-laws (Farideh, Parviz, and Houman), who have always been in close contact with us since the formation of my immediate family.

The ideas expressed in this work are based on the teachings, writings, and insights of Professor Gareth Morgan, to whom the nucleus of this work is owed. Needless to say, I stand responsible for all the errors and omissions. I would like to thank Professor Gareth Morgan, who taught me how to diversely view the world, and accordingly inspired my work.

I am also thankful to the Marist College library staff for their timely provision of the requested literature, which they obtained from various sources. I would additionally like to thank the publishers, referenced in the footnotes, who allowed me to use their materials. Certainly, I would like to thank the respectable people who work at Lexington Books, an imprint of Bloomsbury Publishing Inc., for their recognition of the significance of my work and for their publication of the book with utmost professionalism.

## Notes

1 Ardalan (2008).

2 Ardalan (2008, 2014, 2016, 2018, 2019a, 2019b, 2020, 2021, 2023a, 2023b, 2023c).

3 This parable is taken from Steger (2002).

## References

Ardalan, Kavous (2008), *On the Role of Paradigms in Finance*, Aldershot: Ashgate Publishing Limited, and Burlington, VT: Ashgate Publishing Company.

Ardalan, Kavous (2014), *Understanding Globalization: A Multi-Dimensional Approach*, Piscataway, NJ: Transaction Publishers.

Ardalan, Kavous (2016), *Paradigms in Political Economy*, New York, NY: Routledge.

Ardalan, Kavous (2018), *Case Method and Pluralist Economics: Philosophy, Methodology, and Practice*, New York, NY; and Cham: Springer International Publishing AG.

Ardalan, Kavous (2019a), *Global Political Economy: A Multi-Paradigmatic Approach*, New York, NY; and Cham: Springer International Publishing AG.

Ardalan, Kavous (2019b), *Equity Home Bias in International Finance: A Place-Attachment Perspective*, Abingdon, Oxon; and New York, NY: Routledge.

Ardalan, Kavous (2020), *Understanding Revolution: A Multi-Paradigmatic Approach*, New York, NY; and Cham: Springer International Publishing AG.

Ardalan, Kavous (2021), *Feminist Theories and Feminist Economics: A Multi-Paradigmatic Approach*, Lanham, MD: Lexington Books (Rowman and Littlefield Publishing Group, Inc.).

Ardalan, Kavous (2023a), *A Multi-Paradigmatic Approach to Understanding History*, Newcastle Upon Tyne: Cambridge Scholars Publishing.

Ardalan, Kavous (2023b), *On the Methodology of Financial Economics: A Multi-Paradigmatic Look at Bias in the Mainstream*, Cheltenham: Edward Elgar Publishing.

Ardalan, Kavous (2023c), *Understanding Identity: A Multi-Paradigmatic Approach*, Hauppauge, NY: Nova Science Publishers, forthcoming.

Burrell, Gibson and Morgan, Gareth (1979), *Sociological Paradigms and Organizational Analysis*, Hants, Britain: Gower Publishing Company Limited.

Morgan, Gareth (1983), *Beyond Method: Strategies for Social Research*, Beverley Hills, CA: Sage Publications.

Steger, Manfred B. (2002), *Globalism: The New Market Ideology*, New York, NY: Rowan & Littlefield Publishers, Inc.

# 1

# Four Paradigms

Social theory can usefully be conceived in terms of four key paradigms: functionalist, interpretive, radical humanist, and radical structuralist. The four paradigms are founded upon different assumptions about the nature of social science and the nature of society. Each generates theories, concepts, and analytical tools that are different from those of other paradigms.[1,2]

All theories are based on a philosophy of science and a theory of society. Many theorists appear to be unaware of, or ignore, the assumptions underlying these philosophies. They emphasize only some aspects of the phenomenon and ignore others. Unless they bring out the basic philosophical assumptions of the theories, their analysis can be misleading since by emphasizing differences between theories, they imply diversity in approach. While there appear to be different kinds of theory, they are founded on a certain philosophy, worldview, or paradigm. This becomes evident when these theories are related to the wider background of social theory.

The functionalist paradigm has provided the framework for current mainstream academic fields and accounts for the largest proportion of theory and research in these respective academic fields.

In order to understand a new paradigm, theorists should be fully aware of the assumptions upon which their own paradigm is based. Moreover, to understand a new paradigm, one must explore it from within, since the concepts in one paradigm cannot easily be interpreted in terms of those of another. No attempt should be made to criticize or evaluate a paradigm from the outside. This is self-defeating since it is based on a separate paradigm. All four paradigms can be easily criticized and ruined in this way.

These four paradigms are of paramount importance to any scientist, because the process of learning about a favored paradigm is also the process of learning what that paradigm is not. The knowledge of paradigms makes scientists aware of the boundaries within which they approach their subject. Each of the four paradigms implies a different way of social theorizing.

Before discussing each paradigm, it is useful to look at the notion of "paradigm." Burrell and Morgan (1979)[3] regard the

> four paradigms as being defined by very basic meta-theoretical assumptions which underwrite the frame of reference, mode of theorizing and modus operandi of the social theorists who operate within them. It is a term which is intended to emphasize the commonality of perspective which binds the work of a group of theorists together in such a way that they can be usefully regarded as approaching social theory within the bounds of the same problematic.
>
> The paradigm does . . . have an underlying unity in terms of its basic and often "taken for granted" assumptions, which separate a group of theorists in a very fundamental way from theorists located in other paradigms. The "unity" of the paradigm thus derives from reference to alternative views of reality which lie outside its boundaries, and which may not necessarily even be recognized as existing. (pp. 23–4)

Each theory can be related to one of the four broad worldviews. These adhere to different sets of fundamental assumptions about the nature of science (i.e., the

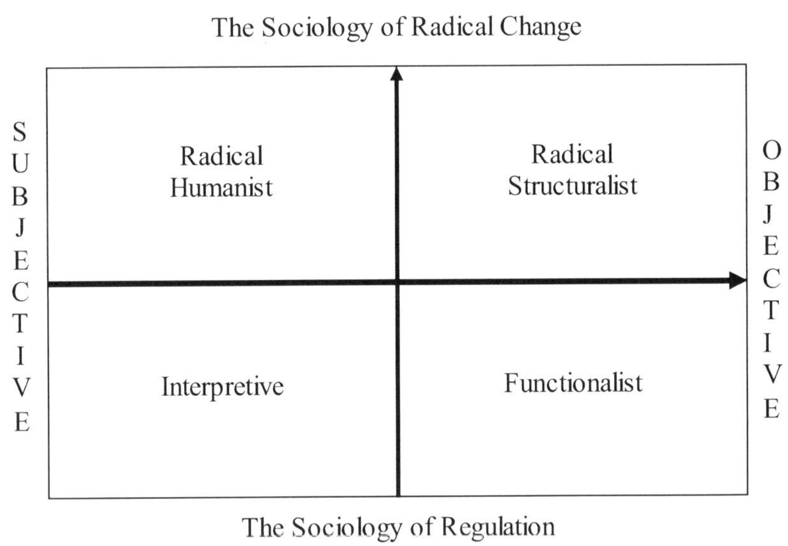


**Figure 1.1** The four paradigms. Each paradigm adheres to a set of fundamental assumptions about the nature of science (i.e., the subjective-objective dimension) and the nature of society (i.e., the dimension of regulation-radical change).

subjective-objective dimension) and the nature of society (i.e., the dimension of regulation-radical change) as in Figure 1.1.[4]

Assumptions related to the nature of science are assumptions with respect to ontology, epistemology, human nature, and methodology.

The assumptions about ontology are assumptions regarding the very essence of the phenomenon under investigation—that is, the extent to which the phenomenon is objective and external to the individual or subjective and the product of the individual's mind.

The assumptions about epistemology are assumptions about the nature of knowledge—that is, assumptions about how one might go about understanding the world and communicate such knowledge to others. For example, what constitutes knowledge and to what extent it is something that can be acquired or must be personally experienced?

The assumptions about human nature are concerned with human nature and, in particular, the relationship between individuals and their environment, which is the object and subject of social sciences—that is, the extent to which human beings and their experiences are the products of their environment or whether human beings are creators of their environment.

The assumptions about methodology relate to the way in which one attempts to investigate and obtain knowledge about the social world—that is, the extent to which the methodology treats the social world as being real, hard, and external to the individual, or as being of a much softer, personal, and more subjective quality. In the former case, the focus is on the universal relationship among elements of the phenomenon; whereas in the latter case, the focus is on the understanding of the way in which the individual creates, modifies, and interprets the situation which is experienced.

The assumptions related to the nature of society are concerned with the extent of regulation of society or radical change in society. Sociology of regulation provides an explanation of society based on the assumption of its unity and cohesiveness. It focuses on the need to understand and explain why society tends to hold together rather than fall apart. Sociology of radical change provides an explanation of society based on the assumption of its deep-seated structural conflict, modes of domination, and structural contradiction. It focuses on the deprivation of human beings, both material and psychic, and it looks toward alternatives rather than the acceptance of the status quo.

The subjective-objective dimension and the regulation-radical change dimension together define four paradigms, which all share common fundamental assumptions about the nature of social science and the nature of society. Each paradigm has a fundamentally unique perspective for the analysis of social phenomena.

## Functionalist Paradigm

The functionalist paradigm assumes that society has a concrete existence and follows a certain order. These assumptions lead to the existence of an objective and value-free social science, which can produce true explanatory and predictive knowledge of the reality "out there." It assumes scientific theories can be assessed objectively by reference to empirical evidence. Scientists do not see any roles for themselves within the phenomenon that they analyze through the rigor and technique of the scientific method. This attributes independence to the observer from the observed—that is, an ability to observe "what is" without affecting it. It assumes there are universal standards of science that determine what constitutes an adequate explanation of what is observed. It assumes there are external rules and regulations governing the external world. The goal of scientists is to find the orders that prevail within that phenomenon.

The functionalist paradigm seeks to provide rational explanations of social affairs and generate regulative sociology. It assumes a continuing order, pattern, and coherence, and tries to explain what is. It emphasizes the importance of understanding order, equilibrium, and stability in society and the way in which these can be maintained. It is concerned with the regulation and control of social affairs. It believes in social engineering as a basis for social reform.

The rationality which underlies functionalist science is used to explain the rationality of society. Science provides the basis for structuring and ordering the social world, similar to the structure and order in the natural world. The methods of natural science are used to generate explanations of the social world. The use of mechanical and biological analogies for modeling and understanding social phenomena is particularly favored.

Functionalists are individualists—that is, the properties of the aggregate are determined by the properties of its units. Their approach to social science is rooted in the tradition of positivism. It assumes that the social world is concrete, meaning it can be identified, studied, and measured through approaches derived from the natural sciences.

Functionalists believe that the positivist methods that have triumphed in the natural sciences should prevail in social sciences as well. In addition, the functionalist paradigm has become dominant in academic sociology. The social world is treated as a place of concrete reality, characterized by uniformities and regularities which can be understood and explained in terms of causes and effects. Given these assumptions, individuals are regarded as taking on a passive role; their behavior is rather determined by the social environment.

Functionalists are pragmatic in orientation and are concerned about understanding society so the knowledge thus generated can be used in society. Functionalism is problem-oriented in approach, as it is concerned with providing practical solutions to practical problems.

In Figure 1.1, the functionalist paradigm occupies the southeast quadrant. Schools of thought within this paradigm can be located on the objective-subjective continuum. From right to left they are objectivism, social system theory, integrative theory, interactionism, and social action theory.[5]

## Interpretive Paradigm

The interpretive paradigm assumes that social reality is the result of the subjective interpretations of individuals. It sees the social world as a process that is created by individuals. Social reality, insofar as it exists outside the consciousness of any individual, is regarded as a network of assumptions and intersubjectively shared meanings. This assumption leads to the belief there are shared multiple realities that are sustained and changed. Researchers recognize their role within the phenomenon under investigation. Their frame of reference is one of participant, as opposed to observer. The goal of the interpretive researchers is to find the orders that prevail within the phenomenon under consideration; however, they are not objective.

The interpretive paradigm is concerned with understanding the world as it is, at the level of subjective experience. It seeks explanations within the realm of individual consciousness and subjectivity. Its analysis of the social world produces sociology of regulation. Its views are underwritten by the assumption that the social world is cohesive, ordered, and integrated.

Interpretive sociologists seek to understand the source of social reality. They often delve into the depths of human consciousness and subjectivity in their quest for the meanings in social life. They reject the use of mathematics and biological analogies in learning about society, and their approach places emphasis on understanding the social world from the vantage point of the individuals who are actually engaged in social activities.

The interpretive paradigm views the functionalist position as unsatisfactory for two reasons. First, human values affect the process of scientific inquiry—that is, the scientific method is not value-free, since the frame of reference of the scientific observer determines the way in which scientific knowledge is obtained. Second, in cultural sciences, the subject matter is spiritual in nature—that is, human beings cannot be studied by the methods of the natural sciences, which aim to establish general laws. In the cultural sphere, human beings are perceived as free. An understanding of their lives and actions can be obtained by the intuition of the total wholes, which is bound to break down by atomistic analysis of the functionalist paradigm.

Cultural phenomena are seen as the external manifestations of inner experience. Cultural sciences, therefore, need to apply analytical methods based on "understanding," through which the scientist can seek to understand human beings, their minds, and their feelings, and the way these are expressed in their outward actions. The notion of "understanding" is a defining characteristic of all theories located within this paradigm.

The interpretive paradigm believes that science is based on "taken-for-granted" assumptions and, like any other social practice, must be understood within a specific context. Therefore, it cannot generate objective and value-free knowledge. Scientific knowledge is socially constructed and socially sustained; its significance and meaning can only be understood within its immediate social context.

The interpretive paradigm regards mainstream social theorists as belonging to a small and self-sustaining community who believe that social reality exists in a concrete world. They theorize about concepts that have little significance to people outside the community who practice social theory and the limited community whom social theorists may attempt to serve.

Functionalist social theorists tend to treat their subject of study as a hard, concrete, and tangible empirical phenomenon that exists "out there" in the "real world." Interpretive researchers are opposed to such structural absolution. They emphasize that the social world is no more than the subjective construction of individual human beings who create and sustain a social world of intersubjectively shared meaning, which is in a continuous process of reaffirmation or change. Therefore, there are no universally valid social rules. Interpretive social research enables scientists to examine social behavior together with ethical, cultural, political, and social issues.

In Figure 1.1, the interpretive paradigm occupies the southwest quadrant. Schools of thought within this paradigm can be located on the objective-subjective continuum. From left to right they are solipsism, phenomenology, phenomenological sociology, and hermeneutics.[6]

## Radical Humanist Paradigm

The radical humanist paradigm provides critiques of the status quo and is concerned to articulate, from a subjective standpoint, the sociology of radical change, modes of domination, emancipation, deprivation, and potentiality. Based on its subjectivist approach, it places great emphasis on human consciousness. It tends to view society as anti-human. It views the process of reality creation as feeding back on itself, such that individuals and society are prevented from reaching their highest possible potential—that is, the consciousness of human beings is dominated by the ideological superstructures of the social system, resulting in their alienation or false consciousness. This, in turn, prevents true human fulfillment. Social theorists regard the orders that prevail in society as instruments of ideological domination. Their major concern is with the way this occurs and how human beings can release themselves from constraints that existing social arrangements place upon the realization of their full potential. They seek to change the social world through a change in consciousness.

Radical humanists believe that everything must be grasped as a whole, because the whole dominates the parts in an all-embracing sense. Moreover, truth is historically specific, relative to a given set of circumstances, so that one should not search for generalizations for the laws of motion of societies.

Radical humanists believe the functionalist paradigm accepts purposive rationality, the logic of science, positive functions of technology, and the neutrality of language and uses them in the construction of "value-free" social theories. Radical humanist theorists intend to demolish this structure, emphasizing its political and repressive nature. They aim to show the role that science, ideology, technology, language, and other aspects of the superstructure play in sustaining and developing the system of power and domination within the totality of the social formation. Their function is to influence the consciousness of human beings for eventual emancipation and formation of alternative social formations.

Radical humanists note that functionalist sociologists create and sustain a view of social reality that maintains the status quo and that forms one aspect of the network of ideological domination of society.

The focus of radical humanists upon the "superstructural" aspects of society reflects their attempt to move away from the economism of orthodox Marxism and emphasize the Hegelian dialectic. It is through the dialectics that the objective and subjective aspects of social life interact. The superstructure of society is believed to be the medium through which the consciousness of human beings is controlled and molded to fit the requirements of the social formation as a whole. The concepts of structural conflict, contradiction, and crisis do not play a major role in this paradigm, because these are a more objectivist view of social reality—that is, one that falls within the radical structuralist paradigm. In the radical humanist paradigm, the concepts of consciousness, alienation, and critique form the key concerns.

In Figure 1.1, the radical humanist paradigm occupies the northwest quadrant. Schools of thought within this paradigm can be located on the objective-subjective continuum. From left to right they are solipsism, French existentialism, anarchistic individualism, and critical theory.[7]

## Radical Structuralist Paradigm

The radical structuralist paradigm assumes that reality is objective and concrete, as it is rooted in the materialist view of the natural and social world. The social world, similar to the natural world, has an independent existence—that is, it exists outside the minds of human beings. Sociologists aim to discover and understand the patterns and regularities that characterize the social world. Scientists do not see any roles for themselves in the phenomenon under investigation. They use scientific methods to find the order that prevails in the phenomenon. This paradigm views society as a potentially dominating force. Sociologists working within this paradigm have an objectivist standpoint and are committed to radical change, emancipation, and potentiality. In their analysis, they emphasize structural conflict, modes of domination, contradiction, and deprivation. They analyze the basic interrelationships within the total social formation and emphasize the fact that radical change is inherent in the structure of society and that radical change takes place through political and economic crises. This radical change necessarily disrupts the status quo and replaces it with a radically different social formation. It is through this radical change that the emancipation of human beings from the social structure is materialized.

For radical structuralists, an understanding of classes in society is essential for understanding the nature of knowledge. They argue that all knowledge is class specific—that is, it is determined by the place one occupies in the productive process. Knowledge is more than a reflection of the material world in thought; it is determined by one's relation to that reality. Since different classes occupy different positions in the process of material transformation, there are different kinds of knowledge. Hence, class knowledge is produced by and for classes and exists in a struggle for domination. Knowledge is thus ideological—that is, it formulates views of reality and solves problems from class points of view.

Radical structuralists reject the idea that it is possible to verify knowledge in an absolute sense through comparison with socially neutral theories or data, but they emphasize that there is the possibility of producing a "correct" knowledge from a class standpoint. They argue that the dominated class is uniquely positioned to obtain an objectively "correct" knowledge of social reality and its contradictions. It is the class with the most direct and widest access to the process of material transformation that ultimately produces and reproduces that reality. Radical structuralists' analysis indicates that the social scientist, as a producer of class-based knowledge, is a part of the class struggle.

Radical structuralists believe truth is the whole and emphasize the need to understand the social order as a totality rather than as a collection of small truths about various parts and aspects of society. The economic empiricists are seen as relying almost exclusively upon a number of seemingly disparate, data-packed, problem-centered studies. Such studies, therefore, are irrelevant exercises in mathematical methods.

This paradigm is based on four central notions. First, there is the notion of totality. All theories address the total social formation. This notion emphasizes that the parts reflect the totality, not the totality the parts.

Second, there is the notion of structure. The focus is upon the configurations of social relationships, called structures, which are treated as persistent and enduring concrete facilities.

The third notion is that of contradiction. Structures, or social formations, contain contradictory and antagonistic relationships within them, which act as seeds of their own decay.

The fourth notion is that of crisis. Contradictions within a given totality reach a point at which they can no longer be contained. The resulting political and economic crises indicate the point of transformation from one totality to another, in which one set of structures is replaced by another of a fundamentally different kind.

In Figure 1.1, the radical structuralist paradigm occupies the northeast quadrant. Schools of thought within this paradigm can be located on the objective-subjective continuum. From right to left they are Russian social theory, conflict theory, and contemporary Mediterranean Marxism.[8]

## Conclusion

This chapter briefly discussed social theory, its complexity, and diversity. It indicated that theorists are not always entirely aware of the traditions to which they belong. The diversity of theories presented in this chapter is vast. While each paradigm advocates a research strategy that is logically coherent, in terms of underlying assumptions, these vary from paradigm to paradigm. The phenomenon to be researched is conceptualized and studied in many different ways, each generating distinctive kinds of insight and understanding. There are many different ways of studying the same social phenomenon, and given that the insights generated by any one approach are at best partial and incomplete, the social researcher can gain much by reflecting on the nature and merits of different approaches before engaging in a particular mode of research practice.

Social knowledge is ultimately a product of the researcher's paradigmatic approach to this multifaceted phenomenon. Viewed from this angle, the pursuit of social knowledge is seen as much as an ethical, moral, ideological, and political activity as a technical one. Researchers can gain much by exploiting the new insights coming from other paradigms.

## Notes

1 For the basic literature on the four paradigmatic framework, see Bottomore (1975); Burrell (2002); Burrell and Morgan (1979); Clark (1985); Denisoff (1974); Eckburg and Hill (1979); Effrat (1973); Evered and Louis (1981); Friedheim (1979); Gioia and Pitre (1990); Goles and Hirschheim (2000); Guba (1985); Guba and Lincoln (1994); Hassard (1988, 1991a, 1991b, 1993, 2013); Holland (1990); Jackson and Carter (1991); Jackson and Carter (2008); Jennings, Perren, and Carter (2005); Jick (1979); Kirkwood and Campbell-Hunt (2007); Knudsen (2003); Kuhn (1962,

1970a, 1970b, 1974, 1977); Lammers (1974); Lehmann and Young (1974); Lewis and Grimes (1999); Lincoln (1985); Martin (1990); Maruyama (1974); Masterman (1970); McKelvey (2008); Mir and Mir (2002); Morgan (1990); Okhuysen and Bonardi (2011); Parsons (1967); Ritzer (1975); Romani, Primecz, and Topcu (2011); Schultz and Hatch (1996); Shapere (1971); Siehl and Martin (1988); Snizek (1976); Steinle (1983); van de Berge (1963); White (1983); and Willmott (1990, 1993).

2 For more recent discussions and applications of the four paradigmatic framework, see Ardalan (2008, 2014, 2016, 2018, 2019a, 2019b, 2020, 2021); Arora and Chakraborty (2020); Bleijenbergh, Booysen, and Mills (2018); Cerin (2003); Deetz (1996); Hoque, Covaleski, and Gooneratne (2015); Ismail and Zainuddin (2013); McGregor (2019); McPhail and Cordery (2019); Mkansi and Acheampong (2012); Nemetz and Christensen (1996); Nielsen and Lassen (2011); Pellegrinelli and Murray-Webster (2011); Romani, Mahadevan, and Primecz (2018); Silva and Santos (2022); Watkins-Mathys and Lowe (2005); and Willmott (2005).

3 This work borrows heavily from the ideas and insights of Burrell and Morgan (1979) and Morgan (1983) and applies them to financial economics. Burrell and Morgan (1979) state "The scope for applying the analytical scheme to other field of study is enormous . . . readers interested in applying the scheme in this way should find little difficulty in proceeding from the sociological analyses . . . to an analysis of the literature in their own sphere of specialised interest" (page 35).

4 This can be used as both a classificatory device, or more importantly, as an analytical tool.

5 For classics in this literature, see Blau (1955, 1964); Buckley (1967); Comte (1953); Durkheim (1938, 1947); James (1890); Mead (1932a, 1932b, 1934, 1938); Merton (1968); Pareto (1935); Simmel (1936, 1955); Skinner (1953, 1957, 1972); and Spencer (1873).

6 For classics in this literature, see Berkeley (1962); Dilthey (1976); Gadamer (1965); Garfinkel (1967); Hegel (1931); Husserl (1929); Schutz (1964, 1966, 1967); Winch (2007); and Wittgenstein (1963).

7 For classics in this literature, see Bookchin (1974); Fichte (1970); Goldmann (1969); Gouldner (1954a, 1954b, 1970, 1973, 1976); Gramsci (1971); Habermas (1970a, 1970b, 1971, 1972, 1974, 1976); Horkheimer (1972); Lukacs (1971); Marcuse (1954, 1964, 1966, 1968); Marx (1975), Meszaros (1970, 1971); Sartre (1966, 1974, 1976); and Stirner (1907).

8 For classics in this literature, see Althusser (1969, 1971); Althusser and Balibar (1970); Bukharin (1965); Colletti (1972, 1974, 1975); Dahrendorf (1959); Marx (1973, 1976); Marx and Engels (1965, 1968); Plekhanov (1974); and Rex (1961, 1974).

## References


Althusser, L. (1969), *For Marx*, Harmondsworth: Penguin.

Althusser, L. (1971), *Lenin and Philosophy and Other Essays*, London: New Left Books.

Althusser, L. and Balibar, E. (1970), *Reading Capital*, London: New Left Books.

Ardalan, Kavous (2008), *On the Role of Paradigms in Finance*, Aldershot: Ashgate Publishing Limited, and Burlington, VT: Ashgate Publishing Company.

Ardalan, Kavous (2014), *Understanding Globalization: A Multi-Dimensional Approach*, Piscataway, NJ: Transaction Publishers.

Ardalan, Kavous (2016), *Paradigms in Political Economy*, New York, NY: Routledge.

Ardalan, Kavous (2018), *Case Method and Pluralist Economics: Philosophy, Methodology, and Practice*, New York, NY; and Cham: Springer International Publishing AG.

Ardalan, Kavous (2019a), *Global Political Economy: A Multi-Paradigmatic Approach*, New York, NY:; and Cham: Springer International Publishing AG.

Ardalan, Kavous (2019b), *Equity Home Bias in International Finance: A Place-Attachment Perspective*, Abingdon, Oxon; and New York, NY: Routledge.

Ardalan, Kavous (2020), *Understanding Revolution: A Multi-Paradigmatic Approach*, New York, NY; and Cham: Springer International Publishing AG.

Ardalan, Kavous (2021), *Feminist Theories and Feminist Economics: A Multi-Paradigmatic Approach*, Lanham, MD: Lexington Books (Rowman and Littlefield Publishing Group, Inc.).

Arora, Swapan Deep and Chakraborty, Anirban (2020), "Consumer Complaining Behavior: A Paradigmatic Review," *Philosophy of Management*, 20:2, 113–34.

Berkeley, G. (1962), *The Principles of Human Knowledge and Three Dialogues between Hylas and Philonous*, London: Collins.

Blau, P. M. (1955), *The Dynamics of Bureaucracy*, Chicago, IL: University of Chicago Press.

Blau, P. M. (1964), *Exchange and Power in Social Life*, New York, NY: John Wiley.

Bleijenbergh, Inge, Booysen, Lize, and Mills, Albert J. (2018), "The Challenges and Outcomes of Critical Diversity Scholarship," *Qualitative Research in Organizations and Management*, 13:3, 206–17.

Bookchin, Murray (1974), *Post-Scarcity Anarchism*, London: Wildwood House.

Bottomore, T. (1975), "Competing Paradigms in Macrosociology," in Inkeles, A. (ed.), *Annual Review of Sociology*, New York, NY: Annual Reviews, 191–202.

Buckley, William (1967), *Sociology and Modern Systems Theory*, Englewood Cliffs, NJ: Prentice-Hall.

Bukharin, N. (1965), *Historical Materialism: A System of Sociology*, New York, NY: Russell and Russell.

Burrell, Gibson (2002), "Organization Paradigms," in Sorge, A. (ed.), *Organization*, London: Thompson Learning, 25–42.

Burrell, Gibson and Morgan, Gareth (1979), *Sociological Paradigms and Organizational Analysis*, Hants: Gower Publishing Company Limited.

Cerin, Pontus (2003), "Sustainability Hijacked by the Sociological Wall of Self-Evidence," *Corporate Social-Responsibility and Environmental Management*, 10:4, 175–85.

Clark, D.L. (1985), "Emerging Paradigms in Organization Theory," in Lincoln, Y. (ed.), *Organizational Theory and Inquiry*, Beverly Hills, CA: Sage.

Colletti, L. (1972), *From Rousseau to Lenin*, London: New Left Books.

Colletti, L. (1974), "A Political and Philosophical Interview," *New Left Review*, 86, 3–28.

Colletti, L. (1975), "Marxism and the Dialectics," *New Left Review*, 93, 3–29.

Comte, Auguste (1953), *The Positivist Philosophy*, Vol. I, London: Chapman.

Dahrendorf, R. (1959), *Class and Class Conflict in Industrial Society*, London: Routledge and Kegan Paul.

Deetz, Stanley (1996), "Describing Differences in Approaches to Organization Science: Rethinking Burrell and Morgan and Their Legacy," *Organization Science*, 7:2, 191–207.

Denisoff, R., Callahan, O., and Levine, M. H. (1974), *Theories and Paradigms in Contemporary Sociology*, New York, NY: Peacock.

Dilthey, Wilhelm (1976), *Selected Writings*, ed. Rickman, H.P., London: Cambridge University Press.

Durkheim, Emile (1938), *The Rules of Sociological Method*, Glencoe, IL: Free Press.

Durkheim, Emile (1947), *The Division of Labour in Society*, Glencoe, IL: Free Press.

Eckburg, D. and Hill, L., Jr. (1979), "The Paradigm Concept and Sociology: A Critical Review," *Annual Sociological Review*, 44:4, 925–37.

Effrat, A. (1973), "Power to the Paradigms," in Effrat, A. (ed.), *Perspectives in Political Sociology*, New York, NY: Bobbs-Merrill, 3–33.

Evered, R. and Louis, M. (1981), *Alternative Perspectives in Organizational Sciences*, *Academy of Management Review*, 6:3, 385–95.

Fichte, J.F. (1970), *Science of Knowledge*, eds. Heath, P. and Lachs, J., New York, NY: Century Philosophy Sourcebooks.

Friedheim, E.A. (1979), "An Empirical Comparison of Ritzer's Paradigms and Similar Metatheories," *Social Forces*, 58:1, 59–66.

Gadamer, H.G. (1965), *Wahrheit und Method*, Tubingen: J.C.B. Mohr.

Garfinkel, Harold (1967), *Studies in Ethnomethodology*, Englewood Cliffs, NJ: Prentice-Hall.

Gioia, D. and Pitre, E. (1990), "Multi-Paradigmatic Perspectives in Theory Building," *Academy of Management Review*, 15, 584–602.

Goldmann, Lucien (1969), *The Human Sciences and Philosophy*, London: Cape.

Goles, T. and Hirschheim, R. (2000), "The Paradigm Is Dead, the Paradigm Is Dead . . . Long Live the Paradigm: The Legacy of Burrell and Morgan," *Omega*, 28, 249–68.

Gouldner, Alvin W. (1954a), *Patterns of Industrial Bureaucracy*, Glencoe, IL: Free Press.

Gouldner, Alvin W. (1954b), *Wildcat Strike*, New York, NY.: Antioch Press.

Gouldner, Alvin W. (1970), *The Coming Crisis of Western Sociology*, London: Heinemann.

Gouldner, Alvin W. (1973), *For Sociology*, Harmondsworth: Allen Lane.

Gouldner, Alvin W. (1976), *The Dialectic of Ideology and Technology*, New York, NY: Macmillan.

Gramsci, Antonio, (1971), *Selections from the Prison Notebooks of Antonio Gramsci*, eds. Hoare, Quinton and Nowell-Smith, Geoffrey, London: Lawrence and Wishart.

Guba, E.G. (1985), "The Context of Emergent Paradigm Research," in Lincoln, Y.S. (ed.), *Organizational Theory and Inquiry*, Beverly Hills, CA: Sage.

Guba, E.G. and Lincoln, Y.S. (1994), "Competing Paradigms in Qualitative Research," in Denzin, N.K. and Lincoln, Y.S. (eds.), *Handbook of Qualitative Research*, Thousand Oaks, CA: Sage Publications, pp. 105–17.

Habermas, Jurgen (1970a), "On Systematically Distorted Communications," *Inquiry*, 13, 205–18.

Habermas, Jurgen (1970b), "Towards a Theory of Communicative Competence," *Inquiry*, 13, 360–75.

Habermas, Jurgen (1971), *Toward a Rational Society*, London: Heinemann.

Habermas, Jurgen (1972), *Knowledge and Human Interests*, London: Heinemann.

Habermas, Jurgen (1974), *Theory and Practice*, London: Heinemann.

Habermas, Jurgen (1976), *Legitimation Crisis*, London: Heinemann.

Hassard, John (1988), "Overcoming Hermeticism in Organization Theory: An Alternative to Paradigm Incommensurability," *Human Relations*, 41:3, 247–59.

Hassard, John (1991a), "Multiple Paradigm Analysis: A Methodology for Management Research," in Smith, C. and Dainty, P. (eds.), *Handbook for Management Researchers*, London: Routledge.

Hassard, John (1991b), "Multiple Paradigm Research in Organizations: A Case Study," *Organization Studies*, 12:2, 275–99.

Hassard, John (1993), *Sociology and Organizational Theory: Positivism, Paradigms, and Postmodernity*, Cambridge: Cambridge University Press.

Hassard, John (2013), "Can Sociological Paradigms Still Inform Organizational Analysis? A Paradigm Model for Post-Paradigm Times," *Organizational Studies*, 34:11, November, 1701–28.

Hegel, G. (1931), *The Phenomenology of Mind*, London: George Allen and Unwin.

Holland, R. (1990), "The Paradigm Plague: Prevention, Cure, and Innoculation," *Human Relations*, 43:1, 23–48.

Hoque, Zahirul, Covaleski, Mark A., and Gooneratne, Tharusha N. (2015), "A Response to 'Theoretical Triangulation and Pluralism in Accounting Research: A Critical Realist Critique," *Accounting, Auditing, and Accountability Journal*, 28:7, 1151–9.

Horkheimer, M. (1972), *Critical Theory: Selected Essays*, New York, NY: Herder.

Husserl, Edmund (1929), "Entry on 'Phenomenology,'" in Garvin, T. L., (ed.), *Encyclopedia Britannica*, 14th ed, New York, NY: Encyclopedia Britannica.

Ismail, Kamisah and Zainuddin, Suria (2013), "Research Paradigms for Accounting: A Review," *Asian Journal of Accounting Perspectives*, 6:1, 50–6.

Jackson, N. and Carter, P. (1991), "In Defense of Paradigm Incommensurability," *Organization Studies*, 12:1, 109–27.

Jackson, N. and Carter, P. (2008), "Baffling Bill McKelvey, the Commensurability Kid," *Epherma*, 8, 403–19.

James, William (1890), *Principles of Psychology*, London: Macmillan.

Jennings, P., Perren, L., and Carter, S. (2005), "Guest Editor's Introduction: Alternative Perspectives on Entrepreneurship Research," *Entrepreneurship Theory and Practice*, 29, 145–52.

Jick, T. (1979), "Mixing Quantitative and Qualitative Methods: Triangulation in Action," *Administrative Science Quarterly*, 24:4, 602–11.

Kirkwood, J. and Campbell-Hunt, C. (2007), "Using Multiple Paradigm Research Methodologies to Gain New Insights into Entrepreneurial Motivations," *Journal of Enterprise Culture*, 15, 219–41.

Knudsen, C. (2003), "Pluralism, Scientific Progress and the Structure of Organization Theory," in Tsoukas, H. and Knudsen, C. (eds.), *The Oxford Handbook of Organization Theory*, Oxford: Oxford University Press, pp. 262–88.

Kuhn, T.S. (1962), *The Structure of Scientific Revolutions*, Chicago, IL: Chicago University Press.

Kuhn, T.S. (1970a), *The Structure of Scientific Revolutions*, Chicago, IL: University of Chicago Press, Second Edition with Postscript.

Kuhn, T.S. (1970b), "Reflections on My Critics," in Lakatos, I. and Musgrave, A. (eds.), *Criticism and the Growth of Knowledge*, Cambridge: Cambridge University Press, 254–67.

Kuhn, T.S. (1974), "Second Thoughts on Paradigms," in Suppe, F. (ed.), *The Structure of Scientific Theories*, Chicago, IL: University of Illinois Press, 459–82.

Kuhn, T.S. (1977), *The Essential Tension*, Chicago, IL: University of Chicago Press.

Lammers, C. (1974), "Mono- and Poly-Paradigmatic Developments in the Natural and Social Sciences," in Whitely, R. (ed.), *Social Processes of Scientific Development*, London: Routledge and Kegan Paul.

Lehmann, T. and Young, R. (1974), "From Conflict Theory to Conflict Methodology: An Emerging Paradigm for Sociology," *Sociological Inquiry*, 44:1, 15–28.

Lewis, M. and Grimes, A. (1999), "Metatriangulation: Building Theory from Multiple Paradigms," *Academy of Management Review*, 24, 672–90.

Lincoln, Y.S. (ed.), (1985), *Organizational Theory and Inquiry: The Paradigm Revolution*, Beverly Hills, CA: Sage Publications.

Lukacs, Georg (1971), *History and Class Consciousness*, London: Merlin.

Marcuse, H. (1954), *Reason and Revolution*, New York, NY: Humanities Press.

Marcuse, H. (1964), *One-Dimensional Man*, London: Routledge and Kegan Paul.

Marcuse, H. (1966), *Eros and Civilisation*, Boston, MA: Beason.

Marcuse, H. (1968), *Negations: Essays in Critical Theory*, London: Heinemann.

Martin, J. (1990), "Breaking up the Mono-Method Monopolies in Organizational Research," in Hassard, J. and Pym, D. (eds.), *The Theory and Philosophy of Organizations*, London: Routledge, 30–43.

Maruyama, M. (1974), "Paradigms and Communication," *Technological Forecasting and Social Change*, 6, 3–32.

Marx, Karl (1973), *Grundrisse: Foundations of the Critique of Political Economy*, Harmondsworth: Penguin.

Marx, Karl (1975), *Early Writings*, Harmondsworth: Penguin.

Marx, Karl (1976), *Capital: A Critique of Political Economy*, Vols. I-III, Harmondsworth: Penguin.

Marx, Karl and Engels, Fredrick (1965), *The German Ideology*, London: Lawrence and Wishart.

Marx, Karl and Engels, Fredrick (1968), *Selected Works*, London: Lawrence and Wishart Ltd.

Masterman, M. (1970), "The Nature of Paradigms," in Lakatos, I. and Musgrave, A. (eds.), *Criticism and Growth of Knowledge*, Cambridge: Cambridge University Press, pp. 59–90.

McGregor, Caroline (2019), "A Paradigm Framework for Social Work Theory for Early 21st Century Practice," *British Journal of Social Work*, 49:8, 2112–29.

McKelvey, B. (2008), "Commensurability, Rhetoric, and Ephemera: Searching for Clarity in a Cloud of Critique," *Epherma*, 8, 420–32.

McPhail, Ken and Cordery, Carolyn J. (2019), "Theological Perspectives on Accounting: Worldviews Don't Change Overnight," *Accounting, Auditing, and Accountability Journal*, 32:8, 2330–52.

Mead, George Herbert (1932a), *Movements of Thought in the Nineteenth Century*, ed. Moore, M.N., Chicago, IL: University of Chicago Press.

Mead, George Herbert (1932b), *The Philosophy of the Present*, ed. Murphy, A.E., Chicago, IL: Open Court Publishing.

Mead, George Herbert (1934), *Mind, Self and Society*, ed. Morris, Charles, Chicago, IL: University of Chicago Press.

Mead, George Herbert (1938), *The Philosophy of the Act*, ed. Morris, Charles, Chicago, Il: University of Chicago Press.

Merton, Robert K. (1968), *Social Theory and Social Structure*, New York, NY: Free Press.

Meszaros, I. (1970), *Marx's Theory of Alienation*, London: Merlin.

Meszaros, I. (1971), *Aspects of History and Class Consciousness*, London: Routledge and Kegan Paul.

Mir, R. and Mir, A. (2002), "The Organizational Imagination from Paradigm Wars to Praxis," *Organizational Research Methods*, 5, 105–25.

Mkansi, Marcia and Acheampong, Edwin Asiamah (2012), "Research Philosophy Debates and Classifications: Students' Dilemma," *Electronic Journal of Business Research Methods*, 10:2, December, 132–40.

Morgan, G., ed. (1983), *Beyond Method: Strategies for Social Research*, Beverly Hills, CA: Sage Publications, Inc.

Morgan, G. (1990), "Paradigm Diversity in Organizational Research," in Hassard, J. and Pym, D. (eds.), *The Theory and Philosophy of Organizations*, London: Routledge, 1–22.

Nemetz, Patricia L. and Christensen, Sandra L. (1996), "The Challenge of Cultural Diversity: Harnessing a Diversity of Views to Understand Multiculturalism," *Academy of Management Review*, 21:2, 434–62.

Nielsen, Suna Lowe and Lassen, Astrid Heidemann (2011), "Images of Entrepreneurship: Towards a New Categorization of Entrepreneurship," *International Entrepreneurship and Management Journal*, 8:1, 35–53.

Okhuysen, G. and Bonardi, J.P. (2011), "Editors' Comments: The Challenge of Building Theory by Combining Lenses," *Academy of Management Review*, 36, 6–11.

Pareto, Vilfredo (1935), *The Mind and Society*, 4 Volumes, New York, NY: Harcourt, Brace, Jovanovich.

Parsons, T. (1967), "A Paradigm for the Analysis of Social Systems and Change," in Demerath, N. and Peterson, R. (eds.), *System, Change, and Conflict*, New York, NY: Free Press, 189–212.

Pellegrinelli, Sergio and Murray-Webster, Ruth (2011), "Multi-Paradigmatic Perspectives on a Business Transformation Program," *Project Management Journal*, 42:6, 4–19.

Plekhanov, G. (1974), *Selected Philosophical Works*, Vol. I, Moscow: Progress.

Rex, J. (1961), *Key Problems in Sociological Theory*, London: Routledge and Kegan Paul.

Rex, J. (1974), *Approaches to Sociology*, London: Routledge and Kegan Paul.

Ritzer, G. (1975), *Sociology: A Multiple-Paradigm Science*, New York, NY: Allyn and Bacon.

Romani, Laurence, Mahadevan, Jasmin, and Primecz, Henriett (2018), "Critical Cross-Cultural Management: Outline and Emerging Contributions," *International Studies of Management and Organization*, 48:4, 403–18.

Romani, L., Primecz, H., and Topcu, K. (2011), "Paradigm Interplay for Theory Development: A Methodological Example with the Kulturstandard Method," *Organizational Research Method*, 14, 432–55.

Sartre, Jean-Paul (1966), *Being and Nothingness*, New York, NY: Washington Square Press.

Sartre, Jean-Paul (1974), *Between Existentialism and Marxism*, London: Pantheon.

Sartre, Jean-Paul (1976), *Critique of Dialectical Reason*, Vol. I, London: New Left Books.

Schultz, M. and Hatch, M.J. (1996), "Living with Multiple Paradigms: The Case of Paradigm Interplay in Organizational Culture Studies," *Academy of Management Review*, 21, 529–57.

Schutz, Alfred (1964), *Collected Papers II: Studies in Social Theory*, The Hague: Martinus Nijhoff.

Schutz, Alfred (1966), *Collected Papers III: Studies in Phenomenological Philosophy*, The Hague: Martinus Nijhoff.

Schutz, Alfred (1967), *Collected Papers I: The Problem of Social Reality*, Second Edition, The Hague: Martinus Nijhoff.

Shapere, D. (1971), "The Paradigm Concept," *Science*, 17, 706–9.

Siehl, C. and Martin, J. (1988), "Measuring Organizational Culture: Mixing Qualitative and Quantitative Methods," in Jones, M., Moore, D., and Snyder, R. (eds.), *Inside Organizations*, Beverly Hills, CA: Sage, 79–103.

Silva, Patricia Araujo and Santos, Ana Cristina Batista dos (2022), "Epistemological Possibilities of Public Administration Theories: From Paradigms to Epistemic Matrices," *Organizacoes and Sociedade*, 29:101, 277–96.

Simmel, Georg (1936), *The Metropolis and Mental Life*, Chicago, IL, University of Chicago Press.

Simmerl, Georg (1955), *Conflict and the Web of Group Affiliations*, Glencoe, IL: Free Press.

Skinner, B.F. (1953), *Science and Human Behaviour*, New York, NY: Macmillan.

Skinner, B.F. (1957), *Verbal Behavior*, New York, NY: Appleton-Century-Crofts.

Skinner, B.F. (1972), *Beyond Freedom and Dignity*, New York, NY: Alfred Knopf.

Snizek, W. (1976), "An Empirical Assessment of 'Sociology: A Multi-Paradigm Science'," *American Sociologist*, 1:2, 217–19.

Spencer, Herbert (1873), *The Study of Sociology*, London: Kegan Paul and Tench.

Steinle, C. (1983), "Organization Theory and Multiple Plane Analysis," *Management International Review*, 23, 31–46.

Stirner, Max (1907), *The Ego and His Own*, New York, NY: Libertarian Book Club.

van de Berge, P. (1963), "Dialectics and Functionalism: Toward a Theoretical Synthesis," *American Sociological Review*, 28:5, 695–705.

Watkins-Mathys, Lorraine and Lowe, Sid (2005), "Small Business and Entrepreneurship Research: The Way through Paradigm Incommensurability," *International Small Business Journal*, 23:6, 657–77.

White, O. (1983), "Improving the Prospects for Heterodoxy in Organization Theory," *Administration and Society*, 15:2, 257–72.

Willmott, Hugh (1990), "Beyond Paradigmatic Closure in Organizational Inquiry," in Hassard, J. and Pym, D. (eds.), *The Theory and Philosophy of Organizations*, London: Routledge, 44–62.

Willmott, Hugh (1993), "Breaking the Paradigm Mentality," *Organization Studies*, 14, 681–719.

Willmott, Hugh (2005), "Theorizing Contemporary Control: Some Post-structuralist Responses to Some Critical Realist Questions," *Organization*, 12:5, 747–80.

Winch, Peter (2007), *The Idea of a Social Science and Its Relation to Philosophy*, London: Routledge and Kegan Paul.

Wittgenstein, L. (1963), *Philosophical Investigations*, Oxford: Blackwell.

2

# Structure of a Paradigm

This chapter focuses on one paradigm, discusses its structure, and relates it to the controversies within the paradigm. It builds on the previous chapter, which examined paradigms, emphasized their diversity, and showed that the functionalist paradigm forms the context of the mainstream of the academic field of economics.

The hierarchical structure of paradigms consists of three consecutive levels: paradigm, metaphor, and puzzle solving. Theories and controversies in mainstream academic economics, despite their apparent diversity, are founded on the functionalist paradigm and are associated with its metaphor level.

This chapter is organized as follows. The first section discusses the structure of a paradigm. The second section discusses a controversy on the balance of payments. The third section concludes that the different views that underlie the balance of payments controversy fall within the mainstream functionalist economic paradigm.

## Structure of a Paradigm

The hierarchical structure of a paradigm consists of three consecutive levels: paradigm, metaphor, and puzzle solving. (See Figure 2.1.)[1]

Paradigm can be regarded as the same as a worldview or way of seeing reality. It refers to both implicit and explicit views of reality. Paradigms are defined and characterized by a set of fundamental assumptions, which, in turn, translate into certain rules and standards for scientific practice. These are common among the theorists and researchers who share the same paradigm, although their work may appear different and sometimes at odds with each other.

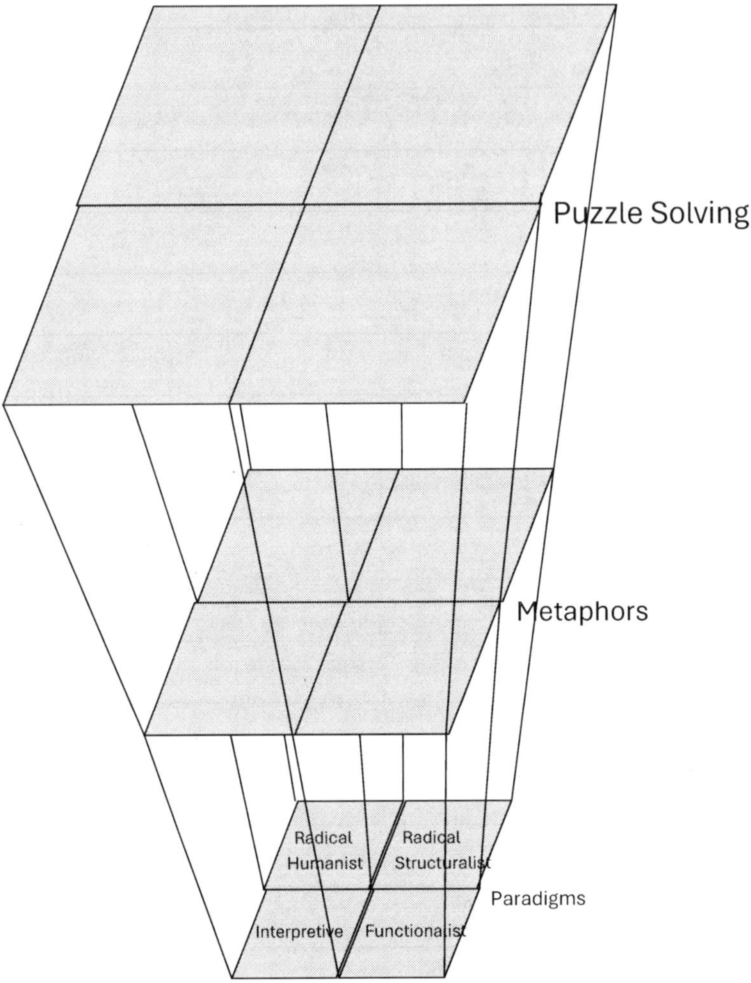


**Figure 2.1** The structure of a paradigm.

Paradigms provide researchers not only with a map but also with directions essential for map-making. Since, in learning a paradigm, the researcher acquires theories, methods, and standards together in a cohesive manner.

Paradigms or worldviews consist of different schools of thought. These are different ways of studying a shared reality. Schools of thought accept and use special metaphors in their studies. The network of commitments—conceptual, theoretical, and methodological—is the principal source of the metaphor[2] that relates paradigms to puzzle solving. Because it provides rules that tell the researchers what both the world and their science are like, they can concentrate with assurance upon the problems that these rules and existing knowledge define for them.

A metaphor creatively produces a crossing of images. It plays an important role in the way human beings conceive conceptions about their reality and, therefore, in the development of the social and natural sciences. In the process of scientific inquiry, scientists view the world metaphorically. This is accomplished through the choice of metaphors. Schools of thought are based on the insights associated with different metaphors, as the logic of metaphor has important implications for the process of theory construction.

A metaphor serves to generate an image for studying a subject. This image provides the basis for detailed scientific research that attempts to discover the extent to which features of the metaphor are found in the subject of inquiry. Much of the puzzle-solving activity of scientists is of this kind. They attempt to examine, operationalize, and measure detailed implications of the metaphorical insight upon which their research is implicitly or explicitly based. Different metaphors capture the nature of the subject of study in different ways. Each generates distinctive, but essentially partial, insight. New metaphors create new ways of viewing the subject of study that overcome the weaknesses of traditional metaphors. They offer supplementary or even contradictory approaches to the analysis of the subject of study.

At the puzzle-solving level of analysis, research activities seek to operationalize the detailed implications of the metaphor defining a particular school of thought. Schools of thought, at their puzzle-solving level, get involved with detailed analysis of specific phenomena or problems, and use specific models and tools. Resolution of a research problem requires the solution of all sorts of complex puzzles. The rules and standards defined by the paradigm limit both the nature of acceptable solutions and the steps by which they are to be obtained. The current theoretical and empirical research in academic economics, and most of the consequent debates and controversies, are at this level.

## Controversies in Economics

Theories and controversies in mainstream academic economics, despite their apparent diversity, are founded on the functionalist paradigm and are associated with its metaphor level. This section considers the balance of payments metaphor and brings out current controversies about it. These controversies are about the assumptions made in mainstream academic economics.

## *Balance of Payments*

Two theories, Keynesian and monetarist, dominate macroeconomics in general and balance of payments theories in particular. Three alternative theories of balance of payments adjustment are reviewed in this section. They are commonly known as the elasticities, absorption approaches (associated with Keynesian theory), and the monetary approach.[3]

### *a. The Elasticities Approach*

The elasticities approach applies the Marshallian analysis of elasticities of supply and demand for individual commodities to the analysis of exports and imports as a whole. It is spelled out by Joan Robinson (1950).

Robinson was mainly concerned with the conditions under which devaluation of a currency would lead to an improvement in the balance of trade. Suppose the trade balance equation is written as:

X = value of exports
IM = value of imports
BT = balance of trade

$$BT = X - IM \quad (1)$$

In this context, it is generally assumed that exports depend on the price of exports, and imports depend on the price of imports. These relations are then translated into elasticities, by differentiating the above equation with respect to the exchange rate. A criterion for a change in the balance of trade in the desired direction can be established, assuming that export and import prices adjust to equate the demand for and supply of exports and imports. In effect, the exchange rate clears balance of payments.

The effect of a devaluation on the trade balance depends on four elasticities: the foreign elasticity of demand for exports, and the home elasticity of supply, the foreign elasticity of supply of imports, and the home elasticity of demand for imports. For the special case where it is assumed that the trade balance is initially zero and that the two supply schedules are infinitely elastic, the elasticities condition for the impact of a devaluation to be an improvement in the trade balance is that the sum of the demand elasticities exceed unity. This has been termed the "Marshall-Lerner condition."

This special case and the assumptions behind it should be viewed against the background of the time they were developed, the Great Depression of the 1930s. The theory adopted Keynesian assumptions of wage and price rigidity and mass unemployment and used these to extend the Keynesian analysis to the international sphere.

Under Keynesian assumptions of sticky wages and prices, devaluation changes the prices of domestic goods relative to foreign goods, that is, a change in the terms of trade, in foreign and domestic markets, and causes alterations in production and consumption. This in turn has an impact on the balance of trade.

It is important to note the following two characteristics of the special case of the elasticities approach: (1) Any impact of the devaluation on the demand for domestic output is assumed to be met by variations in output and employment rather than relative prices, with the repercussions of variations in output on the balance of payments regarded as secondary. This is made possible by the assumption that supply elasticities are infinite. The assumption of output and employment being variable proved highly unsatisfactory in the immediate postwar period of full and over-full employment. (2) The connections between the balance of payments and the money supply, and between the money supply and the aggregate demand, are ignored. This is made possible by the assumed existence of unemployed resources, as well as by the Keynesian skepticism regarding the influence of money. As will be shown later, the monetary approach differs from the elasticities approach on both these grounds.

A notable shortcoming of the elasticities analysis is its neglect of capital flows. Even though the adherents of the elasticities approach were attempting to guide the policy maker in improving the country's balance of payments, their focus, nevertheless, was on the balance of trade (net exports of goods and services). For the special case mentioned above, this is traceable to the emphasis in Keynesian analysis given to aggregate demand (of which net exports are a component).

Before we close this section, one important point has to be mentioned. In the literature, the elasticities approach is often mistakenly referred to as being a partial equilibrium analysis. This type of argument is based on the fact that in the special case, elasticities of supplies of exports and imports are assumed to be infinite; the effect of changes in the quantity of goods and services exported and imported are independent of, or are not sensitive to, the happenings elsewhere in the economy; for example, the change in income that results from the change in exports does not have an effect on imports. The important point to note is that, whereas the special case of infinitely elastic supplies of exports is a partial equilibrium analysis, the general case is not. In general, the elasticities approach considers the usual demand and supplies for imports and exports where they are obtained on the basis of the production possibilities curve of domestic economies; like any usual general equilibrium analysis, everything depends on the happenings elsewhere in the economy, that is, general equilibrium analysis.

### *b. The Absorption Approach*

The absorption approach was first presented by Alexander (1968). He sought to look at the balance of trade from the point of view of national income accounting:

Y = domestic production of goods and services
E = domestic absorption of goods and services, or domestic total expenditure
BT = balance of trade

$$BT = Y - E \tag{2}$$

The above identity is useful in pointing out that an improvement in the balance of trade calls for an increase in production relative to absorption.

When unemployed resources exist, the following mechanism is visualized: the effect of a devaluation is to increase exports and decrease imports. This in turn causes an increase in production (income) through the multiplier mechanism. If total expenditure rises by a smaller amount, there will be an improvement in the balance of trade. Thus, the balance is set to be identical with the real hoarding of the economy, which is the difference between total production and total absorption of goods and services (in effect, income or expenditure clears the balance of payments), and therefore equal to the accumulation of securities and/or money balances (as will be shown later, the monetary approach concentrates on the accumulation of money balances only). In the presence of unemployment, therefore, devaluation not only aids the balance of payments but also helps the economy move toward full employment and is, therefore, doubly attractive.

Suppose, however, that the country is at full employment to begin with. It cannot hope to improve its trade balance by increasing real income. Here, it has to depend on its ability to reduce absorption. How can a devaluation achieve this? Alexander argued that the rise in the price level consequent upon the devaluation would tend to discourage consumption and investment expenditures out of a given level of income. One way this will happen is through the "real balance effect"—a reference to the public's curtailment of expenditure in order to rebuild their stock of real cash balances that was diminished by the increase in the price level. The real balance effect will be seen to play an important role in the monetary approach as well.

However, under conditions of full employment, a devaluation cannot be expected to produce, by itself, the desired extent of change in the overall balance. The reduction in the public's expenditure in order to build their money balances will have to be supplemented by domestic deflationary policies, the so-called "expenditure-switching" and "expenditure-reducing" policies. This, of course, is because the balance of trade cannot be improved through a rise in the output level.

The absorption approach can be said to work only in the presence of unemployed resources. The absorption approach is a significant improvement over the special case of the elasticities approach in one important sense: this is its view of the external balance via national income accounting. In this manner, the approach relates the balance to the happenings elsewhere in the economy rather than taking the partial equilibrium view of the special case of the elasticities approach in analyzing the external sector in isolation.

### *c. The Monetary Approach*

The "monetary approach" is so called because it considers disequilibrium in the balance of payments to be essentially, though not exclusively, a monetary phenomenon. To say that something is essentially a monetary phenomenon means that money plays a vital role but does not imply that only money plays a role. The monetary approach takes explicit account of the influence of real variables such as levels of income and interest rates on the behavior of the balance of payments.

The elasticities and absorption approaches are concerned with the balance of trade, while the monetary approach concerns itself with the deficit on monetary account. In principle, this balance consists of the items that affect the domestic monetary base. In practice, the monetary approach uses the nearest approximation, usually the official settlements concept of imbalance, because the theoretical concept is relatively new and is not published in official statistics.

In general, the approach assumes full employment and emphasizes the budget constraint imposed on the country's international spending. It views the current and capital accounts of the balance of payments as the "windows" to the outside world, through which an excess of domestic stock demand for money over domestic stock supply of money, or of excess domestic stock supply of money over domestic stock demand for money, is cleared. Accordingly, surpluses in the trade account and the capital account, respectively, represent excess flow supplies of goods and of securities and excess domestic demand for money. Consequently, in analyzing the money account, or more familiarly, the rate of increase or decrease in the country's international reserves, the monetary approach focuses on the determinants of the excess stock demand for, or supply of, money.

This theory divides the country's monetary base into foreign assets and domestic assets of the monetary authorities. An increase in the foreign assets of the central bank is achieved when the central bank purchases foreign exchange or gold. Under pegged exchange rates, the central bank buys foreign exchange in order to prevent the national currency from appreciating in the foreign exchange market. The central bank's purchase of foreign assets increases its domestic monetary liabilities by the same amount.

An increase in domestic assets of the central bank is achieved when the central bank purchases bonds from the fiscal branch of the government (the treasury) or from the public. The central bank's purchases of domestic assets (e.g., bonds) increase its domestic monetary liabilities, that is, the monetary base, by the same amount. The excess supply of money has to be matched by an equivalent excess demand for goods and/or securities. This is because the budget constraint deems that the public's flow demand for goods, securities, and money—assuming that these three encompass all that the public demands—should add up to the public's total income. Therefore, with an unchanged level of income, an excess supply of money has to be matched by an equivalent excess demand for goods and/or securities. Viewing the economy as a whole, what does the excess demand for goods and securities imply? In a closed economy, an excess demand for goods would lead to an increase in the domestic price level and a consequent fall in the real money balances the public holds. An excess demand for securities would increase their price (decrease the interest rate), increasing desired money balances. Price and interest rate changes eventually cause the existing nominal money supply to be willingly held by the public. However, in a small open economy with fixed exchange rates, the domestic price level has to maintain parity with the price level in the rest of the world, and the domestic price of securities (and therefore the interest rate) is determined by the price of securities (and therefore the interest rate) in the world as a whole. So, in the absence of sales of domestic assets by the central bank, the desired level of real money balances is achieved by importing goods and/or securities from abroad. This creates a deficit in the money account, resulting in a fall in foreign assets of the central bank and, therefore, in the money supply.

The monetary approach is seen to have an appreciation of the interrelated nature of the various markets. The monetary approach insists that when one market is eliminated from a general equilibrium model by Walras's law, the behavioral specifications for the included markets must not be such as to imply a specification for the excluded market that would appear unreasonable if it were made explicit. The monetary approach focuses on stock and flow equilibrium, with emphasis on stock equilibrium for money. In this way it considers interrelationships among various markets and, therefore, the inter-relationship between stock and flow equilibrium. The stock-flow consideration of the monetary approach is in fact the essential difference between the monetary approach and the elasticities and absorption approaches, where the latter two consider the flow equilibrium only.

The monetary approach, like the absorption approach, stresses the need for reducing domestic expenditure relative to income in order to eliminate a deficit in the balance of payments. However, whereas the absorption approach looks at the relationship between real output and expenditure on goods, the monetary approach concentrates on deficient or excess nominal demand for goods and securities and the resulting accumulation or decumulation of money.

The monetary approach looks at the balance of payments as the change in the monetary base less the change in the domestic component:

H = change in the quantity of money demanded
D = domestic credit creation
BP = H − D

Putting just monetary assets rather than all assets "below the line" contributes to the simplicity of the monetary approach. Other things being equal, growth in demand for money, and of factors that affect it positively should lead to a surplus in the balance of payments. Growth in domestic money, other things being equal, should worsen it. Thus, the growth of real output in a country with constant interest rates causes its residents to demand a growing stock of real and nominal cash balances. This means that the country will run a surplus in the balance of payments. In order to avoid a balance of payments surplus, the increase in money must be satisfied through domestic open market operations. To produce a deficit, domestic money stock must grow faster than the growth of real income.

This analysis suggests that if a country is running a deficit, then assuming that the economy is growing at its full-employment growth rate with a given rate of technological progress, it should curtail its rate of domestic monetary expansion. The use of other measures like the imposition of tariffs, devaluation, or deflation of aggregate demand by fiscal policy can succeed only in the short run.

Looking at the balance of payments as the change in the monetary base less the change in the domestic component has led to charges that the monetary approach is not a theory but a tautology. It has also been argued that the relationships among credit creation, money supply, and the balance of payments can be expressed through identities, but it is impossible to identify the model in a general way to distinguish the independent from the dependent variables.

The two points above are related. We shall see how the monetary view answers them. First, even though the monetary approach starts with an identity, it can be falsified (and therefore shown to be a theory rather than a tautology) if the demand for money is not a stable function of a few variables: If money demand were passive (i.e., if the economy was in a liquidity trap), the monetary approach would have no predictive power. The cumulative balance of payments surplus would be whatever was dictated by exclusively non-monetary considerations, and the demand for money would simply adjust to that fact. A non-monetary approach to the balance of payments would not only be justified, but it would also be required.

Just as the Keynesian analysis starts out with the income-expenditure identity and develops a theory by assuming stability of the consumption function, the monetary approach becomes a testable proposition due to its assumed stability of the demand for money function. Evidence from estimating the demand for money in the context of a closed economy indicates that the demand for money is stable. This suggests that the monetary approach should be given a chance in a trial of its validity.

The decision on which variables are exogenous and which are endogenous is made in the following manner: real income is assumed exogenous in the long run. Also, in the long run, prices and interest rates are exogenous for small countries. Thus, the quantity of money demanded is exogenous. The monetary approach assumes that the domestic assets component of the monetary base is unaffected by balance of payments flows. This (the domestic assets) is the variable that the monetary authorities control and, thereby, indirectly control the balance of payments.

This is the well-known "non-sterilization" assumption. The monetary approach considers the non-sterilization assumption to be realistic because of its view of the overall balance as a symptom of excess demand for money. Thus, a deficit indicates the presence of a negative excess demand. The deficit also removes the disequilibrium in the money market. Any attempt by the monetary authorities to make up for the decline in money supply is doomed to failure, since credit creation will only prolong the payments deficit.

The monetary approach often sets its eyes toward long-run analysis and assumes full employment. Also, assuming an integrated world, markets are believed to work as well internationally as they do domestically. This approach believes that under fixed exchange rates, we can talk about the world price level and interest rate, just as we talk about the price level and interest rate for a large country.

An historical inference from the assumption of a unified world market is that, under the gold standard, the United States, the United Kingdom, and the other countries had little control over their money supply. Money, like any other good, could be exported or imported to adjust to the demand for it; that is, the money stock of any one country in an interdependent world is endogenous. This view contrasts with the monetarist's closed economy view, namely, the determinants of a nation's demand for money (prices, interest rates, and income) have to adjust to the supply, which in turn is determined by the domestic monetary authorities. The monetarist's international view, which is a rediscovery of Hume's price-specie-flow mechanism, would apply the quantity theory of money only to the world as a whole—and not to an individual country—if fixed exchange rates characterize its nation-states. The theory for a closed economy is applicable to an individual economy only under perfectly flexible exchange rates, for only then do monetary authorities have the ability to set the quantity of money.

Finally, a discussion of the monetary approach's price assumptions may be in order. In contrast to some earlier theories that assumed changes in the price of exports relative to imports, or of tradable goods relative to non-tradable goods, affect the balance of payments, the monetary approach assumes a world price level. This assumption is defendable on the grounds that (1) effective arbitrage would see to it that traded goods prices are equalized in the integrated world, and (2) the relative price changes between traded and non-traded goods can be ignored when we realize that even for the goods that are not traded, the factors used to build them, in a sense, can be traded. Thus, if the barber does not obtain hourly earnings comparable to the domestic wheat exporter, he/she will switch to the higher-paying job of producing traded goods. Also, the prices of traded and non-traded goods are linked on the demand-side through consumers' tastes.

Once again, the reasonableness of the assumptions is dependent on the theory's concern with the long run.

The concentration on the absolute, rather than relative, price level is a notable point of departure from the Humean monetary approach that long preceded Keynes. In Hume, the domestic price level can vary from purchasing power parity due to stock disequilibrium in the domestic money market. Such a variation in relative price levels gives rise to changes in trade flows, which affect the balance of payments, and hence the domestic money stock in the long run. The monetary approach, on the other hand, often relies on the excess demand for money to directly affect the overall balance rather than via a change in relative price levels. It should be pointed out that both the Humean adjustment process and the monetary approach have the same implications with respect to the price level in the long run.

According to the monetary as well as the absorption approach, accumulation or decumulation of assets depends on the aggregate relationship between domestic expenditure and income rather than on the composition of expenditure between exportables and importables or between goods that, given the price structure, are classified into tradable and non-tradable goods. Consequently, though relative prices influence the composition of expenditures, they play a secondary or negligible role in the monetary approach (as in the absorption approach). On the other hand, in the monetary approach, the general price level plays a central role since it equalizes the real value of existing nominal assets (money and possibly fixed-interest debt traded internationally) with the corresponding real demand for them. It should be noted that, contrary to the monetary approach, the absorption approach either ignores the price level or assumes the price level to be constant.

Under fixed exchange rates, a small country controls neither its price level nor quantity of domestic money in anything but the short run. Its money supply is endogenous, and what it controls by open market operations is simply the international component of the monetary base. In a system of flexible exchange rates, the focus of analysis shifts from determination of the balance of payments to the determination of the exchange rate.

The preceding pages present a review of the three major approaches to the balance of payments—elasticities, absorption, and monetary. Ignoring capital flows, the three views can be summarized with the following equations:

Y = real income
*D*H = change in the quantity of money demanded

$DD$ = domestic credit creation

BT = X − IM (Elasticities) (3)

BT = Y − E (Absorption) (4)

BT = $DH - DD$ (Monetary) (5)

where the "italic D," that is, *D*, appearing in front of a variable designates the "change" in that variable. That is, *D* is the first difference operator: $DX = X_{(t)} - X_{(t-1)}$.

Mundell (1968) cautions that the three approaches are all correct and assert identical propositions, even if capital movements are included when all variables are defined as ex post, realized entities. This can be shown by the following three equations:

$DR$ = increase in international reserves

$DK$ = net capital outflow

Y = E + BT (6)

$DH = DD + DR$ (7)

$DR$ = BT − $DK$ (8)

From national income accounting, we have equation (6); from banking accounts, equation (7) follows; balance of payments accounts give us equation (8). The ex post identity of the three approaches is seen when we note that:

$DR$ = BT − $DK$ = Y − E − $DK$ = $DH - DD$ (9)

Though it is true that "an improvement in the balance of payments must imply an increase in Y–E–*DK*, an increase in *DR*, an increase in *DH*–*DD* provides additional checks on the logic of balance of payment policies," it should be remembered that the assumptions behind the three approaches differ. So do their views of the process of adjustment in the balance of payments. Differences in the approaches become apparent when we conceive of the categories as ex ante—that is, as representative of intentions.

### *d. Summary*

This section reviewed three alternative theories of balance of payments adjustments. These theories were the elasticities and absorption approaches (associated with Keynesian theory) and the monetary approach. In the elasticities and absorption approaches, the focus of attention is on the trade balance with unemployed resources. The elasticities approach emphasizes the role of the relative prices (or exchange rate) in balance of payments adjustments by considering imports and exports as being dependent on relative prices (through the exchange rate). The absorption approach emphasizes the role of income (or expenditure) in balance of payments adjustments by considering the change in expenditure relative to income resulting from a change in exports and/or imports. In the monetary approach, on the other hand, the focus of attention is on the balance of payments (or the money account) with full employment. The monetary approach emphasizes the role of the demand for and supply of money in the economy.

## Conclusion

The second section provided an example of the current prominent controversies in mainstream academic economics. Other examples, such as controversies on the efficient market and the capital asset pricing theories, are Haugen (1995) and Shanken and Smith (1996), who provide two alternate views. Brav and Heaton (2002) show that both the "rational finance" and the "behavioral finance," despite their differing theoretical foundations, share remarkable mathematical and predictive similarities and differ mainly in the labels they attach to similar modeling techniques and in the interpretations they give to resulting predictions. In academic finance, Bettner, Robinson, and McGoun (1994) show that indeed the mainstream academic finance is based in the functionalist paradigm. In other words, theories and controversies in mainstream academic finance, despite their apparent diversity, are founded on the functionalist paradigm.

These and other controversies in mainstream academic economics and finance are the natural outcome of the progress within a paradigm. They are all based on the same basic and fundamental assumptions that define the paradigm. Furthermore, they use similar metaphors, which are the products of the same paradigm. Even when these different schools of thought tend to debate each other's metaphors, they do not debate the fundamental assumptions of their common paradigm.

Any adequate analysis of the role of paradigms in social theory must recognize the assumptions that underwrite that paradigm or worldview. Social theory can usefully be conceived in terms of four key paradigms: functionalist, interpretive, radical humanist, and radical structuralist. The four paradigms are founded upon different views of the social world. Each generates theories, concepts, analytical tools, and controversies that are different from those of the other paradigms.

Most mainstream academic economics theories are located within the bounds of the functionalist paradigm. They leave the other paradigms unexplored. Despite the apparent diversity in theories, the issues that separate them are of minor significance. The larger issues are rarely discussed, lying hidden beneath the commonality of perspectives and assumptions.

Knowledge of economics is ultimately a product of the researcher's paradigmatic approach to this multifaceted phenomenon. Viewed from this angle, the pursuit of economic knowledge can be seen as much an ethical, moral, ideological, and political activity as a technical one. Academic economics can gain much by exploiting the new insights coming from other paradigms.

## Notes

1 See Morgan (1980) for a discussion of paradigms, metaphors, and puzzle solving.

2 For discussions and examples of metaphors in finance, such as: "abnormal return," "market for corporate control," and "signaling," see Bettner, Robinson, and McGoun (1994) and Frankfurter and McGoun (1993, 1995). For discussions and examples of other metaphors, such as "efficiency," "system," "asset pricing," "equilibrium," "structure," "hierarchy," "work," "leisure," "scarcity," and "profitability," see Burrell and Morgan (1979) and Morgan (1980).

3 For this literature, see Alexander (1968); Bickerdike (1920); Collery (1971); Frenkel and Johnson (1976); Johnson (1958, 1976, 1972); Kindleberger (1973); Kreinin and Officer (1978); Magee (1976); McClosky and Zecher (1976); Mundell (1968); Mussa (1974, 1976); Robinson (1950); and Whitman (1975).

## References

Alexander, Sidney (1952), "Effects of a Devaluation on a Trade Balance," *International Monetary Fund Staff Papers*, 2:2, April, 263–78.

Bettner, M.S., Robinson C., and McGoun E. (1994), "The Case for Qualitative Research in Finance," *International Review of Financial Analysis*, 3:1, 1–18.

Bickerdike, C.F. (1920), "The Instability of Foreign Exchange," *Economic Journal*, 30, March, 118–22.

Brav, A. and Heaton, J.B. (2002), "Competing Theories of Financial Anomalies," *Review of Financial Studies*, 15:2, 575–606.

Burrell, G. and Morgan, G. (1979), *Sociological Paradigms and Organizational Analysis*, Hants: Gower Publishing Company Limited.

Collery, Arnold (1971), "International Adjustment, Open Economies, and the Quantity Theory of Money," *Princeton Studies in International Finance*, 28, June, Princeton University Press.

Frankfurter, G.M. and McGoun, E.G. (1993), "The Event Study: An Industrial Strength Method," *International Review of Financial Analysis*, 2:2, 121–41.

Frankfurter, G.M. and McGoun, E.G. (1995), "The Event Study: Is It Either?," *Journal of Investing*, 4:2, 8–16.

Frenkel, Jacob and Johnson, Harry G. (1976), "The Monetary Approach to the Balance of Payments: Essential Concepts and Historical Origins," in Frenkel, Jacob and Johnson, Harry G. (eds.), *The Monetary Approach to the Balance of Payments*, Toronto, Canada, and Buffalo, NY: University of Toronto Press, 1–25.

Haugen, R.A. (1995), *The New Finance: The Case against Efficient Markets*, Upper-Saddle River, NJ: Prentice Hall.

Johnson, Harry G. (1958), "Towards a General Theory of the Balance of Payments," in Johnson, Harry G. (ed.), *International Trade and Economic Growth*, London: George Allen and Unwin. Reprinted in Frenkel, Jacob and Johnson, Harry G., eds. (1976), *The Monetary Approach to the Balance of Payments*, Toronto, and Buffalo, NY: University of Toronto Press, 153–68.

Johnson, Harry G. (1972), "The Monetary Approach to Balance of Payments Theory," *Journal of Financial and Quantitative Analysis*, Papers and Proceedings, 7, March, 1555–72.

Kindleberger, Charles (1973), *International Economics*, Homewood, IL: Richard D. Irwin, Inc.

Kreinin, Mordechai E. and Officer, Lawrence H. (1978), "The Monetary Approach to the Balance of Payments: A Survey," *Princeton Studies in International Finance*, 43, November, 3–4.

Magee, Stephen (1976), "The Empirical Evidence on the Monetary Approach to the Balance of Payments and Exchange Rates," *American Economic Review: Papers and Proceedings*, 66:2, May, 163–70.

McCloskey, Donald and Zecher, Richard (1976), "How the Gold Standard Worked, 1880–1913," in Frenkel, Jacob and Johnson, Harry G. (eds.), *The Monetary Approach to the Balance of Payments*, Toronto, and Buffalo, NY: University of Toronto Press, 357–85.

Morgan, G. (1980), "Paradigm, Metaphors, and Puzzle Solving in Organization Theory," *Administrative Science Quarterly*, 25:4, December, 605–22.

Mundell, Robert A. (1968), "Balance of Payments," in Sills, David L. (ed.), *International Encyclopedia of the Social Sciences*, Vol. 8, NY: Crowell Collier and Macmillan, Inc, 1–11.

Mussa, Michael (1974), "A Monetary Approach to Balance of Payments Analysis," *Journal of Money, Credit and Banking*, 6:3, August, 333–51.

Mussa, Michael (1976), "Tariffs and the Balance of Payments: A Monetary Approach," in Frenkel, Jacob and Johnson, Harry G. (eds.), (1976), *The Monetary Approach to the Balance of Payments*, Toronto, and Buffalo, NY, University of Toronto Press, 187–221.

Robinson, Joan (1950), "The Foreign Exchanges," in Ellis, Howard and Metzler, Lloyd (eds.), *Readings in the Theory of International Trade*, Homewood, IL: Irwin, 157–76.

Shanken, J. and Smith, C.W. (1996), "Implications of Capital Markets Research for Corporate Finance," *Financial Management*, 25:1, 98–104.

Whitman, Marina V.N. (1975), "Global Monetarism and the Monetary Approach to the Balance of Payments," *Brookings Papers on Economic Activity*, 3, 491–536.

# 3

# Human Nature

## A Multi-Paradigmatic View

Any explanation of human nature is based on a worldview. The premise of this book is that any worldview can be associated with one of the four broad paradigms: functionalist, interpretive, radical humanist, and radical structuralist. This chapter takes the case of human nature and discusses it from the four different viewpoints. It emphasizes that the four views expressed are equally scientific and informative; they look at the phenomenon from their certain paradigmatic viewpoint; and together they provide a more balanced understanding of the phenomenon under consideration. In this chapter, the first through the fourth sections present the four perspectives, and the fifth section concludes the chapter.

## Functionalist View

The "economic" approach can be used to understand human behavior in a variety of contexts and situations. The intention here is to spell out the principal attributes of the economic approach that distinguish it from sociological, psychological, anthropological, political, and genetical approaches to the understanding of human behavior.[1]

It is helpful to start with the definitions of different fields. For economics, there are at least three definitions that are conflicting. Economics is defined as the study of: (1) the allocation of material goods to satisfy material wants, (2) the market sector, and (3) the allocation of scarce means to satisfy competing ends.

The definition of economics that is based on material goods is the narrowest and least satisfactory. This is because it does not adequately describe the market sector. For instance, recently in the United States, the production of tangible goods has provided less than half of all market employment, and the intangible outputs of the service sector have been larger in value than the outputs of the goods sector. In addition, economists have been as successful in understanding the supply and demand for retail trade, films, or education as they have been for those of autos or meat. The persistence of the definition of economics which is based on material goods might be due to a reluctance to subject certain types of human behavior to the "frigid" calculus of economics.

The definition of economics that is based on scarce means and competing ends is the most general one. It defines economics with reference to the nature of the problem to be solved and goes far beyond the market sector. Scarcity and choice characterize all resource allocation problems faced by politicians (e.g., which industries to tax, how fast to increase the money supply, and whether a war should be initiated); by families (e.g., decisions about a marriage mate, family size, the frequency of church attendance, and the allocation of time between sleeping and waking hours); by scientists (e.g., decisions about allocating their thinking time and allocating mental energy to different research problems); and by many others.

These most common definitions of economics simply define the scope of economics, and none of them specify what the "economic" approach is. For instance, they do not specify whether the "economic" approach stresses tradition and duty, impulsive behavior, maximizing behavior, or any other human behavior when analyzing the market sector or the allocation of scarce means to competing ends.

Similarly, definitions of sociology and other social sciences do not distinguish their approaches from others. For instance, the definition of sociology as "the study of social aggregates and groups in their institutional organization, of institutions and their organization, and of causes and consequences of changes in institutions and social organization" distinguishes neither the subject matter nor the approach of sociology from other social sciences, such as economics. Or the definition of comparative psychology as being "concerned with the behavior of different species of living organisms" is as general as the definitions of economics and sociology.

Therefore, the focus of attention should be turned away from definition and be placed on approach. This is because what most distinguishes the discipline of economics from other disciplines in the social sciences is not its subject matter but its approach. As a matter of fact, various types of behavior are studied by several disciplines. For instance, fertility behavior falls within the subject matter of sociology, anthropology, economics, history, and politics. The unique power of the economic approach is that it can integrate a wide range of human behavior.

The economic approach assumes maximizing behavior and consequently maximizes the utility or wealth function of the household, firm, union, and government bureau. In addition, the economic approach assumes that markets exist and that, with varying degrees of efficiency, they coordinate the actions of different market participants—individuals, firms, and nations—such that their behavior becomes consistent. Moreover, since economists are not aware of how preferences are formed, they assume that preferences are stable, that is, preferences do not change substantially over time, preferences are not very different between wealthy and poor persons, and preferences are not very different among persons raised in different societies and cultures. Prices and other market instruments that allocate the scarce resources within an economy act as constraints on the desires of participants and coordinate their actions. In the economic approach, these market instruments perform most, if not all, of the functions that "structure" performs in sociological theories.

The assumed stable preferences are not defined with respect to market goods and services—for example, oranges, automobiles, or medical care—but, are defined with respect to underlying objects of choice that each household produces by the use of a combination of their own time, market goods and services, and other inputs. These underlying preferences are defined with respect to fundamental aspects of life—for example, health, prestige, sensual pleasure, benevolence, or envy—that do not always hold a stable relation to market goods and services. The assumed stable preferences provide a stable foundation for making predictions about human responses to various changes and help the analyst avoid postulating a shift in preferences to "explain" apparent contradictions to his predictions.

The economic approach relentlessly uses the combination of the following three assumptions: maximizing behavior, market equilibrium, and stable preferences. The economic approach uses these assumptions in order to produce many of its theorems. Some such theorems are: (1) an increase in price, decreases quantity demanded, for example, an increase in the market price of eggs decreases the quantity demanded for eggs; an increase in the "shadow" price of children decreases the quantity demanded for children; and an increase in the office waiting time for physicians—which is one of the constitutive components of the full price of physician services—decreases the quantity demanded for their services; (2) an increase in price, increases the quantity supplied, for example, an increase in the market price of beef increases the number of cattle raised and slaughtered; an increase in the wage rate offered to married women increases their labor force participation; and a decrease in "cruising" time increases the effective price received by taxicab drivers and thereby increases the supply of taxicabs; (3) competitive markets satisfy consumer preferences more effectively than monopolistic markets, for example, in the market for aluminum; and in the market for ideas; and (4) a tax on the output of a market decreases that output, for example, an excise tax on gasoline decreases the use of gasoline; punishment of criminals (which is a "tax" on crime) decreases the amount of crime; and a tax on wages decreases the labor supplied to the labor market.

The economic approach is not restricted to either material goods and wants, or the market sector. Prices—whether they are the money prices of the market sector or the "shadow" imputed prices of the non-market sector—represent the opportunity cost of using scarce resources, and the economic approach predicts the same type of reaction to shadow prices as to market prices. For instance, a utility-maximizing person whose only scarce resource is his limited amount of time can use this time to produce various commodities that enter his preference function. In the absence of a market sector, each commodity has a marginal "shadow" price, that is, the time required to produce an additional unit of that commodity. In equilibrium, the ratio of these "shadow" prices must equal the ratio of the marginal utilities of the corresponding goods or services. Most importantly, as per the prediction of the economic approach, an increase in the relative price of any commodity—that is, an increase in the time required to produce a unit of that commodity—decreases the consumption of that commodity.

The economic approach does not assume that all market participants necessarily have complete information or engage in costless transactions. The economic approach has led to a theory of the optimal or rational accumulation of costly information that implies, for instance, that market participants make greater investments in information when they undertake major decisions—for example, when they intend to purchase a house or enter into marriage versus when they intend to purchase a sofa or bread.

When a firm, worker, or household does not exploit an apparently profitable opportunity, the economic approach does not resort to irrationality, contentment with wealth already acquired, or a shift in values (i.e., preferences). Instead, the economic approach postulates the existence of monetary or psychic costs—costs that are not easily observable by outsiders—of taking advantage of these opportunities that eliminate the apparent profitability of such opportunities. In fact, postulating the existence of costs closes or "completes" the economic approach in the same way that postulating the existence of (sometimes unobserved) uses of energy "completes" and preserves the law of the conservation of energy. Systems of analysis in chemistry, genetics, and other fields are completed similarly.

The economic approach does not necessarily assume that decision-makers are either conscious of their maximization efforts or can describe the reasons for their systematic patterns of behavior. Thus, the economic approach is consistent with both modern psychology—that emphasizes the subconscious—and sociology—that distinguishes between manifest and latent functions. Furthermore, the economic approach does not distinguish between major and minor decisions—for example, decisions with respect to life and death versus decisions with respect to a brand of coffee—or between decisions involving strong emotions and decisions involving little emotions—for example, decisions with respect to choosing a mate or the number of children versus decisions with respect to buying paint—or between decisions made by persons with different income, education, or family background.

The economic approach is a comprehensive approach because it is applicable to all human behavior, for example, the behavior involving money prices or imputed shadow prices; repeated or infrequent decisions; large or minor decisions; emotional or mechanical ends; rich or poor persons; men or women; adults or children; brilliant or stupid persons; patients or therapists; businessmen or politicians; and teachers or students. The applications of the economic approach are as broad as the scope of economics as defined by the allocation of scarce means to competing ends.

The economic approach to human behavior has a long history. Adam Smith frequently used the economic approach to understand political behavior. Jeremy Bentham explicitly expressed his belief that the pleasure-pain calculus is applicable to all human behavior. According to Bentham, pleasure and pain are two sovereign masters that govern mankind. They determine what man ought to do, as well as what man shall do. They govern man in all he does, says, and thinks—without restriction to monetary decisions, repetitive choices, unimportant decisions, etc. Bentham applied his pleasure-pain calculus to a wide range of human behavior, for example, criminal sanctions, prison reform, legislation, usury laws, and jurisprudence, as well as the markets for goods and services.

The economic approach has been applied to understand racial discrimination, fertility, education, use of time, crime, marriage, child-rearing, labor force participation, social interactions, evolution of language, church attendance, capital punishment, legal system, extinction of animals, incidence of suicide, and other "sociological," "legal," and "political" problems. The rapid growth of the related work has shown that the economic approach is indeed applicable to all human behavior.

For example, with respect to intellectual and artistic careers, the economic approach reasons that people choose to follow scholarly or other intellectual or artistic pursuits only if they expect the benefits—both monetary and psychic—would exceed those of alternative occupations. Since the criterion that people apply to the choice of an intellectual and artistic career is the same as the criterion that they apply to the choice of other occupations, there is no reason to believe that intellectuals would be less concerned with personal rewards, be more concerned with social well-being, or be more honest than others. Furthermore, according to the economic approach, when there is an increase in demand by different interest groups or constituencies for particular intellectual arguments and conclusions, then there would be an increase in the supply of these types of arguments. This reasoning is based on the economic theorem that an increase in price leads to an increase in quantity supplied. Similarly, the economic approach predicts that a flow of funds from a foundation or government into particular research topics—even "ill-advised" topics—would generate more proposals for research on those same topics. This reasoning, again, is based on the economic theorem that an increase in price leads to an increase in quantity supplied.

As for another example, good health and a long life are important aims for most people, but they are not the only aims. Therefore, somewhat better health or somewhat longer life may be given up in exchange for other aims. According to the economic approach, a person has an "optimal" expected length of life, at which the utility of an additional year of life is less than the utility forgone by using time and other resources to obtain that year. For instance, a person may continue his heavy smoking habit because the lifespan forfeited is not worth the cost to him of quitting smoking.

The economic approach recognizes that many non-economic variables also significantly affect human behavior. For instance, the laws of mathematics, chemistry, physics, and biology tremendously affect human behavior through their effect on preferences and production possibilities. The economic approach acknowledges that the human body ages, that the rate of population growth equals the birth rate plus the migration rate minus the death rate, that children of more intelligent parents tend to be more intelligent than children of less intelligent parents, that people need to breathe to live, that a hybrid plant has a particular yield under one set of environmental conditions and a very different yield under another set, that gold and oil are located only in certain parts of the world and cannot be made from wood, that an assembly line operates according to certain physical laws, etc. The economic approach recognizes that all of these and many more factors influence choices, the production of people and goods, and the evolution of societies.

This does not mean, for instance, that the rate of population growth is "non-economic" because birth rate, migration rate, and death rate cannot be analyzed by the economic approach. Similarly, the above does not mean that the rate of adoption of new hybrid corn is "non-economic" because it cannot be examined by the economic approach. As a matter of fact, the application of the economic approach has had useful implications about the number of children in different families by assuming that families maximize their utility from stable preferences subject to prices and their resources. Where, prices and resources are partly determined by the gestation period for pregnancies, the abilities of children, and other non-economic variables. Similarly, the rate of adoption of hybrid corn in different parts of the United States has been explained by assuming that farmers maximize profits. That is, the new hybrid corn was more profitable and was adopted earlier in some parts of the country because weather, soil, and other physical conditions were more favorable.

The economic approach not only uses many non-economic variables for understanding human behavior but also benefits from the contributions of other fields, such as sociology, psychology, socio-biology, history, anthropology, political science, and law. The economic approach provides a useful framework for understanding all human behavior, but it does not intend either to downgrade the contributions of other social scientists or to suggest that the contributions of economists are more important. For instance, the economic approach assumes that preferences are both given and stable, and on this basis makes predictions. It recognizes that such preferences are analyzed by the sociologist, psychologist, and the socio-biologist. How preferences are formed, and how slowly they evolve over time, are obviously important in predicting and understanding behavior.

The economic approach provides a useful unified framework for understanding all human behavior. According to the economic approach, all human behavior can be viewed as involving utility maximization based on a stable set of preferences that would lead to the accumulation of an optimal amount of information and other inputs in a variety of markets. Of course, much behavior has not yet been explained by the economic approach. Furthermore, non-economic variables and the techniques and findings from other fields contribute significantly to the understanding of human behavior. That is, although the economic approach has provided a comprehensive framework, many of the important concepts and techniques are provided and will continue to be provided by other disciplines.

## Interpretive View

The Enlightenment viewed man as wholly of a piece with nature and complying with the general uniformity of composition which Baconian and Newtonian natural science had discovered there. That is, there is a human nature which is regularly organized, thoroughly invariant, and marvelously simple as Newton's universe. Some of its laws may be different, but there are laws; some of its regularities may be obscured by the trappings of local fashion, but it is regular. Men are men under any guise and against any backdrop.[2]

According to the Enlightenment view, all the differences among men, in beliefs and values, in customs and institutions, both over time and across place, do not play any role in defining human nature. These differences are nothing but mere accretions, distortions, overlaying, and obscuring the truth in human nature: the constant, the general, and the universal. In general, anything of which the intelligibility, verifiability, or actual affirmation is limited to men of a special age, race, temperament, tradition, or condition lacks truth, value, or importance to a reasonable man.

In contrast to the Enlightenment type of view, a constant human nature independent of time, place, circumstance, studies and professions, transient fashions, and temporary opinions does not exist. What man is, indeed, depends on where he is, who he is, and what he believes, because man is so entangled with them and so is inseparable from them. These considerations have given rise to the cultural view of man, which stands in contrast to the uniformitarian view of man. The former strongly believes that men unmodified by the customs of their particular places do not exist, have never existed, and cannot exist. To use the metaphor of performing actors, there is, and there can be, no backstage where one can go to see the "real persons" who are relaxing in their casual clothes and are disengaged from their profession, displaying their spontaneous desires and unprompted passions. This is because they only change their roles, their styles of acting, and their play's drama; that is, they are always performing.

This makes the distinction between what is natural, universal, and constant in man and what is conventional, local, and variable extraordinarily difficult. Any attempt to make such a distinction falsifies the human situation. What can one conclude about human nature from the thousand peculiar things that people in different cultures do, which anthropologists discover, investigate, and describe? That people living in a specific culture are peculiar? That they are just the same as other people living in totally different cultures, but with some peculiar and incidental customs? That they are innately different or instinctively led in certain directions rather than others? Or, that human nature does not exist; and men are pure, and they are simply what their culture makes them?

All of these interpretations are unsatisfactory. A more viable concept of man would take into account not only culture and the variability of culture but also the basic unity of mankind. This more viable concept of man would not totally leave the uniformitarian view of human nature. It, at the same time, would not adhere to the idea that the diversity of customs across time and space is not a mere matter of garb and appearance and of stage settings and comedic masques, because such adherence would mean that human nature is as various in its essence as it is in its expression.

Attempts to locate man within his customs have taken several directions and have followed diverse tactics. But, almost all of them have proceeded along a single overall intellectual strategy, which may be called the "stratigraphic" conception of the relations between biological, psychological, social, and cultural factors in human life. In this conception, man is composed of several "levels," each of which is superimposed upon those beneath it, and, at the same time, underpins those above it. In the analysis of man, these layers are peeled off one after another. Each of these layers is complete and irreducible in itself. After one layer is peeled off, underneath it is another layer, which is of a quite different type. Beneath the layer designated for the motley forms of culture, there is the layer designated for structural and functional regularities of social organization. After these two layers are peeled off, there is the layer designated for the underlying psychological factors—that is, "basic needs"—that support them and make them possible. After the layer for psychological factors is peeled off, there is the layer designated for the biological foundations—that is, anatomical, physiological, and neurological—of the whole edifice of human life.

This type of conceptualization not only has guaranteed the independence and sovereignty of established academic disciplines but also has avoided stating that man's culture is all there is to him and has stated that culture is an essential, irreducible, and paramount ingredient in his nature. According to this type of conceptualization, cultural facts can be interpreted against the background of non-cultural facts, without either dissolving cultural facts into that background or dissolving that background into the cultural facts. In this conceptualization, man is a hierarchically stratified being, and at each of his various levels—organic, psychological, social, and cultural—he has an assigned and incontestable place. In order to see what he really is, it is necessary to superimpose findings from the various relevant sciences—anthropology, sociology, psychology, and biology—upon one another. When this is done, the cultural level, which is distinctive to man, would contribute, in its own right, to the understanding of what man really is. In this way, the eighteenth-century image of man as pure "reasoner"—that is, when he took off his cultural costumes—was replaced, in the late nineteenth and early twentieth centuries—by the image of man as the stratified being—that is, when he put on his cultural costumes.

This grand strategy, at the level of concrete research and specific analysis, translates into two steps. First, a search for universals in culture, that is, for empirical uniformities that, despite the diversity of customs across time and space, can be found everywhere in almost the same form. Second, relating such universals in culture to the established constants of human biology, psychology, and social organization. If some customs can be found as common to all local variants of it, and if these can then be related in a determinate manner with certain invariant points of reference on the subcultural levels, then progress can be made toward specifying which cultural traits are essential to human existence and which are merely adventitious, peripheral, or ornamental. In this way, cultural dimensions of a concept of man can be determined such that they are commensurate with dimensions similarly determined by biology, psychology, and sociology.

Of course, this is not a new idea. It is the notion of a "consensus gentium" (a consensus of all mankind), which states that there are some things that all men agree upon as right, real, just, or attractive, and, therefore, in fact, these things are right, real, just, or attractive. This notion was present in the Enlightenment, and perhaps, some form of it has been present in all ages. The question is whether this research project would work.

The answer depends on whether it is possible to establish and sustain the dualism between empirically universal aspects of culture rooted in subcultural realities, on the one hand, and empirically variable aspects of culture not rooted in subcultural realities, on the other hand. This requires: (1) that the universals can be found and that they be substantial; (2) that they be closely and directly intertwined with particular biological, psychological, or sociological processes; and (3) that they can be defended as core elements in the characterization of human nature such that the much more numerous cultural particularities are of secondary importance. On all of these three counts, the "consensus gentium" approach fails. That is, rather than moving closer to the essentials of human nature, it moves away from it.

The major reason for the search for universals and shying away from cultural particularities in defining human nature is that the enormous variation in human behavior haunts them with a fear of historicism, of becoming lost in cultural relativism that deprives them of any fixed bearings at all. The notion that only an empirically universal cultural phenomenon can reflect something about the nature of man is not logical. This is because this notion has the same logic as the notion that because sickle-cell anemia is, fortunately, not universal, it cannot tell us anything about human genetic processes. In science, what is critically important is not whether phenomena are empirically common, but whether phenomena can reveal the enduring natural processes that underlie them. For instance, this is why Becquerel had been so interested in the peculiar behavior of uranium.

Therefore, there should be a search for systematic relationships among diverse phenomena, instead of a search for substantive identities among similar ones. For this purpose, the "stratigraphic" conception of the relationships among the various aspects of human existence should be replaced with a synthetic one. In this one, biological, psychological, sociological, and cultural factors are treated as variables within unitary systems of analysis. This does not mean that the establishment of a common language in the social sciences is either a matter of coordination of terminologies or of creating new ones, or that it is a matter of imposing one set of categories upon the whole area. But it is a matter of integrating different types of theories and concepts in order to formulate meaningful propositions embodying findings that are now compartmentalized in separate fields of study.

In order for such an integration to provide a more accurate image of man, it would be useful to account for the following two ideas. The first idea is that culture should be viewed not as complexes of concrete behavior patterns—customs, usages, traditions, habit clusters—as has been done up to now, but as a set of control mechanisms—plans, recipes, rules, instructions (or "programs," as in the parlance of computer engineers)—for the governing of behavior. The second idea is that man is most desperately dependent upon such cultural programs that would act as extra-genetic, outside-the-skin control mechanisms for ordering his behavior.

The "control mechanism" view of culture assumes that the foundation of human thought is both social and public. That is, the natural habitat of human thought is the house yard, the marketplace, and the town square. Thinking does not consist of "happenings in the head," although what happens in the head and elsewhere are necessary for thinking to occur. Thinking consists of traffic in "significant symbols"—that is, words (for the most part), gestures, drawings, musical sounds, mechanical devices (e.g., clocks), or natural objects (e.g., jewels). These significant symbols are, indeed, composed of anything that is disengaged from its mere actuality and used to impose meaning upon experience. Each individual takes such symbols as given. When the individual is born, he finds such symbols already current in the community. During his life, some of the existing symbols remain in place, some of the existing symbols are partially altered, some of the existing symbols are discarded, and some new symbols are added. The individual may or may not have had a role in these changes. After the individual dies, these symbols remain in circulation with their relevant changes. During his life, the individual uses some or all of the symbols either deliberately and with care, or spontaneously and with ease. The individual always uses the symbols to put a construction upon the events of his life and to orient himself with respect to his life experiences.

Man needs these symbolic sources of illumination in order to find his bearings in the world. This is because the non-symbolic sources, which are constituted in his body, provide only a diffused light. For lower animals, their behavior patterns, to a much larger extent, are given to them by their physical structure. Their genetic sources of information order their behavior within much limited ranges of variation. The narrower and more completely their behavior is determined by the genetic sources, the lower the animal. For man, on the other hand, genetic sources provide only extremely general response capacities. Although these innately given capacities allow for far greater plasticity, complexity, and effectiveness of behavior (under certain perfect conditions), they leave human behavior much less precisely regulated. Therefore, if man's behavior is undirected by culture patterns—that is, organized systems of significant symbols—it would be virtually ungovernable. There will be a mere chaos of pointless acts and exploding emotions, such that man's experience will be virtually shapeless. Culture, the accumulated totality of such symbolic patterns, is not merely an ornament of human existence but the principal basis of the specificity of human existence; that is, culture is an essential condition for human existence.

The most crucial support for such cultural position comes from recent advances in knowledge and evidence with respect to the emergence of "Homo sapiens" out of his general primate background. Of these advances, three are most important: (1) the replacement of a sequential view of the relations between the physical evolution and the cultural development of man with an overlap or interactive view; (2) the discovery that the major biological changes that produced modern man out of his most immediate progenitors took place in his central nervous system and most especially in his brain; (3) the understanding that, in physical terms, man is an incomplete and unfinished animal; that what distinguishes him most graphically from non-men is not so much his sheer ability to learn (great as that is), but how much and what specifically he has to learn before he is enabled to function. Let me take each of these points in turn.

The traditional view of the relations between the biological and the cultural advance of man was that at some point in time the biological development was completed and exactly at that time the cultural development began. According to the evidence, such a moment in time did not exist. The transition to the cultural mode of life took the genus Homo more than one million years to accomplish. Over such a long period of time, complex and closely ordered sequences of genetic changes took place.

In the current view, the evolution of "Homo sapiens"—that is, modern man—from his immediate pre-sapiens counterpart started nearly two million years ago with the emergence of Australopithecines—that is, the ape men of southern and eastern Africa—and culminated with the appearance of sapiens himself one to two hundred thousand years ago. Thus, as at least basic forms of cultural, or proto-cultural, activity (e.g., simple toolmaking and hunting) were present among some of the Australopithecines, there was an overlap of more than one million years between the beginning of culture and the appearance of the current man. This overlap was an extended one. The final phases (i.e., final as of today) of the phylogenetic development of man took place in the same grand geological era—that is, Ice Age—as the initial phases of his cultural development.

This means that culture was not added to a finished animal but was a crucial ingredient in the production process of that animal itself. The slow and steady growth of culture through the Ice Age played a major directive role in man's evolution. The development of tools, the adoption of organized hunting and gathering practices, the beginnings of true family organization, the discovery of fire, and the increasing use of systems of significant symbols (language, art, myth, ritual) for orientation, communication, and self-control all created a new environment for man, who had to adapt to them. As culture slowly accumulated and developed, an advantage was given to those individuals in the community who were most able to benefit from it—for example, the effective hunter, the persistent gatherer, the adept toolmaker, and the resourceful leader—until the small-brained, proto-human "Homo Australopithecus" became the large-brained, fully human "Homo sapiens." Among the cultural pattern, the body, and the brain, a feedback system came into being such that each shaped the progress of the other. For instance, in this system, the interaction among increasing tool use, the changing anatomy of the hand, and the expanding representation of the thumb on the cortex represents how the feedback system worked. By adopting symbolically mediated programs for producing artifacts, organizing social life, or expressing emotions, man determined, perhaps unknowingly, the final stages of his own biological development. Quite literally, but quite inadvertently, man created himself.

This suggests that human nature is not independent of culture. As man's central nervous system—and most particularly its crowning curse and glory, the neo-cortex—developed in great part in interaction with culture, it cannot direct man's behavior or organize his experience without the guidance generated by systems of significant symbols. In the Ice Age, man was obliged to replace the regularity and precision of detailed genetic control over his conduct with the flexibility and adaptability of a more generalized genetic control over his conduct. To receive the additional information that was necessary to be enabled to act, man was forced to increasingly rely on cultural sources—that is, the accumulated significant symbols. Thus, such symbols are not mere expressions, instrumentalities, or correlates of man's biological, psychological, and social existence; but, they are prerequisites for it. Without men, there is no culture; and without culture, there are no men. Men are incomplete animals who complete themselves through culture, and they complete themselves not through culture in general but through highly particular forms of it. Men's ideas, values, acts, emotions, and nervous systems are cultural products, products which are manufactured out of tendencies, capacities, and dispositions with which men were born, but manufactured, nonetheless.

## Radical Humanist View

Man is a recognizable and ascertainable being. Man has an entity that is not only biological, anatomical, and physiological, but also psychological. Human nature is not identical to the specific expression of human nature that is prevalent in the society in which he lives. That is, human nature in general is not identical to the human nature that is modified in each historical period. The concept of human nature is not an abstraction. The essence of man is not identical to the various forms of his historical existence. The essence of man is not an abstraction and is inherent in each individual.[3]

In line with this distinction between general human nature and the specific expression of human nature in each culture, a distinction can be made between two types of human drives and appetites: (1) the constant or fixed appetites—for example, hunger and sexual urge—that are an integral part of human nature, and only their form and direction can be changed in various cultures; and (2) the "relative" appetites, which are not an integral part of human nature but whose origin is in specific social structures and specific conditions of production and communication. For instance, in the capitalistic structure of society, the need for money is the need created by the modern economy, and it is the only need that it creates. This is a subjective matter, partly due to the fact that the expansion of production and of needs becomes an ingenious and always calculating subservience to inhuman, depraved, unnatural, and imaginary appetites.

Man's potential is a given potential. Man has always been the human raw material which cannot be changed. However, man changes in the course of history. Man develops himself. Man transforms himself. Man is the product of history. Because man makes his history, he is his own product. History is, indeed, the history of man's self-realization. History is man's self-creation through the process of his work and his production. World history is the creation of man by human labor, and the emergence of human nature. Therefore, man has the evident and irrefutable proof of his self-creation, and of his origins.

The concept of man is rooted in the insight that appearance and essence do not coincide. A dialectical thinker needs to distinguish between the essential and the apparent processes of reality and to grasp their relationship, that is, the relationship between essence and existence. The process of existence entails the realization of the essence, while existing means a return to the essence. When man gains self-consciousness, he learns about the truth of himself and his world. His learning of truth leads to his action, which makes the world what it essentially is, that is, the fulfillment of man's self-consciousness. Knowledge is not obtained in the context of the subject-object split, in which the object of learning is treated as separate from and opposed to the thinker. Man and things are in constant flux. Therefore, a thing is for itself only when it has expressed all its characteristics and made them moments of its self-realization. Thus, in all changing conditions, it is always returning to itself, that is, its essence. This essence is the unity of being and is the identity throughout change. In this process, everything deals with its inherent contradictions and unfolds as a result. Thus, the essence is both historical and ontological. Things realize their essential potentialities in the same process that they establish their existence. The essence can "achieve" its existence when the potentialities of things are realized in and through the conditions of reality. This is the process of transition to actuality. Man is characterized by the "principle of movement." This principle is not mechanical, but it is a man's drive, creative vitality, energy for his object. This emphasizes the active process within man, that is, man's productivity.

A productive man is an individual who is himself because he is not passive-receptive but actively related to the world. This man, through this process, grasps the world productively, and thus makes it his own. The development of an individual's powers, capacities, and potentialities is possible only through continuous action, not by mere contemplation or receptivity. In this productive process, man realizes his essence and returns to his essence.

The concept of productivity, in contrast to that of receptivity, can be understood more easily when it is applied to the phenomenon of love. Assume man is man and his relation to the world is a human one. Accordingly, love can only be exchanged for love, trust for trust, and so on. If a man wishes to influence other people, he must have a stimulating and encouraging effect upon others. Each of his relations to other humans and to nature must correspond to the object of his will, that is, of his real individual life. If his love does not invoke love in return, then his love is impotent and a misfortune. What is of central significance is that the love between man and woman should be regarded as the immediate relationship of human being with human being. If the relationship with woman is expressed as the prey and the handmaid of communal lust, it shows the infinite degradation of man that he has created for himself. This is because the conception of the relation of man to woman underlies the way in which natural species' relationship is conceived. The immediate, natural, and necessary relation of human being to human being is no different from the relation of man with woman. In this natural species' relationship, man's relation with nature is reflective of his relationship with man, and his relation with man is reflective of his relation with nature, that is, with his own natural function. From this relationship, man's extent of development can be assessed. This relationship shows how far man has become, and to what extent he has understood himself as a human being, that is, a species-being. The relation of man with woman is a natural relation that mirror-images that of human being with human being. It shows, therefore, to what extent man's behavior has become human, to what extent his human essence has become a natural essence for him, and to what extent his human nature has become nature for him. It also indicates to what extent man's needs have become human needs, and consequently to what extent other humans, as humans, have constituted his needs, and to what extent his individual existence is congruent with his social being.

To understand the concept of activity, it is of utmost importance to understand the relationship between subject and object. Man's senses, to the extent that they are crude animal senses, have only a limited meaning. For a starving man, the human form of food does not exist, but either the abstract character of food or the crudest form of food exists. And this feeding activity would most likely be very similar to the feeding of animals. The needy man, who is burdened with cares, cannot appreciate the most beautiful spectacle. Man's senses need to be formed by the objects outside of them. Any object can only be the confirmation of one of the faculties of man. This is because in addition to the five senses, there are spiritual senses, the practical senses (e.g., desiring and loving). For a human, the character of his senses comes into being through the existence of an object, that is, through humanized nature. The objects confirm and realize man's individuality. The specific characterization of objects by man's senses depends on the nature of the object and the nature of his corresponding faculty. The distinctive character of each faculty constitutes both its characteristic essence and its characteristic mode of objectification, of its objectively real, living being. Therefore, it is not only in thought, but also through all the senses that man is affirmed in the objective world.

Communism entails the abolition of private property, which means the abolition of human self-alienation, and leads to the real appropriation of human nature through and for man. It is the complete and conscious return of man as a really social human being, who assimilates all the wealth of previous development. Communism as a fully developed naturalism is humanism and as a fully developed humanism is naturalism. It is the complete resolution of the antagonism between man and nature, on the one hand, and between man and man, on the other hand. It is the definitive solution of the conflict between existence and essence, between objectification and self-affirmation, between freedom and necessity, between individual and species. It is the solution of the puzzle of history, and it is aware that it is the solution. This active relationship to the objective world is called "productive life," which is life creating life. In the productive life resides the whole character of a species, that is, its species-character. For human beings, free and conscious activity is the species-character. Where, the "species-character" means the essence of man. It represents that which is universally human and which is realized by man through his productive activity in the process of history.

This concept of human self-realization leads to a new concept of wealth and poverty. In contrast to the wealth and poverty defined in political economy, there is a wealthy man who has plenitude of human needs. The wealthy man is in need of a complex of human manifestations of life, and whose inner necessity and need is his self-realization. In a socialist perspective, both the wealth and the poverty of man acquire a human meaning that translates into a social meaning. Poverty is the passive bond that leads man to feel a need for the greatest wealth, that is, the other person. Man's passion reflects both the expression of the objective entity within him and the sensuous outbreak of his life-activity that becomes the activity of his being. The existence of what a man truly loves—for example, freedom of the press—gives him a feeling of necessity and need, without which his essence cannot be fulfilled, satisfied, and complete.

It is the society that at its beginnings finds—through the development of private property that entails wealth and poverty (both intellectual and material)—the materials necessary for the cultural development of the fully constituted society—that produces man in all the plenitude of his being and the wealthy man endowed with all the senses—as an enduring reality. Society is the only context in which subjectivism and objectivism, spiritualism and materialism, and activity and passivity cease to remain as antinomies. Theoretical contradictions can be resolved only through practical means, that is, only through the practical energy of man. They cannot be resolved through knowledge because they are real problems of life. Philosophy was unable to resolve such problems precisely because it viewed them as purely theoretical problems.

Closely related to the concept of the wealthy man is the conceptual difference between man's sense of having and man's sense of being. Private property has made people so nonsensical and partial that an object is theirs only when they have it, when they use it as capital, or when they directly utilize it, for example, eat it, drink it, wear it, or inhabit it. Private property conceives these forms of possession as means of life, but the life for which they serve as means is the life of private property, that is, labor and the creation of capital. Private property alienates the physical and intellectual senses and replaces these senses with the sense of having. The human being has been reduced to this absolute poverty in order to be enabled to gain access to all his inner wealth.

The science of the capitalistic economy, which is a worldly and pleasure-seeking science, is a truly moral science, which can be regarded as the most moral of all sciences. Its principal thesis is the renunciation of human life and human needs. It states that the less man eats, drinks, buys books, goes to the theater, goes to balls, goes to bars, thinks, loves, theorizes, sings, paints, fences, and so on, the more he will be able to save and the greater will become his treasure, that is, his capital. The less man is, the less he expresses his life, and the more he has, the greater is his alienated life, and the greater is the saving of his alienated being. What the economist takes away from man in the way of human life and humanity, he returns to man in the form of money and wealth. Everything which man is unable to do, his money can do for him: it can eat; drink; go to the ball; go to the theater; travel; and acquire art, learning, historical treasures, and political power. Money can appropriate all these things for man, and it can purchase everything for man, therefore, according to the economist, it is the true opulence. But the point is: although money can do all this for man, its only desire is to create itself and to buy itself; and everything else is subservient to it. When one owns the master, one also owns the servant, but one no longer needs the master's servant. This means that all human passions and activities must be directed toward avarice. The worker must have just what is necessary for him to want to live, and he must want to live only in order to have this.

The aim of society is not the production of useful things as an aim in itself. In other words, maximum production and consumption are not the unquestionable goals of society. This is because the production of too many useful things results in too many useless people. The contradictions between prodigality and thrift, luxury and abstinence, wealth and poverty, are only apparently different, because all these antinomies are truly equivalent. A distinction has to be made between the aim of overcoming the abysmal poverty that interferes with a dignified life, and the aim of an ever-increasing consumption that carries the supreme value for capitalism. The proper position favors the conquest of poverty and is equally against consumption as a supreme end.

Man's independence and freedom are based on his act of self-creation. A man does not regard himself to be independent unless he is his own master, which is when he owes his existence to himself. A man does not regard himself to be independent when he lives by the favor of another man, which is when he owes the other man not only the continuance of his life but also its creation; that is, when the other man is the source of man's life. Man's life necessarily has a source of life outside itself if it is not his own creation. A man is independent only if he affirms his individuality in each of his relations to the world: seeing, hearing, smelling, tasting, feeling, thinking, willing, and loving. A man is independent only if he affirms and expresses all organs of his individuality. When he is independent, he is not only free from but also free to. The aim of socialism is the emancipation of man. The emancipation of man is his self-realization, which takes place in the process of productive relatedness and oneness with man and nature. The aim of socialism is the development of the personality of the individual.

The concept of the self-realization of man can be fully understood only in connection with the concept of work. Labor and capital are not only economic categories but also anthropological categories, imbued with value judgments rooted in humanistic position. Capital, which represents what has already been accumulated over time, represents the past. In contrast, labor is, or ought to be, free and is the expression of life. In bourgeois society, the past dominates the present. In communist society, the present dominates the past. In bourgeois society, capital is independent and has individuality, while man is dependent and has no individuality. Labor is the act of man's self-creation. Labor is an activity, not a commodity. Man's function is "self-activity," not labor. Indeed, the abolition of labor is the aim of socialism. Alienated labor through the "emancipation of labor" becomes free.

Labor is the process of participation of both man and nature that man starts, regulates, and controls the material reactions between himself and nature. He treats nature as one of his own forces and utilizes arms and legs, head and hands, and the natural forces of his body in order to make nature's productions suitable for his wants. When man acts on nature to change it, at the same time he changes his own nature. He develops his influential powers and compels nature to act in accordance with his will. At the current stage of man's development, he has far passed those primitive instinctive forms of labor that are similar to those of animals. An immeasurable interval of time separates the current state of human life—in which a man sells his labor power as a commodity in the market—from the primitive state of human life—in which human labor was still in its first instinctive stage. The concept of labor refers to man's activity, which is exclusively human. A spider's operational conduct resembles that of a weaver, and a bee performs much better than many architects in the construction of her cells. But the distinguishing aspect of the worst architect from the best bees is that the architect raises the structure in his imagination before he erects it in reality. That is, the end result of a typical labor process already existed in the imagination of the laborer at the commencement of the labor process. Man not only changes the form of the material on which he works, but also he realizes his own purpose, which sets his modus operandi, and his will is subjected to it. And this subjection is not a momentary phenomenon. The labor process demands not only the exertion of the bodily organs but also that the man's will be steadily in accordance with his purpose during the whole operation. This requires man's close attention. More specifically, the less man is attracted by the nature of the work and the mode of carrying out such work, and, therefore, the less he enjoys the work as something that gives play to his bodily and mental powers, the more close his attention is forced to be.

Labor is the process of the self-expression of man. Labor is the process of the expression of man's individual physical and mental powers. Labor is a process of genuine activity, in which man develops himself and becomes himself. Work is not only a means to an end—that is, the product—but also an end in itself. Work is the meaningful expression of human energy; therefore, work is enjoyable. The central criticism of capitalism is not the inequality in the distribution of wealth, but it is the perversion of labor into forced, alienated, meaningless labor that transforms man into a "crippled monstrosity." The concept of labor as the self-expression of man leads to the vision of the complete abolition of the lifelong subjection of man to one occupation. Because the aim of the development of man is the development of the total, whole human, man must be emancipated from the crippling effects of specialization. In all previous societies in history, man has been a hunter, a fisherman, a shepherd, or a critical critic; and he has to continue doing so in the future in order to maintain his means of livelihood. However, in a communist society, nobody has one exclusive area of activity, and each man can excel in any field he wishes. Furthermore, society regulates the general production and accordingly makes it possible for each man to do one thing today and another tomorrow. It is even possible for each man to hunt in the morning, fish in the afternoon, rear cattle in the evening, and criticize after dinner, without anyone ever becoming a hunter, a fisherman, a shepherd, or a critic.

## Radical Structuralist View

The purpose here is to correctly explain the essence of man and scientifically deal with the interrelationships between man and nature. The essence of man and the interrelationships between man and nature can be understood only on the basis of a materialistic philosophy. Nature can be interpreted as meaning the universe, which is matter in all its diverse manifestations. It is the objective reality that exists outside, and it is independent of consciousness, and it had existed before any consciousness appeared.[4]

Man is a product of nature. Man is nature's highest manifestation and creation. Man is the highest stage of living organisms on the Earth. Man appeared on the Earth due to the self-development of nature based on the natural laws of evolution. In this sense, it can be said that in man and through man, nature seems to gain knowledge about itself. Man subdues nature and adapts it to his goals. Man subordinates nature to his conscious activity on the basis of his knowledge of the laws of the development of nature. At the same time, man remains part of nature, that is, a profoundly natural creature. In the process of the development of society, man increasingly becomes more separate from nature, increasingly becomes more independent of natural conditions, but increasingly attains closer ties and harmony with nature. Man "harmonizes" nature and improves the conditions of his life.

Man lives in a natural environment and uses its products in his life. He actively affects it, changes it, and transforms it. Only man succeeded in leaving his imprint on nature. The consequences of his activities can disappear only with global extinction. Man derives the means of his existence only from nature. This underlies the most fundamental understanding of the mutual relations between man and nature. These mutual relations are of the same nature as the metabolism between man and nature. Man's labor is considered to be the process of metabolism between man and nature. In this process, man appropriates the matter of nature for himself; he uses nature for his own aims and interests; and he uses nature to support and reproduce himself, his life, and his life's conditions.

Thus, production becomes an important connection between man and nature. It becomes the basic driving force for human progress. The real essence of man is in social labor, in a productive relation with nature, in social relations with other men, and in the cognition of objective reality. The more man becomes knowledgeable about the secrets of nature, the more successfully he will be able to regulate nature's processes based on a plan that he has made in advance, the more man will feel and know himself to be with nature, and the more meaningless the idea of a contradiction between mind and matter, man and nature, and soul and body becomes.

Man, animals, and plants use the substances of nature. Whereas animals use only those products of nature that exist in ready form, man not only uses the substances of nature but also remakes them and adapts them to his aims and needs. Man's work distinguishes him from animals and makes him a human being. In this sense, it can be said that work created man. It is only due to his labor applied in the work process that man gradually becomes transformed into a human being in the real sense of the word. Man's labor develops his body, enriches his mind, and improves his intellect. Work is an eternal and natural need of man. Production is a permanent condition for the existence of man. Without production, neither the metabolism between man and nature nor the human life would be possible.

The metabolism between man and nature should not be regarded as a one-sided process. That is, not all the phenomena of nature should be considered only from the viewpoint of man's needs. This view is very limited and regards the history of man as a list of needs that arise and those that are satisfied. This view evaluates the activities of man as constantly exhausting the sources of nature and regressing nature's development.

This view that depicts man only as an exploiter of nature loses sight of an important concept: that the history of man is both an integral part of the history of nature and the formation of nature by man. That is, man himself, his social organization, and the rest of nature should be regarded as the context in which man's productive activity imparts new motion to it. The creation of qualitatively new forms of bodies and new processes—both for man and for nature—reflects the progress of both man and nature.

The character and degree of man's effect on nature are different in different historical epochs. This is because people organize themselves differently—in socio-economic terms—in different epochs for their struggle with nature. The form and character of these socio-economic relations are determined not by the wishes of people but by the objective conditions of their life. The objective conditions of human life depend most crucially on the level of the development of the productive forces in a given epoch and consequently on the dominant method of production. The different socio-economic structures that have existed in the history of mankind are characterized by the manner in which goods were produced, that is, by the character of the means of production and the implements of labor.

In the history of human society, there have been many technical revolutions, which constituted turning points and significant landmarks that have affirmed the domination of man over nature. The transformation from the stone axe to implements of labor made of bronze, the transition to agriculture, the invention of the steam engine, the discovery of electricity and its application in industry, and the use of atomic energy must be regarded as great technical revolutions. These technical revolutions provided new opportunities for human advancement and for the development of his culture.

The process of subordinating nature to man has been in effect throughout man's history. However, due to the historically established social relations that have involved exploitation (i.e., slavery, feudalism, capitalism), man became dependent on the elemental forces of social development. On the one hand, man has become an increasingly stronger and more powerful ruler of nature; on the other hand, as a result of the consequent social relations, man has become the slave of blind necessity, that is, the elements dominating his society. The laborers have created all material values, but have not enjoyed equal rights and have been subjected to exploitation. This tragedy of men of labor is the greatest of all known tragedies in the history of mankind.

The archaic and unorganized nature of the social structure of capitalism has resulted in a lack or deficiency in the use of technical advances for the improvement of the well-being of people. In contrast, under socialism, all social production takes place for the sake of man and for the benefit of the whole society. Under socialism, production is not made for the sake of production, but for the sake of man. In a socialist society, the highest goal is the welfare of the people, which shows the truly humanist content of socialist social relations.

The public ownership of the means of production creates the context for the development of the creative activity of personality and for its initiative. It is in the collective and through the medium of the collective that personality finds and attains real freedom. In a society where the private ownership of the means of production is dominant, the scope of activity is in the monopoly of the person who possesses the means of production. Consequently, such a person finds himself in a position against society. In a society where the social ownership of the means of production is dominant, the interests of the collective are harmonized with the interests of the individuals, and the necessary conditions are created for the complete emancipation of personality, that is, for the manifestation of the talents and abilities of each individual.

The harmony between man and nature requires the equality of conditions for all people in using the benefits of nature and the right to participate in the collective endeavor to affect nature. This means no privileged social groups should exist in society. This is because if some individuals or social groups have the opportunity to appropriate the products of the labor of other people, then the outcome is not only unjust but also results in the consolidation of their privileges by political means. This prevents the harmony between the personal and the social. The social organization should be such that every individual gets the opportunity to take part in labor, to work in his specialty, and to reveal his abilities and talents. When all people are involved in creative work, the life of each will be better, richer, and more joyful.

The scientific solution to the problem of man and society can be founded on the theory of historical materialism. According to this theory, the social aspect of society is based on the material production aspect of the society, which follows its own specific laws. According to historical materialism, the so-called natural and eternal needs of man, which in anthropological analysis are used as a measure for evaluating existing social relations and also used as a criterion for subsequent social development, are indeed a product of the existing level of the development of production and the material relations that already exist. Thus, historical materialism does not support the idea that human nature is universal. It does not support the idea that the nature of man is a passive, because it explains the real definition of man by his object-practical activity.

Historical materialism does not mean that man presents to society a list of his eternal and natural needs that reflect his wretched and insignificant state of being, to which he has been brought by the existing social system. Historical materialism states that man does not need philanthropy. He can be the master of his destiny, he can create marvels, and he can set gigantic forces into motion if his labor and creative energy are liberated. This requires the exploitation of labor to be ended. The prerequisite for an understanding of man and the point of reference for real humanism is an analysis of the objective process by means of which man distinguishes himself from nature, that is, an analysis of work and material production. When in the attempt to understand human nature the focus is placed on the analysis of work and material production, the purpose is not to ignore man's individuality, man's inner world, man's spiritual potentials, and man's moral qualities; the purpose is to reveal man's real, and not illusory, essence.

In the study of human beings, it is necessary to study the concrete conditions of their existence, and more importantly, to study how to change the conditions of man's existence, both the natural and social, in order to create real possibilities for the harmonious development of human personality. The study of how to change the conditions of man's existence leads to a theory of revolution, which is a program for the transformation of social relations, the program for the building up of communism. This program is aimed at exalting man, toward creating normal living conditions for his existence, conditions under which his personal individuality and essence can be genuinely revealed.

The source of all existing calamities lies in the current labor process. Man is potentially omnipotent, and with his energetic forces, he has brought life to the labor process, which has many-sided social consequences, the most important of which is the opposition to man as alien forces. Behind the existing poverty and misery of the masses, and their future resolution, is the tremendous latent force and the constructive principle of history.

Over the course of history, the development of productive forces, which are created by man, greatly exceeds everything that he needs. In any era in history, the tools and forms of the social combination of labor, which are created for the production of one particular product, contain many more possibilities than the creation of just the given type of product. In this process, it can metaphorically be said that the plow is much more important than the grain that is produced with its aid. In addition, the liberation of all the internal possibilities of material production and the full development of man's creative and active forces would constitute the basis on which the diversity of man's personality and the richness of his needs and tendencies can be developed.

The focus should be placed on the man-the-creator, the man-the-worker, and investigate the ways of liberating his active, creative, constructive potentialities. This means that the man of the future is not something ready, given naturally, available within the limits of the existing society, and isolated from that society.

The historical process of the transition from the present to the future is subject to objective laws. In this process, man enters into an active struggle for the reorganization of the world. Marx's understanding of man's personality and man's consciousness is inseparably connected with the concrete socio-historical process of the decomposition of the old and the birth of a new social formation.

This is in contrast to the idea that there is an abstract, timeless, natural essence of man. The role of the active historical action of the masses is the real basis for a correct understanding of man's personality and his freedom, that is, the understanding of the all-round development of man.

The starting point for the understanding of man is to consider a live, concrete person living and working in a definite historical environment. This starting point is real people, who are involved in their real, vital, active processes, based on which they develop their ideological reflections. This regards the spiritual aspect of man's activity as man consciously and purposefully transforming the world. Human nature is not an abstraction inherent in each single individual, but it is the ensemble of social relations.

The individual is a social creature. Any manifestation of the individual's life is a manifestation and affirmation of social life. Even those manifestations of the individual's life that do not appear to be directly related to collective life, that is, accomplished jointly with others, are nevertheless manifestations and affirmations of social life. The individual and the social life of a person are not separate things, despite the fact that they have different forms of expression. They are two sides of man's life, and they are interconnected, and each of them is manifested in the other to some higher or lower extent.

Based on the preceding idea, it can be concluded that the personality of man can achieve full development only in the collective. It is only in the collective that the individual receives the means that enable him to develop his inclinations in every respect, and, therefore, it is only in the collective that the individual achieves his real freedom. In the substitutes for collectivity—that is, divided society—that have existed until now, personal freedom has been enjoyed by individuals who belonged to the dominating class. Sham collectivity has pretended that it is independent of its members; and as a union of one class against another, it is regarded by the subordinated class as not only absolutely illusory collectivity, but also new fetters. In a real collectivity, the individuals gain their freedom in their association with the collectivity and through it.

Man can settle down only in society, and his individuality can be revealed only in society and in accordance with social conditions. In the entire historical development of human society, three stages in the mutual relations of society and the person have unfolded: (1) Personal dependence (primitive) is the first major form of society in which the productivity of people develops only very slowly and only in certain places. (2) Personal independence, which is based on eternal dependence, is the second major form of society in which there is a system of universal metabolism, of universal relations, of comprehensive needs and universal abilities. (3) Free individuality, based on the universal development of individuals, based on individuals' subordination to the collective, and based on regarding social productivity as their social property.

Under communism—in contrast to the bourgeois society, in which there are classes and class antagonisms—there is harmony between personal and social interests, such that the free development of each is the condition for the free development of all. In other words, society cannot free itself without freeing every individual person. The harmonious union of the individual and the social, of the person and the collective, entails the flourishing of the spiritual side of the individual and society. This organic interaction leads to a high level of development in the material productivity of man.

There is an exceptionally great role for consciousness, thought, ideas, and the spiritual life of man. The significance of social consciousness in the development of human society cannot be exaggerated. There is an inspiring role for progressive ideas in the life of man and human society, and in their development. Spiritual life exists, and the basis of spiritual life is objective, material existence. That is, first there is matter and then consciousness. Consciousness is the other side of matter, but it is its derivative.

## Conclusion

This chapter briefly discussed four views expressed with respect to human nature. The functionalist paradigm believes that humans are maximizers. The interpretive paradigm believes that what man is depends on where he is, who he is, and what he believes, because man is so entangled with them and so is inseparable from them. The radical humanist paradigm believes that man has an entity that is not only biological, anatomical, and physiological, but also psychological. The radical structuralist paradigm believes that the real essence of man is in social labor, in a productive relation with nature, in social relations with other men, and in the cognition of objective reality.

Each paradigm is logically coherent—in terms of its underlying assumptions—and conceptualizes and studies the phenomenon in a certain way, generating distinctive kinds of insight and understanding. Therefore, different paradigms in combination provide a broader understanding of the phenomenon under consideration. An understanding of different paradigms leads to a better understanding of the multifaceted nature of the phenomenon.

## Notes

1 For this literature, see Alhadeff (1982); Crouch (1979); Doucouliagos (1994); Friedman (1953); Jaggar (1983); Kaufman (1989); Simon (1957); Steen (1996); Thaler (2000); Vyverberg (1989); and Wilson (1978). This section is based on Becker (1976).

2 For this literature, see Brown (1988); Cooley (1992); Coutu (1949); Dewey (1957); Granovetter (1985); Jensen (1987); Midgley (2002); Montagu (1957); Sperry (1965); and Thomas (1997). This section is based on Geertz (1973).

3 For this literature, see Habermas (2003); Held (2004); Horkheimer (1974); Jaggar (1983); Kellner (1977); Lewontin, Rose, and Kamin (1984), Sayers (1998); and Williams (1999). This section is based on Fromm (2004).

4 For this literature, see Berry (1986); Fromm and Xirau (1968); Geras (1983); Jaggar (1983); Kupperman (2010); Marx (1969); Plamenatz (1975); Stevenson (1981); Stevenson and Haberman (2008); and Venable (1966). This section is based on Mitin (1966).

## References

Alhadeff, David A. (1982), *Microeconomics and Human Behavior: Toward a New Synthesis of Economics and Psychology*, Berkeley, CA: University of California Press.

Becker, Gary S. (1976), *The Economic Approach to Human Behavior*, Chicago, IL: University of Chicago Press.

Berry, Christopher J. (1986), *Human Nature, Atlantic Highlands*, NJ: Humanities Press International.

Brown, Donald E. (1988), *Hierarchy, History, and Human Nature: The Social Origins of Historical Consciousness*, Tucson, AZ: University of Arizona Press.

Cooley, Charles Horton, (1992), *Human Nature and the Social Order*, New Brunswick, NJ: Transaction Publishers.

Coutu, Walter (1949), *Emergent Human Nature: A Symbolic Field Interpretation*, New York, NY: A.A. Knopf.

Crouch, Robert L. (1979), *Human Behavior: An Economic Approach*, North Scituate, MA: Duxbury Press.

Dewey, John (1957), *Human Nature and Conduct: An Introduction to Social Psychology*, New York, NY: Random House.

Doucouliagos, Chris (1994), "A Note on the Evolution of Homo Economicus," *Journal of Economic Issues*, 28:3, September, 877–83.

Friedman, Milton (1953), *Essays in Positive Economics*, Chicago, IL: University of Chicago Press.

Fromm, Erich (2004), *Marx's Concept of Man*, New York, NY: Continuum.

Fromm, Erich and Xirau, Ramon, ed. (1968), *The Nature of Man*, New York, NY: Macmillan.

Geertz, Clifford (1973), "The Impact of the Concept of Culture on the Concept of Man," in Geertz, Clifford (ed.), *The Interpretation of Cultures*, New York, NY: Basic Books, Inc., Publishers, Chapter 2, pp. 33–54.

Geras, Norman (1983), *Marx and Human Nature: Refutation of a Legend*, London: NLB and Verso.

Granovetter, Mark (1985), "Economic Action and Social Structure: The Problem of Embeddedness," *American Journal of Sociology*, 91:3, November, 481–510.

Habermas, Jurgen (2003), *The Future of Human Nature*, Cambridge: Polity.

Held, David (2004), *Introduction to Critical Theory: Horkheimer to Habermas*, Cambridge: Polity Press.

Horkheimer, Max (1974), *Critique of Instrumental Reason: Lectures and Essays since the End of World War II*, New York, NY: Continuum.

Jaggar, Alison M. (1983), *Feminist Politics and Human Nature*, Totowa, NJ: Rowman and Allanheld Publishers.

Jensen, Hans E. (1987), "The Theory of Human Nature," *Journal of Economic Issues*, 21:3, September, 1039–73.

Kaufman, Bruce E. (1989), "Models of Man in Industrial Relations Research," *Industrial and Labor Relations Review*, 43:1, October, 72–88.

Kellner, Douglas (1977), "Adam Smith and Karl Marx on Capitalism and Human Nature," in Schwartz, Jesse (ed.), *The Subtle Anatomy of Capitalism*, Santa Monica, CA: Goodyear Publishing Company, Inc.

Kupperman, Joel J. (2010), *Theories of Human Nature*, Indianapolis, IN: Hackett Publishing Company, Inc.

Lewontin, Richard C., Rose, Steven, and Kamin, Leon J. (1984), *Not in our Genes: Biology, Ideology, and Human Nature*, New York, NY: Pantheon Books.

Marx, Karl (1969), "Theses on Feuerbach," in *Marx and Engels Selected Works*, Volume One, Moscow, USSR: Progress Publishers, pp. 13–15.

Midgley, Mary (2002), *Beast and Man: The Roots of Human Nature*, New York, NY: Routledge.

Mitin, Mark (1966), "The Concept of Man in Marxist Thought," in Radhakrishnan, S. and Raju, P.T. (eds.), *The Concept of Man*, Lincoln, NE: Johnsen Publishing Co., Chapter 8, pp. 476–535.

Montagu, Ashley (1957), *Anthropology and Human Nature*, Boston, MA: Porter Sargent Publishers.

Plamenatz, John (1975), *Karl Marx's Philosophy of Man*, New York, NY: Oxford University Press.

Sayers, Sean (1998), *Marxism and Human Nature*, New York, NY: Routledge.

Simon, Herbert A. (1957), *Models of Man: Social and Rational*, New York, NY: John Wiley and Sons.

Sperry, Roger W. (1965), "Mind, Brain and Humanist Values," in Platt, John Rader (ed.), *New Views of the Nature of Man*, Chicago, IL: University of Chicago Press, Chapter 4, pp. 71–92.

Steen, R. Grant (1996), *DNA and Destiny: Nature and Nurture in Human Behavior*, New York, NY: Plenum Press.

Stevenson, Leslie, ed. (1981), *The Study of Human Nature*, New York, NY: Oxford University Press.

Stevenson, Leslie and Haberman, David L. (2008), *Ten Theories of Human Nature*, Oxford: Oxford University Press.

Thaler, Richard H. (2000), "From Homo Economicus to Homo Sapiens," *Journal of Economic Perspectives*, 14:1, winter, 133–41.

Thomas, Robert Murray (1997), *Moral Development Theories – Secular and Religious: A Comparative Study*, Westport, CT: Greenwood Press.

Venable, Vernon (1966), *Human Nature: The Marxian View*, Cleveland, OH: Meridian Books.

Vyverberg, Henry (1989), *Human Nature, Cultural Diversity, and the French Enlightenment*, New York, NY: Oxford University Press.

Williams, David (1999), "Constructing the Economic Space: The World Bank and the Making of Homo Oeconomicus," *Millennium: Journal of International Studies*, 28:1, 79–99.

Wilson, Edward O. (1978), *On Human Nature*, Cambridge, MA: Harvard University Press.

# 4

# Rationality

## A Multi-Paradigmatic View

Any explanation of rationality is based on a worldview. The premise of this book is that any worldview can be associated with one of the four broad paradigms: functionalist, interpretive, radical humanist, and radical structuralist. This chapter takes the case of rationality and discusses it from the four different viewpoints. It emphasizes that the four views expressed are equally scientific and informative; they look at the phenomenon from their specific paradigmatic viewpoint; and together they provide a more balanced understanding of the phenomenon under consideration. In this chapter, the first through the fourth sections present the four perspectives, and the fifth section concludes the chapter.

## Functionalist View

Economics has been defined as the science that studies the relationship between means and ends, where means are scarce and have alternative uses. It has applied rational choice theory for a very general science of practical reason, which accurately describes, successfully predicts, and powerfully explains. A rational choice says that an agent would do well to make it under the given circumstances. If an agent does not make the rational choice, then that agent is at fault.[1]

Although the origin of the history of rational choice theory can be traced back to Plato and Aristotle, modern theory started with the scientific aspirations of the Enlightenment. More specifically, it was initiated with the ambitious but conflicting attempts at a moral science of mind made by Hobbes, Hume, and Kant; then it was given a mathematical structure by Bentham and the utilitarians; and finally, it was abstracted and turned into a formal exercise in epistemic logic.

According to Hobbes, the driving force behind humans' actions is their appetites and aversions. Their will is their last appetite or aversion that immediately turns into an action or inaction. Reason plays a role when a person faces conflicting appetites and aversions, and therefore the person confronts mutually exclusive courses of action. The person enters a deliberation mode, in which passion and reason play distinct roles. The person deliberates subjunctively and with suppositions with respect to the action's consequences. It takes the following form: if action "a" is undertaken, then the consequence "b" will follow. The person applies reason to the particular situation, while desire and aversion play their imperative role. Reason may be able to tell a person how best to satisfy his/her given desires, but reason cannot do the same with respect to setting those desires. Good is subjective by its very nature. Something is regarded as good by a person only if that thing is an object of his/her desires. The person's desires determine whether something is good, evil, or contemptible (i.e., neither good nor bad). Nothing is absolutely good, evil, or contemptible. These are all determined relative to the person's desires.

According to Hobbes, "felicity" refers to a situation where a person continually succeeds in obtaining those things which he/she desires. Felicity does not refer to a specific good and does not have a common currency in which different desires can be measured. Felicity involves an open-ended and dynamic process that is separate from calculating how to maximize some given index of desire-satisfaction. Felicity does not refer to a state of a satisfied mind, but it refers to a continual progress of satisfying desires, from one object to another, from the attainment of the former on the way to the attainment of the latter. It involves a perpetual and restless attainment of desires that ceases only in death.

According to Hobbes, all persons, nevertheless, follow "precepts" or "general rules," which can be found out by reason. These rules exist because some passions—especially the desire to survive—are common to all humans. Based on reason, humans can discover that they can best survive by following some general rules, such as "to seek peace and follow it" and "to defend themselves by all means they can." Based on reason, humans follow these rules in order to satisfy their most urgent desires. Furthermore, based on reason, humans can understand the need to make and maintain commonwealths. This tends to remove the constant fear of violent death and secures a peace that allows a desired living. In the state of nature, human life consists of a war of every man against every man. But, rational humans can avoid it by creating a common power to maintain mutual respect among humans. Meanwhile, in the spirit of

Enlightenment, Hobbes declares that: reason is the pace; increase of science is the way; and the benefit of mankind is the end.

Hume, a century after Hobbes, expressed skepticism with respect to the high status that Reason attained in the seventeenth century as a superior guide to science and as an ultimate benefit to mankind. But Hume sees good prospects for Reason in an empirical science of mind. Like Hobbes, Hume believes that all human actions are produced as a result of two elements: passion and reason. Passion has an original existence and acts as the motivating force. Reason, by itself, can never act as a motive to any action because Reason follows, serves, and obeys the passions. Thus, ultimate ends cannot be subjected to rational criticism. In this way, Hobbes and Hume have similar basic views on practical reason.

Hume has a somewhat different view of human nature than that of Hobbes. Hume believes that humans have kinder passions, such as a natural sympathy for people who are in distress. However, like Hobbes, Hume believes that humans have some basic desires that are constant across time and across societies. Various passions—ambition, avarice, self-love, vanity, friendship, generosity, public spirit—have always been the sources of all actions and enterprises. These passions, from the beginning of the world, have been mixed in various degrees, have been distributed through society, and have been observed among mankind. Humans have been so much the same across times and across places that history informs us of nothing new or strange in this regard. On this basis, Hume argues—like Hobbes—that there are some rules of action that can be used as means for satisfying desired ends, which are common to all humans. Hume argues that, based on Reason, humans need to adhere to the institution of property because that institution tends to satisfy universal human desires and therefore works to everyone's benefit. Hume then adds that nature remedies the judgment and understanding caused by irregular and incommodious affections.

Kant's moral psychology stands in sharp contrast to Hobbes's and Hume's instrumental notion of rational action. In Kant's view, reason can be and ought to be a motive to the will. This underlies Kant's moral philosophy and his rationalization of the categorical imperative: Act only on the basis of that maxim which you can, and at the same time will that it should become a universal law. A morally right action is right for anyone and is thus impersonal and impartial. The moral and ideally rational agent is autonomous because he/she is freed from personal inclinations and biases. Such an agent respects the autonomy of others and never treats others as a means to his/her own ends. A morally right action is based on the right motives without regard to its consequences—even if its consequences are for human happiness. Kant believed that a moral action is a rational action. Rational agents recognize that there is a moral reason for a right action; therefore, they make that moral reason their own and act on it. Kantian moral psychology is impersonal and impartial. It leads agents to distance themselves from their own inclinations and creates non-instrumental rationality. It becomes attractive when the theory of rational choice starts to run into paradoxes because agents who strictly adhere to their preferences cannot escape foreseeably inferior consequences. Scholars who have followed the line of thinking of Hume have remained skeptical about Kant's views. In general, the mainstream of economic thinking has mostly followed Hume rather than Kant.

Bentham gave a new slant to economic thought. According to Bentham, rationality is expressed through the "principle of utility." This approves or disapproves of every action depending on whether the action increases or decreases the happiness of the agent whose interest is under consideration. It defines "utility" as that property of an object that produces benefit, advantage, pleasure, good, or happiness (where all of these terms come to the same thing) to the agent whose interest is being considered. An action is in the interest of an agent when it adds to the sum total of his/her pleasures.

Bentham considers rational actions in terms of the mental states which result from those actions, and not in terms of the desires that, according to Hume, provide the motivational force for those actions. This assigns to reason a more active role. According to Bentham, a rational agent takes those actions that maximize his/her happiness over the rest of his/her life, even if the agent's current desires require different actions. Reason can overrule passion in order to achieve a greater overall benefit, advantage, pleasure, good, or happiness. Pleasure (and hence utility) is a quality which all actions generate, it is measurable, and such measured quantities of pleasure can be added together. Therefore, every problem of rational choice is indeed an exercise in maximization. This is the crucial feature of Bentham's utilitarianism, which is not an implication of Hume's theory of practical reason. According to Hume, reason is the slave of passions, which has an original existence. Therefore, reason cannot require that passions be subjected to any particular mathematical representation. In other words, an agent's desires do not need to satisfy the property of "consistency" required for reason to identify a best action. In order to arrive at a maximizing theory of rational choice, Bentham adds a psychological hypothesis about the nature of desires or pleasures.

Bentham's utilitarian approach was favored in economics until well into the twentieth century. Bentham's idea that rationality requires the maximization of utility was treated with greater mathematical sophistication from the 1870s. This happened through the development of the theory of marginal utility and the application of the mathematics of calculus. However, the psychological underpinnings of utilitarianism were the subject of continual controversy. The initial dispute was about which one of the five psychological concepts (benefit, advantage, pleasure, good, or happiness) specified by Bentham best characterizes the general human motivation, if the quintet does not boil down to the same thing. J. S. Mill selected "happiness" as the most general human motivation term and made a distinction between "higher" and "lower" pleasures, by which he raised the question of whether all motivating factors are commensurable. In the ensuing debate, "neoclassical" economists of the late nineteenth century defended their psychological assumptions not as universal truths but as simplifications that are sufficiently realistic for economic analysis. For instance, Jevons accepted that higher and lower pleasures are incommensurable and added that economics could safely confine its attention to the lower pleasures. Similarly, Edgeworth started with the claim that the first principle of economics is that every agent is motivated solely by self-interest and qualified his claim with the remark that this principle is especially applicable to commerce, even though it is less applicable to other realms of behavior.

Later economists removed the dependence on psychological assumptions but retained the mathematical structure of utilitarian theory. Pareto derived the theory of consumer choice without reference to any psychological assumptions about utility. Pareto started with indifference curves, which are bundles of consumption goods among which a consumer is indifferent. Pareto claimed that the notion of indifference is directly confirmed by experience. A person being indifferent between two bundles of goods means that he/she is willing to exchange one for the other. This does not require anything to be stated about the person's desire or pleasure. A family of indifference curves can be drawn and a numerical index can be assigned to each curve. The mathematical function that assigns numerical indices to the indifference curves is a representation of the person's preferences. These indices can be called indices of "utility" (Pareto preferred "ophelimity"), and the person's behavior can be described as utility maximization. This expresses the idea that the person chooses in accordance with his/her set of preferences. Through this approach, the theory of economic science acquires the rigor of rational mechanics, because it obtains its results based on experience, without reference to any metaphysical entity.

Samuelson's theory of revealed preference carried further the work of Pareto. Samuelson derived a consumer theory from a compact set of axioms about behavior in situations of choice. In Samuelson's theory, the central axiom is the consistency between choices. That is, in any given choice situation, if x is revealed preferred to y (i.e., if x is chosen when y could have been chosen), then there is no other choice situation in which y is revealed preferred to x. Von Neumann and Morgenstern extended Pareto's work to choice under conditions of risk. They derived the expected-utility theory from known probabilities and axioms about preferences. Ramsey, furthermore, derived subjective probabilities from axioms about choice among gambles.

Savage synthesized this body of work into the generally regarded most satisfactory statement of the foundations of the theory of rational choice. Savage refers to his theory as a quasi-logical analysis of choice under uncertainty. He is concerned with the role of reasoning in decision-making. He extends the principles of logic to bear more fully on decision-making under uncertainty. Savage's theory can be used in the same way that logic can be used to detect inconsistencies among an agent's beliefs and to derive new beliefs from existing ones. That is, Savage's theory can be used to check one's own decisions for consistency and possibly translate complicated decisions into simpler ones. Savage considers rationality in terms of the consistency among decisions.

Savage's theory starts with three concepts: "states of the world," "consequences," and "preferences." "States of the world" are mutually exclusive and represent uncertainty. One and only one of these states of the world will materialize. Sets of states of the world are called events. A "consequence" is what may happen to the agent who makes the choice. The agent makes a choice among acts, where an act is a list of conceivable consequences, one for each state of the world. For instance, in gambling on the toss of a coin, "Heads" and "Tails" are the events; and the payoff in each event is the consequence for that event. Then a typical choice is between the acts "if heads, gain nothing; if tails, gain nothing" and "if heads, gain $10; if tails, lose $10." The choice that the agent makes between the acts is the agent's preference between the acts.

Savage formalizes rational choice by four main postulates—and three technical ones. The first postulate is that a rational agent has a complete and consistent preference ordering over all possible acts. The second and third postulates lead to the specification of the agent's preference between any pair of acts, conditional on any given event's happening. Furthermore, such preferences are dependent only on the consequences of those acts in that event and are independent of the description of the event itself. The fourth postulate leads to the generation of a relation of "subjectively more probable than" between events. That is, one event is subjectively more probable than another if the agent prefers to choose the first over the second.

Savage proved that an agent, with preferences satisfying all the postulates, chooses as if he/she maximizes his/her expected utility. For such an agent, it is possible to assign to each event a number between 0 and 1 such that these numbers have the standard properties of probabilities. These numbers can be treated as the "subjective probabilities" of the corresponding events. It is also possible to assign to every consequence a number, such that the ranking of consequences by these numbers is the same as the agent's preference ranking. These numbers can be treated as the "utilities" of the corresponding consequences. And it is possible to choose these numbers such that for every pair of acts, the ranking of the acts in terms of expected utility corresponds to their ranking in the agent's preference ordering.

Savage has obtained these results without making any assumptions about desires or beliefs. His only requirement has been that the agent's decisions be consistent in a certain way. Therefore, this is not a theory of instrumental rationality. An agent whose decisions are consistent as per Savage's postulates acts as if he/she makes complicated utilitarian calculations, using measures of utility and probability to calculate the expected utility of each of the acts, one of which he is to choose. However, these utility and probability measures, and the expected utility thus calculated, do not explain or justify the choices that the agent makes. Rather, these are all derived from the choices that the agent makes. Savage retains utilitarian mathematics but abandons both the utilitarian psychology and the broadly Humean theory of practical reason on which this mathematics previously relied. Savage purged the notion of rationality of all psychological content and replaced it with an abstract scheme of quasi-logical relations.

The theory of rational choice, as discussed above, considers a single agent making choices based on a set of parameters determined by an independent environment. Game theory takes the next step to consider rational decision-making when there are at least two agents involved. Game theory considers rational choice where the outcome depends on the choices of more than one agent, and the agents are aware of each other's rationality. Game theory begins with the hope that it can make progress in analysis without making any psychological assumptions and without much reliance on the theory of practical reason. This orientation is attractive in its resulting elegance and economy but has run into some difficulties, indicating that some psychological assumptions would be necessary. Game theory's view of social life as strategic interaction is proving immensely fertile but has encountered paradoxes. Game theory is based on an elegant, universal logic of practical reason. Its rationality is instrumental, and its view of the social world is individualist. But it faces paradoxes even of coordination, trust, and the keeping of promises. There seems to be something amiss with its abstraction from all "moral psychology" and considering a world of fully transparent agents with common knowledge of rationality and alignment between preferences and choices.

## Interpretive View

In order to understand rationality, consider, for instance, some questions about what justice requires and permits. Does justice allow inequality of income and ownership? Does justice require people who have been the subject of inequalities due to past injustice to be compensated, even if those who are required to pay for such compensation played no role in that injustice? Does justice agree with the imposition of the death penalty and, if yes, for which offences? Is justice served when abortion is legalized? When is justice served by going to war? Justice involves a long list of such questions, to which alternative and incompatible answers are provided by different individuals and groups.[2]

Different answers to particular types of questions are supported by different reasons, which emanate from different conceptions of justice. Some conceptions of justice make the concept of desert central, while others ignore its relevance altogether. Some conceptions of justice appeal to inalienable human rights, while others appeal to the concept of social contract, while still others appeal to the notion of utility. Furthermore, different theories of justice not only generate different conceptions of justice but also generate different conceptions of the relationship of justice to other human goods; of the type of equality that justice requires; of the kind of transactions to which and the kind of persons to whom the concept of justice is applicable; and of the relationship between the knowledge of justice and the knowledge of God's law.

This means that, in search of good reasons for making proper judgments on some particular issue, some people made a move from the arena of everyday social life—in which groups and individuals argue about what serves justice in particular situations—to the arena of theoretical inquiry—in which systematic conceptions of justice are elaborated and debated. But they only find themselves to have moved from one arena of diverse and conflicting views to another. They may realize that in their society there are divisions and conflicts, rather than consensus. They may also recognize not only that there are divisions and conflicts regarding the nature of justice, but also that there are divisions and conflicts within themselves. This is because people are not ordinarily taught to think and judge in a coherent way, but their thinking and judging are constructed by some combination of social and cultural components. These social and cultural components are inherited from past traditions. They are derived, in the case of the United States, from the origin of their culture—that is, Puritan, Catholic, Jewish—and from different stages in and aspects of the development of modernity—that is, the French Enlightenment, the Scottish Enlightenment, the nineteenth-century economic liberalism, and the twentieth-century political liberalism. These differences lead to disagreements and conflicts within a person, as well as between the person and others. Therefore, each person or group of persons confronts the following question: How should people decide with respect to different and incompatible accounts of justice that compete for their moral, social, and political allegiance?

A typical contemporary response to the above question is that a person would accept that systematic account of justice which meets the standards of rationality. It may seem that in order to determine what justice is, people must first determine what rationality in practice requires of them. Yet, any attempt to learn this faces immediately the fact that the determination of the nature of rationality in general and practical rationality in particular is as manifold, disputable, and intractable as the determination of justice. More specifically, practical rationality is viewed differently by different groups of people. One group holds that practical rationality requires one to act on the basis of calculations and comparisons of the costs and benefits to oneself of each possible alternative course of action and its consequences. A second group holds that practical rationality requires one to act under the constraints imposed by an impartial person, who accords no particular privileges to one's own interests. A third group holds that practical rationality requires one to act in such a way as to achieve the ultimate and true good of human beings. These differences in the determination of rationality introduce a third level of difference and conflict in the discussion.

So, how should one proceed with respect to an issue such as justice if one desires to act rationally? According to one group of academic philosophers, rationality requires that the person first set aside his/her allegiance to any specific theory and abstract himself/herself from all social relationships that the person has been accustomed to understanding his/her responsibilities and interests. This group of academic philosophers further suggests that only by doing so can the person arrive at a genuinely neutral, impartial, and universal point of view. This point of view is purged of the partisanship, partiality, and one-sidedness that otherwise affect the person. This group of academic philosophers concludes that it is only in this way that the person will be able to evaluate the contending accounts of justice rationally.

One problem with this account of rationality is that the people who agree with following this procedure then get into disagreement about the precise conception of justice which is rationally acceptable. A major problem that arises, even before this problem emerges, is that this account of rationality is contentious in two related ways. First, although it requires disinterestedness, it implicitly supports and justifies a specific account of justice, that of liberal individualism. This means that its apparent neutrality is only its appearance. Secondly, its requirement for a person to become a socially disembodied being in order to decide rationally in fact ignores the historical and social character that any substantive rationality, whether theoretical or practical, is bound to have.

Foundational disagreements about the character of rationality are almost impossible to resolve. This is because those who proceed in one way rather than another to approach the disputed questions have already assumed that their particular procedures are the ones that are rational to follow. There is a certain degree of circularity built into the disputed character of rationality. This degree of circularity becomes even more intense when disagreements between contending views are sufficiently fundamental—for example, disagreements about practical rationality as applied to the determination of the nature of justice—those disagreements also extend to the choice of a procedure to resolve those same disagreements.

Aristotle argued that anyone who denies the basic law of logic—the law of non-contradiction—and who intends to defend his/her position through an argumentative debate will actually rely on the same law. Aristotle added that similar defenses can be constructed for other laws of logic. Aristotle showed that it is not possible for anyone who understands the laws of logic to remain rational while rejecting them. But adherence to the laws of logic is only a necessary and not a sufficient condition for either theoretical or practical rationality.

Disagreements regarding the nature of rationality arise in response to what has to be added to the observance of the laws of logic to justify ascriptions of rationality—whether to oneself or to others, whether to modes of inquiry or to justifications of belief, or to courses of action and their justification. Such disagreement extends to disagreement regarding what is the rational procedure to follow in order to discuss these disagreements. The resources provided by modern academic philosophy have redefined, but not resolved, the problems which a person faces when he/she confronts the rival claims made by protagonists of conflicting accounts of justice and of practical rationality.

Another resource available to such a person is obtained by participation in the life of one of those groups whose thought and action are informed by the group's settled conviction with regard to justice and practical rationality. The people who choose academic philosophy acquire a set of sound arguments to assure themselves and others of the rational justification for their views. The other people who choose instead to participate in a group's life acquire a set of beliefs embodied in the life of the group by placing their trust in persons rather than in arguments. These people are often subjected to the charge of arbitrariness in their commitments. These people, however, attach little weight to such charges.

The reason these charges carry little weight is partly that these people do not believe in the power or relevance of rational argument to sufficiently fundamental matters. Fideism has a large, not always articulate, body of adherents among both religious and secular groups. Furthermore, the reason these charges carry little weight is partly that these people have a strong suspicion of their opponents that they have subjected these people to the charges not so much because they themselves are genuinely moved by rational argument, but because by appealing to rational argument they are able to exercise some power that favors their own interests and privileges, or the interests and privileges of a class that has come up with an effective use of rhetorical argument for its own purposes.

In other words, this group of people regards their opponents' arguments not as expressions of rationality but as weapons used to protect their own interests. This group of people regards the techniques deployed by their opponents' professionally skilled lawyers, academics, economists, and journalists as helping to dominate those who are not fluent and are not articulate. Thus, there is a remarkable mutual understanding among very different social and cultural groups with respect to each other's commitments. For instance, the people who share the presuppositions of the affluent and self-congratulatory liberal

Enlightenment regard the congregations of evangelical fundamentalism as unfashionably unenlightened. Conversely, the members of those congregations regard the enlightened liberals as a community of pre-rational faith—as they themselves are—but they regard the enlightened liberals—unlike themselves—as failing to recognize what they are, and therefore, they regard enlightened liberals as not being in a privileged position to level charges of irrationality at them or anyone else.

Thus, people live in a culture in which contending social groups appeal to competing and conflicting convictions that are unsupported by rational justification. In this culture, people are unable to agree on rationally justified conclusions regarding the nature of justice and of practical rationality. Neither the efforts of academic philosophy—or any other academic discipline—nor those of the various subcultures have offered ordinary people the opportunity to unite conviction on such matters with rational justification. The public realm for debates concerning issues related to justice and practical rationality transforms into an arena for the assertion and counter-assertion of alternative and incompatible sets of premises.

This came about as a result of the Enlightenment and its subsequent history. A central aspiration of the great achievement of the Enlightenment was to provide for use in public debates standards and methods of rational justification in order to judge alternative courses of action in every sphere of life as just or unjust, rational or irrational, enlightened or unenlightened. In this way, reason was expected to displace authority and tradition. Rational justification was based on principles that were expected to be undeniable by any rational person, and therefore be independent of all the social and cultural particularities, which the Enlightenment thinkers regarded as mere accidental phenomena in particular times and places. Rational justification was, according to the Enlightenment thinkers, what was accepted by the vast majority of educated people in the post-Enlightenment cultural and social orders.

Unfortunately, both the Enlightenment thinkers and their successors could not agree on the precise constitution of those principles which they expected to be found undeniable by all rational persons. Different answers were provided by different thinkers: the authors of the *Encyclopedie*, Rousseau, Bentham, Kant, Scottish philosophers of common sense, and their French and American successors. The extent of their disagreements has not only remained undiminished during their subsequent history but has rather enlarged. Thus, the legacy of the Enlightenment, which has been the provision of rational justification, has been impossible to attain. This has created an inability in Western culture to unite conviction and rational justification. Within that group of academic philosophy, who consider themselves as the heirs to the philosophies of the Enlightenment, the discussion of the nature of rational justification has continued increasingly with refinements but with undiminishing disagreements. In the cultural, political, moral, and religious life, post-Enlightenment conviction has actually acquired a life of its own and has become independent of rational inquiry.

Therefore, it seems that the Enlightenment not only propagated its distinctive doctrines that led to its achievements, but also it succeeded in excluding other doctrines from people's views. It is possible that some other mode of understanding—which was excluded from the Enlightenment's vision of the world—can provide the conceptual and theoretical resources for reuniting conviction—concerning such matters as justice—and rational inquiry and justification. In search of this alternative mode of understanding, it is important not to fall into the trap of continuing to accept the standards of the Enlightenment. It is known in advance that the provision of any radically different alternative standpoint will be found rationally unsatisfactory from the standpoint of the Enlightenment. This means that such an alternative standpoint will be unacceptable to and rejected by people whose allegiance is to the prevailing intellectual and cultural modes.

The Enlightenment made people blind to a conception of rational inquiry which was embodied in a tradition. From this conception, the standards of rational justification themselves emerged. These standards were vindicated because they transcended the limitations of and provided remedies to the shortcomings of their predecessors within the history of that same tradition. Of course, not all traditions embodied rational inquiry as their constitutive component. The Enlightenment thinkers dismissed tradition because they regarded it as the antithesis of rational inquiry. But, in this way, they obscured from themselves and their successors the nature of the traditional systems of thought.

To the members of a social and intellectual tradition, the facts of their tradition—that is, the presuppositions of their activities and inquiries—may never become the objects of attention and inquiry. In general, only when traditions either fail and disintegrate, or are challenged, do their members become aware of them and begin to theorize about their tradition. In order to adequately understand the major moral and metaphysical thinkers of the ancient, medieval, and even early modern world, they should be placed within the context of their traditions, of which rational inquiry was a central and constitutive component. This does not mean that these thinkers were concerned with, let alone provided an adequate explanation of the nature of their traditions. The thinkers who explicitly treated this tradition as their subject matter were later thinkers. These thinkers were aware of the antithesis to tradition. This antithesis was unavailable to the earlier inhabitants of the tradition under consideration.

In this alternative tradition, the concept of rational inquiry is inseparable from the intellectual and social tradition in which it is embodied. The concept of rational justification is essentially historical. In the tradition under consideration, justification means to narrate how the argument has gone so far. Within this tradition of inquiry and justification, theoreticians construct theories within a structure that certain theses have the status of first principles, and other claims within such a theory are derived from these first principles. But what justifies the first principles and the whole structure of the theory is the rational superiority of that particular structure to all its predecessors. This does not mean that these first principles are acceptable to all rational persons, unless through a circular requirement such condition is included in advance.

Within this tradition, the mode of rational justification is very different from that of the Enlightenment. In addition, the subject of justification is conceived very differently. According to the theories of the Enlightenment, rival doctrines contend, even though such doctrines have been elaborated in particular times and places. They are judged by the timeless criteria of truth and rational justification. By contrast, from the standpoint of tradition-constituted and tradition-constitutive inquires, the claims of a particular doctrine are always considered as a matter of how precisely they were advanced; of what linguistic particularities were used in its formulation; of what at that time and place had to be denied, if it was asserted; of what was at that time and place presupposed by its assertion, and so on. Doctrines, theses, and arguments have to be understood within their historical context.

So, the concept of rationality itself, whether theoretical or practical, has a history. Indeed, since the traditions of inquiry are diverse, with their own histories, there are rationalities rather than rationality; in the same way that there are justices rather than justice. The proper characterization of the diverse traditions provides an informed explanation of the diverse standpoints. The acknowledgment of the diversity of traditions of inquiry—each with its own specific mode of rational justification—helps to rationally resolve the differences between rival and incompatible traditions. How and under what conditions they can be resolved will be known only after an understanding of the nature of such traditions has been achieved. This means that in the traditions of rational inquiry the existence of diversity is not ignored, but it is used to make it amenable to solution.

## Radical Humanist View

Rationality pervades individual behavior, government policies, the structure of social systems, and the assumptions and strategies of scientists who study these phenomena. Rationality, since the Enlightenment, has developed two main characteristics. The first characteristic is effective instrumental action or instrumental rationality, which may be defined as the capacity to devise, select, and effect appropriate means to reach specified ends. The second characteristic is objectivism, which refers to the criterion that rational choices concerning theories and beliefs—about fact, values, and morals—should be made based on objective standards that are equally applicable and accessible to all individuals.[3]

Instrumental rationality and objectivism form a duo. Instrumental rationality governs rational behavior, and objectivism governs rational belief and morality. Together, they provide a complete guide for becoming a rational individual. In social life, objectivism coordinates the actions of a large number of instrumental rationalists such that it becomes instrumentally rational with respect to any goals which the social system has set for itself. Instrumental rationality and objectivism together create a clean and orderly world where modern science, technology, and economics flourish. However, modernity also allows alternative formations in polity, economy, and society.

Instrumental rationality is more prevalent than objectivism. Indeed, economists—and increasing numbers of political scientists, even a few sociologists—believe that instrumental rationality underlies all human behavior. Most international relations scholars and analysts assume that instrumental rationality captures the foreign policy behavior of whole states. Professional policy analysts, advisors to governments, and critics of governments' actions recommend governments pursue instrumentally rational policies with a set of clear goals.

Some criticisms of instrumental rationality are as follows.

1. Instrumental rationality does not recognize and consequently destroys the more congenial, spontaneous, egalitarian, and intrinsically meaningful aspects of human association. This criticism has a history. At the turn of the twentieth century, Max Weber argued that instrumental rationality (together with objectivist systems of rules) provided justification and organizing principles for bureaucracy. Weber further argued that instrumental rationality that underlies bureaucratization erects an "iron cage" around human existence. More recently, Jurgen Habermas has extended Weber's analysis from bureaucracy to the "colonization" of the "lifeworld" of culture and social interaction by the administration, ministration, influence, and control of technical expertise in the interest of private profit or political power. Administrators, marketing consultants, police, social workers, counselors, physicians, lawyers, and clinical psychologists are at the forefront of this invasive process which used to be constructed and conducted by ordinary people. Moreover, in an instrumentally-rationalized world, individuals act like economic men—that is, like calculating machines with a lack of subjectivity and no sense of self and community.
2. Instrumental rationality has an anti-democratic nature. Max Weber argued that bureaucratization involves the concentration of political power. This tendency is weakened to the extent that instrumental rationality is applied while free criticism is allowed, which is called "piecemeal social engineering" in the "open society." However, even in the open society the risk to democracy still persists, especially in its real-world variants, such as liberal polyarchies. This is because even if the representatives are elected, someone (or some group) must still perform the social engineering, that is, they still exercise power over others. Therefore, in open societies, there is a tension between the desire for rationality and egalitarian principles. Furthermore, there is another threat to democracy because individuals who are reduced to calculating machines are susceptible to totalitarian promises to restore meaning to their lives.
3. Instrumental rationality represses people. On the one hand, instrumental rationality provides people with the power and technology to develop the material conditions for human freedom. On the other hand, the focus

on instrumental rationality suppresses the playfulness and creativity that allow humans to realize this freedom. Horkheimer and Adorno call this paradox the dialectic of Enlightenment, from which there is no escape, except perhaps artistic expressions. A similar position with respect to repression is taken by contemporary feminists, who argue, for instance, that reproductive technology and population control ideology submit the control of the female body to technical experts. That is, the control of a woman's own fertility is given to others.

4. Instrumental rationality—and its corresponding political institutions—cannot effectively solve complex social problems. Instrumental rationality involves analytic sensibility, which requires complex phenomena be disaggregated into their component parts in order for the phenomena to be best understood. Then, each of these component parts should be understood and any problematic aspects of them resolved instrumentally, in a piecemeal fashion. Indeed, such decomposition is used as the organizing principle for bureaucratic division of labor.
5. Instrumental rationality makes it impossible to effectively and appropriately analyze public policies. This criticism applies to the interdisciplinary field of public policy analysis. This field is still mostly dominated by the idea that public policies should make instrumental interventions in society, economy, and polity. If the preceding four counts are accepted, then mainstream policy analysts' recommendations lead to ineffective public action.
6. Instrumental rationality that informs social science produces inappropriate and unfruitful social science instruments and methods. The widespread acceptance and use of such instruments and methods function in a very subtle way to reinforce some undesirable aspects of the dominant political order.

Some criticisms of objectivity are as follows.

1. Objectivism idolizes a false account of science. Post-empiricist philosophy of science has shown that there is no universally applicable "logic of scientific inquiry." Any set of universally applicable scientific rules fails when it is tested against the history of science, especially in relation to exemplary episodes in the history of science. The competition among rival theories and research programs and their outcome rejects objectivist standards.

2. Objectivism has a repressive nature. It imposes its standards and practices on traditions and ways of life that adhere to alternative viewpoints. It does it either by argument in its own terms, or by force. Its victims include indigenous cultures, non-scientific medical practices, and dissenting epistemologies, for example, feminism. One of the protagonists of objectivism congratulates ancient Athens for its application of "some form of imperialism" to defeat "tribalist exclusiveness and self-sufficiency."
3. Objectivism retards the progress of social science, political science, and politics. The extent to which the social and political world is informed by purely objectivist ideas about cognitive rationality grows against defensible social and political science and to authentic political reflection more generally.

Given these counts against instrumental and objectivist rationality, it can be argued that instrumental rationality will always be with us, but it deserves to occupy a more limited domain than it currently does. Objectivism, on the other hand, can be removed entirely. The spaces that are thus vacated can be allocated to a different kind of rationality: discursive and democratic, instead of instrumental and authoritarian. This discursive and democratic rationality can regulate the remainder of instrumental rationality and replace objectivism.

Instrumental rationality and objectivism do not have the sole claim on reason, as there are alternative rationalities. Around the middle of the twentieth century, Max Horkheimer compared and contrasted ancient conceptions of what he called "objective" reason (which is different from objectivism) with the Enlightenment's "subjective" (i.e., instrumental) rationality. Horkheimer appreciates "objective reason" and defines it as a comprehensive system, or hierarchy, consisting of all beings, including man and his aims. Moreover, the degree of reasonableness of a man's life is determined by the extent to which it is in harmony with this totality. Furthermore, there is no manipulation of objects by (human) subjects, but only the harmonization of subjects.

Horkheimer appreciates the role of Aristotle in his objective reason. But he does not do justice to Aristotle's notion of harmonization, especially in relation to politics and practical reason. Aristotelian practical reason entails persuasion, reflection on values, prudential judgment, and free expression of one's ideas. Aristotle's practical reason is clearly grounded in collective life. Accordingly, an isolated individual cannot be rational, because rationality comes into play only in collective interaction. For Aristotle, practical reason, but not power, defines the very idea of politics. That is, politics entails people's deliberate efforts to order, direct, and control their collective affairs and activities; to establish ends for their community; and to implement and evaluate such ends.

This "classical" conception of politics and rationality had been eclipsed by the definition of politics as power and the instrumental pursuit of interest by individuals or states. It was Hannah Arendt who revived this classical ideal, although in a nostalgic fashion. Arendt argues that the classical ideal of unconstrained and egalitarian political debate about principles can materialize in the modern world, but only briefly around the time of revolutions. For instance, spontaneously republican "councils" take form in the French Revolution, the Paris Commune, the Soviets of the Russian Revolution, and the Hungarian Revolt of 1956. In all cases, these councils are soon destroyed by armed forces or subverted by instrumental rationalists.

The work of Arendt belongs to a movement that is sympathetic to practical reason. This movement is called "beyond objectivism and relativism" and is celebrated by Bernstein. He argues that the objectivist search for overarching criteria and universal decision rules for (instrumentally) rational choices is being repudiated in a wide spectrum of areas such as philosophy of science, textual interpretation, and political theory. The alternative, however, does not require resorting to the relativism of closed systems of thought or culture in which no rational choices can be made. This is because rational persuasion can be made across the boundaries of scientific paradigms, political theories, cultures, or normative positions, even without universal criteria. For Bernstein, criteria are always multiple, changeable, open to criticism and defense, and susceptible to selective justification and differential weighting in different cases. That is, they act as resources in the construction of rational arguments to be expressed in debates among proponents of alternative views. Such debates become possible when systems of thought meet on some common ground. If there is no common ground, there is no competition, and there is nothing to disagree about. For instance, scientific paradigms enter a competition among respective communities that each of them shares some values about what it means to do science with respect to the same set of objects.

Bernstein praises Jurgen Habermas, who shares Horkheimer's concern with the Enlightenment legacy. However, Habermas has a somewhat different position on this matter compared to Horkheimer (and Arendt), who condemns post-Enlightenment conceptions of reason. Habermas argues that modernity brings not only the kind of reason that Horkheimer (and Arendt) criticizes, but also it brings increased potential for a more attractive kind of reason. Habermas shares Horkheimer, Adorno, and Weber's denunciation of instrumental rationality on the grounds that it has institutionalized restrictions and constraints through bureaucratization, administration, and social control; despite the fact that instrumental rationality was once very liberating. Furthermore, Habermas argues that modernity also has the potential for communicative rationality that entails uncoerced and undistorted interaction among competent individuals.

According to Habermas, both instrumental and communicative rationalities are created in processes through which the "lifeworld" is increasingly subjected to modern forms of consciousness. Habermas uses the term "lifeworld" to refer to the symbolic network in which people interact, where culture, social relations, and individual personalities are constructed and maintained. Modern consciousness helps to liberate the lifeworld from unthinkingly conforming to traditional values, customs, and other normative constraints; therefore, it helps to release individuals to take instrumentally rational action. Habermas further argues that through these same processes the discursive and critical reconstructions of the lifeworld are enabled. People can coordinate their actions through talk rather than unthinkingly complying with norms, and it is through talk that criticisms can be launched against instrumental rationality. Since the Enlightenment, instrumental rationality has been the dominant side of this conflict, mostly due to the support of the state and capital. Instrumental rationality has also received support from the cultural impoverishment of the lifeworld, whereby expert cultures have monopolized science, technology, art, law, and other activities from which resistance might otherwise benefit. Notwithstanding the above, the possibility still remains for resistance based on reflection, talk, and communicative action.

This is, therefore, why the potential for communicative rationalization increases with that of its opposite, that is, instrumental rationalization. There is another link between these two forms of rationalization. Instrumentally rational action, in a setting that involves other human beings, is only as effective as the individual can comprehend and deploy language in order to recognize and make offers, threats, and bluffs. These uses of language require a commitment to the rules of linguistic interaction. Moreover, coordinated instrumentally rational action by a group of people (e.g., a team of scientific investigators, a task force, or a committee) requires effective communication within that group. In the practice of science, there is a requirement for a "meta-scientific rationality of inter-subjective discourse" within communities of practitioners. The same requirement applies to communities of technologists, whose work is more clearly instrumental than that of scientists. Technologists help in the control of both human and nonhuman nature; or more specifically the instrumental domination of individuals and objects external to them. Therefore, one task for communicative rationalization is the destruction of such privilege and its implicit hierarchy.

Communicative rationality is based on the interaction of social life. Communicative action is based on intersubjective understanding, the coordination of actions through discussion, and the socialization of members of the community. Communicative rationality requires this action to be characterized by the reflective understanding of competent actors. Communicative action should be free from deception, self-deception, strategic behavior, and domination through the exercise of power. Communicative rationality entails intersubjective discourse—not individual maximization—and it pertains to the generation of normative judgments and action principles—not the selection of means to ends. Since communication is in part related to the coordination of actions, communicative rationality cannot totally replace instrumental rationality; rather communicative rationality can only restrict the domain of instrumental rationality.

There are major differences among the figures whose views were introduced above. Nonetheless, the commonalities among their ideas and possibilities should be apparent. A coherent set of ideas is formed by classical politics, practical reason, critical theory, Horkheimer's objective reason, and communicative rationality. Opposed to this first set of ideas are modern politics, deductive-nomological theory, Horkheimer's subjective reason, objectivism, and instrumental rationality. Both sets of ideas exist not only in the world of philosophy, social theory, and political theory but also in the real world.

This second set of ideas is a companion to both bureaucratic-authoritarian and liberal-democratic political forms. In contrast, the first set of ideas is most compatible with the political form which is more participatory democracy, called "strong democracy." Liberal democracy and participatory democracy can be regarded as two major democratic possibilities that form two poles of a spectrum. As one moves toward the participatory-democracy pole of the spectrum, politics becomes increasingly discursive, educational, truly public-interests oriented, and needful of active citizenship. In contrast, as one moves toward the liberal-democracy pole of the spectrum, politics becomes dominated by voting, strategy, private interests, bargaining, exchange, spectacle, and limited involvement. The second set is currently dominant in the real world. However, the first set—which may be called "discursive democracy"—is not lost. Currently, this first set has gained momentum in a variety of political movements, such as Green, feminist, and peace-oriented communitarian, and in a variety of institutional experiments.

## Radical Structuralist View

Rationality changes as social formations change over time. As society moves from feudalism, to capitalism, and toward socialism; rationality changes from traditional rationality to instrumental rationality, and toward dialectical rationality, or dialectical materialism.[4]

Dialectical materialism is "the communist world outlook," that is, the way communists think and act in their life. Engels was the chief founder of dialectical materialism. "Dialectical materialism" is distinct from but related to "historical materialism." Marx's distinctive intellectual work was a theory of society known as historical materialism. Generally, historical materialism is a social theory that regards economics as the basis of society, and in particular, economics as the basis of the capitalist social system. Accordingly, historical materialism is regarded as social science.

Dialectical materialism is a rational logic that people can use in their encounter with reality as a whole, that is, both nature and society. According to dialectical materialism, the same laws that govern nature also govern social history. Thus, the basic laws of dialectical materialism have universal applications: governing nature, society, and thought. Based on its universal applicability, dialectical materialism is generally regarded as a philosophy and provides a general account of the structural relations of the special sciences.

Dialectical materialism as a philosophy is a "world outlook." It provides a synoptic view of the totality of reality, and it supplies special sciences with a common content and an underlying general conception of reality that they all share and express. This philosophy is itself scientific, as it is reflected in the special sciences, and it is supported by the findings of the special sciences as they investigate their own limited domains within the wider reality.

The scientific nature of dialectical materialism, which was emphasized by Engels, has a special political advantage for Marxism. The emphasis was placed on the quality that historical materialism shares with the natural sciences—not only the same method of inquiry, but more importantly, the same "world outlook." The scientific nature of historical materialism is of crucial importance to its promotion. Marxism rejects as unscientific both other social theories—such as bourgeois social theories—and other forms of socialism—such as ethical or utopian socialism. It takes advantage of the cognitive authority of science and distinguishes itself from other socialists as, Engels called, "scientific socialism."

During the rise of the bourgeoisie, the Scientific Revolution and Enlightenment resulted in the establishment of the natural sciences of astronomy, physics, and chemistry. But it was later, in the late eighteenth and early nineteenth centuries that the social sciences started to develop. In this process, social theory began its own transformation from philosophy into science. In the 1840s, Marx and Engels started their work toward a unified and comprehensive social science. They rejected the logical rationality of both the existing bourgeois social theory—such as classical political economy—and the earlier modern natural sciences. In their view, each major social revolution—that is, a revolution in the dominant mode of production—entails an ideological revolution—that is, a revolution in world outlook, logic, and rationality. Thus, the transition from feudalism to capitalism entailed the transition from the religion-dominated ideology of the Middle Ages to a natural-science conception of reality. At the core of this "natural philosophy" of the bourgeois era was "mechanical philosophy." It stated that the objective reality, which is the subject of investigation by science, is a mechanism of matter in motion, a kind of cosmic clockwork, and to understand this reality requires the understanding of the laws that govern the mechanism. Between this world outlook of the bourgeoisie and the new world outlook of the rising working class, there would be both continuities and breaks, which would be generated in bourgeois society. Thus, Marx and Engels noted that, in the latter part of the eighteenth century, the natural sciences had already begun their significant change, developing one of the most basic and characteristic aspects of the new communist point of view.

Newton stated that the planetary system started when God threw the planets around the sun, creating processes that were subject to the laws of motion and gravity, and such processes of movement were repetitive or cyclical within a system that remained unchanged and unchanging. But the Kant-Laplace nebular hypothesis rejected this static conception and offered a new theory stating that the present solar system is the latest stage in a long and continuing evolution. For Marx and Engels, this showed that "nature has a history" and that the natural sciences were themselves evolving from a static conception of nature toward the recognition of a nature that has history. Lyell's geology and Darwin's biology confirmed this tendency.

Marx and Engels noted that the key to understanding this mode of non-cyclical, progressive change had already been prepared within philosophy by Hegel's dialectic. They believed, however, that Hegel's dialectic suffers from a deformation characteristic of philosophy, especially bourgeois philosophy. More specifically, they believed that Hegel's dialectic is idealist, not materialist. That is, for Hegel, reality is ideal, the activity and product of the spirit in mind, so that the nature of his dialectic is an essentially non-material process.

Dialectical materialism, then, resulted from combining two bourgeois philosophies: (1) Hegel's dialectical idealism and (2) the mechanistic materialism of the Scientific Revolution and Enlightenment. Hegel's idealism is incompatible with materialism, and the mechanistic nature of traditional materialism is incompatible with dialectic. Dialectical materialism therefore rejected both and obtained a conception of reality that is both dialectical and materialist.

In the process of the unification of dialectic and materialism, both doctrines are transformed. Traditional materialism, which is non-dialectical, is reductive, that is, a theory of "nothing but." More specifically, it states that reality is nothing but matter in motion and that any process that seems to be otherwise is really not so because it is "reducible" to matter in motion. Furthermore, it states that ideas are reducible to and ultimately identical with material processes. According to this view, change—that is, the development of difference and novelty—is really nothing but the continuation of the same basic processes and laws. In contrast, the dialectical point of view states that concrete reality, which is apparently a unity, is indeed a differentiated unity, in which the components are all interrelated and integrated but not reducible to one another. These differentiated components constitute opposition and contradiction. For instance, the material and the ideal are different and opposed; they are interrelated within a unity, but the material is basic: matter can exist without mind but not mind without matter. For example, epistemologically, physics generates objective knowledge of an objective reality and forms the base of a unified system of the special sciences that are not reducible to physics. Moreover, differentiation is an active process, not a static condition. Reality is a unity, but contradictory; and this conflict of opposites within unity drives reality forward in a historical process of progressive change. This change is both evolutionary and revolutionary, that is, both quantitative and qualitative. The revolutionary or discontinuous moments entail genuine novelty, that is, a qualitative change. In this view, the mind itself is such an emergent novelty.

The logic of dialectical rationality can be represented by three fundamental laws: (1) the law of the unity of opposites: that concrete reality is a unity which is contradictory and in conflict; (2) the law of the negation of the negation: that in the conflict of opposites, one component negates the other but preserves something of the negated component, and then the component itself is negated in a historical process, and in this way, the component rises to ever higher levels; (3) the law of the transformation of quantity into quality: that in the evolutionary process of gradual quantitative change, contradictions intensify to the extent that at some point a revolutionary qualitative change occurs. The popularized version of these laws represents the logic of dialectical rationality as a triadic process of thesis, antithesis, and synthesis. The logic of dialectical rationality is in contrast to the logic of instrumental rationality, which is cause and effect.

Dialectics starts with the axiom that everything is in a constant state of change and flux. Dialectics explains that change and motion involve contradiction, and that change and motion take place through contradictions. In contrast to formal logic—according to which there is a smooth, uninterrupted line of progress—dialectical logic states that progress involves sudden and explosive periods of interruption, in which slow, accumulated changes (quantitative change) become increasingly rapid, leading to the transformation of quantity into quality.

At first encounter, the world is usually seen as an immense and amazingly complex series of phenomena with seemingly endless change, cause and effect, action and reaction. Scientific investigation is motivated by the desire for a rational insight into this complex and confusing world in order to understand it and conquer it. Scientific investigation searches for laws that can distinguish the general from the particular, the accidental from the necessary, and provides an understanding of the forces that give rise to the phenomena which people confront.

In nature, there is nothing that stays constant. Everything perpetually moves, changes, and transforms. Everything surges up out of its antecedents that existed before. Everything turns into something else, and it is impossible for something to disappear without a trace. In summary, everything comes from other things and gives rise to still other things.

The laws of dialectics were originally worked out in detail by Hegel, although in a mystified, idealist form. Marx and Engels gave dialectics a scientific, that is, materialist, basis. Hegel operated with ideological shadows, that is, the "Absolute Idea," as the ultimate reality. Marx demonstrated that the movement of these ideological shadows was a reflection of the movement of material bodies.

Dialectic claims that it revolutionizes thinking at all levels—particularly, at the most intellectually fundamental level of logic. Among the most controversial elements of dialectic is the logical category of contradiction. Dialectic presupposes that there are contradictions in reality. This implies that traditional formal logic, whose central principle is non-contradiction, must be replaced by dialectical logic. In traditional formal logic, two ideas can be contradictory, but both ideas cannot be true, because reality is not contradictory. Hegel rejects this distinction between ideas and reality but ultimately, through his idealism, views contradiction as a relation between ideas. The distinctive feature of dialectical materialism is that it regards the logical category of contradiction as applicable to material reality.

The logic of dialectical materialism can be applied to economics. Accordingly, economic theory identifies major contradictions within the processes of production, exchange, and distribution and uses them to explain the laws of historical change in society. Most importantly, these laws explain the way in which the gradual intensification of contradictions leads to a crisis and ultimately to a revolution, which leads to the establishment of a qualitatively new economic system.

The logic of dialectical materialism has implications not only for economic theory per se, but also for the relationship between economics and other social sciences, such as political science. First, the logic of dialectical rationality emphasizes totality. This means that all things are very closely integrated, to the extent that they can be understood only based on their interrelationships. Therefore, this rejects the treatment of economics as a specialist social science that can understand its domain within social phenomena independently of other social domains and other social sciences. From the point of view of the logic of dialectical rationality, economics is not a specialist social science, but it is an integral part of social science, which is a comprehensive and unified theory about a unified, but contradictory, social totality. Second, materialism states that, within the social totality, economic processes play the overriding role. Materialism, which has been associated with the rise of natural sciences, in the contrast between matter, on the one hand, and mind and ideas, on the other hand, states that matter is the most fundamental, or the only ultimate, component of reality. When materialism is applied to society, as distinct from nature, in its contrast between ideas and theory, on the one hand, and practice, on the other hand, it holds that the most fundamental aspect of any social system is its most material practice, that is, its economic practice, and more fundamentally its mode of material production. Thus, in general, dialectical materialism ultimately explains social structure and social change in terms of economic structure and economic change. According to dialectical materialism, economics is the most foundational part of social science.

Within Marxism, some exaggerate the dialectical materialism doctrine to the point of vulgarization. In emphasizing the scientific nature of historical materialism—that is, by showing that it shares a world outlook with the natural sciences—they lead dialectical materialism to represent historical materialism as a natural science of society. This type of combining dialectic and materialism based on the general perspective of natural science has been associated with the idea that the communist world outlook should be purged of any unreconstructed residues from the bourgeois world outlook. The result has been an influential vulgar version of Marxism that Lenin called "economism."

On the side of dialectic, the orthodox view states that contradiction, as a logical relation, is a relation between ideas, and therefore, it cannot be applied to material reality. Accordingly, the logical category of contradiction has been identified with conflict (i.e., conflict of forces) and has become devoid of logical and critical content. This has helped to undermine the possibility of making the social science of historical materialism a social critique.

On the side of materialism, classical scientific materialism is reductive and determinist, and presupposes "matter" as an object of the "iron laws" of nature. Within Marxism, for those who are under the influence of this tendency, the political and theoretical superstructure are byproducts of society's material base. This means that only the material base, that is, the economy, and, in turn, its most material aspect, that is, technology, act as the driving force of society. The implication of this for socialist strategy is the concentration on working-class action within the economic base, rather than the inclusion of politics and the state. Even this limited focus on the working class can be regarded as either impossible or unnecessary in light of the conception of the science of economics founded on the materialism of the natural science type. Although

Engels was chiefly behind the idea of dialectical materialism, Marx was, at times, supportive of this version of economics. For instance, he referred to the natural laws of capitalist production that necessarily work toward inevitable results. Furthermore, he agreed that the social movement is a process of natural history; and it is governed by laws which are independent of human will, consciousness, and intelligence; and these laws determine human will, consciousness, and intelligence. This view does not leave any possibility for socialist action and any revolutionary class war. Lenin, who was a committed believer in dialectical materialism, persistently argued against the anti-revolutionary tendencies of economism.

Marxism took shape after Marx's death and among the first generation of his followers, in the period that resulted in the Russian Revolution. These followers learned Marxism mainly from the two most well-known books of the founders: Marx's *Capital* and Engels's *Anti-Duhring*. The former provided the basic economic science of historical materialism, and the latter did it with respect to dialectical materialism. Dialectical materialism constituted an essential component of Marxism for that first generation, that is, the generation of the Second International. It was also central to Soviet communism and to the Soviet-led Communist Party orthodoxy. Between the two world wars, Soviet communism was taken over by the Stalinist dictatorship and party bureaucracy. As a result, this first Marxist philosophy, that is, dialectical materialism, came under attack from Marxists outside the USSR. Consequently, it began to lose its position to a second form of Marxist philosophy, that is, Marxist humanism, which has become the characteristic form of "Western Marxism." Its chief theorists are Lukacs, Korsch, and Gramsci, other thinkers of the Frankfurt School, and Sartre, who attempted to marry Marxism with Existentialism. These theorists attacked the materialism of the natural science kind, emphasized Marx's debt to Hegel and dialectic, and insisted on the necessary roles of politics and ideology in social change. Their Marxism was found to be in line with Marx's early writings, especially his *Economic and Philosophical Manuscripts of 1844*, which were rediscovered in the 1920s and 1930s. However, since the 1960s, these Hegelianizers themselves have come under attack, chiefly from Althusser and his followers. But "diamat" (which was the abbreviation of dialectical materialism used in the USSR) remained mainly in Soviet communism and the Soviet-led Communist Parties.

## Conclusion

This chapter briefly discussed four views expressed with respect to rationality. The functionalist paradigm applies rational choice theory as a very general science of practical reason, which accurately describes, successfully predicts, and powerfully explains phenomena. The interpretive paradigm believes that different answers to particular types of questions are supported by different reasons. The radical humanist paradigm believes that instrumental rationality and objectivism are repressive and do not have sole claim on reason, as there are alternative rationalities. The radical structuralist paradigm believes that as society moves from feudalism, to capitalism, and toward socialism; rationality changes from traditional rationality to instrumental rationality, and toward dialectical rationality, or dialectical materialism.

Each paradigm is logically coherent—in terms of its underlying assumptions—and conceptualizes and studies the phenomenon in a certain way, generating distinctive kinds of insight and understanding. Therefore, different paradigms in combination provide a broader understanding of the phenomenon under consideration. An understanding of different paradigms leads to a better understanding of the multifaceted nature of the phenomenon.

## Notes

1 For this literature, see Arrow (1951); Becker (1976); Drichoutis and Nayga (2020); Gigerenzer (2021); Gillespie (2023); Hahn (2022); Hertwig, Leuker, Pachur, Spiliopoulos, and Pleskac (2022); Hogarth and Reder (1987); Hollis and Sugden (1993); Hsu (2022); Mallard (2020); Nozick (1993); Petracca (2021); Pothos and Pleskac (2022); Sent (2018); Simon (1982); Sugden (1991); Thagard (2004); and Weirich (2004). This section is based on Hollis and Sugden (1993).

2 For this literature, see Bergamaschi Ganapini (2020); Cabantous, Gond, and Johnson-Cramer (2008); Chater et al. (2018); Felin, Koenderink, and Krueger (2017); Friedland and Robertson (1990); Geertz (1973); Granovetter (1985); Halevy and Mayraz (2022); MacIntyre (1988); Mirowski (1988); Rojot (2008); Viale, Gallagher, and Gallese (2023); Weber (1968); and Winch (1958). This section is based on MacIntyre (1988).

3 For this literature, see Blau (2021); Dryzek (1990); Gorz (1989); Habermas (1983); Horkheimer (1947); Horkheimer and Adorno (1944); Jones (2004); Kravchenko

and Morozov (2021); Lash and Whimster (1987); Losonc (2020); Marcuse (1964); Munroe (2021); Nieswandt (2023); Ostapiuk (2019); Ozdemir (2021); Raz (2017); Singh (2022); and Zafirovski (2008). This section is based on Dryzek (1990).

4 For this literature, see Casal (2020); Colletti (1975); Edgley (2010); Engels (1877); Foley (2004); Grinin and Grinin (2023); Jordan (1967); Lenin (1908); Lettow (2017); Lukojanov and Sherikhova (2018); Marx (1873/1976); Noonan (2021); Novack (1971); Rupert and Smith (2016); Xu (2019); and Wetter (1952). This section is based on Edgley (2010).

## References

Arrow, Kenneth J. (1951), "Alternative Approaches to the Theory of Choice in Risk-Taking Situations," *Econometrica*, XIX, 404–37, October.

Becker, Gary (1976), *The Economic Approach to Human Behavior*, Chicago, IL: University of Chicago Press.

Bergamaschi Ganapini, Marianna (2020), "Belief's Minimal Rationality," *Philosophical Studies*, 177:11, 3263–3282.

Blau, Adrian (2021), "Defending Instrumental Rationality against Critical Theorists," *Political Research Quarterly*, 74:4, 1067–80.

Cabantous, Laure, Gond, Jean-Pascal, and Johnson-Cramer, Michel (2008), "The Social Construction of Rationality in Organizational Decision Making," in Hodgkinson, Gerard P. and Starbuck, William H. (eds.), *The Oxford Handbook of Organizational Decision Making*, Oxford: Oxford University Press, Chapter 21, 399–417.

Casal, Paula (2020), "G.A. Cohen's Historical Materialism: A Feminist Critique," *Journal of Political Ideologies*, 25:3, 316–33.

Chater, Nick, Felin, Teppo, Funder, David C., Gigerenzer, Gerd, Koenderink, Jan J., Krueger, Joachim I., Noble, Denis, Nordli, Samuel A., Oaksford, Mike, Schwartz, Barry, Stanovich, Keith E., and Todd, Peter M. (2018), "Mind, Rationality, and Cognition: An Interdisciplinary Debate," *Psychonomic Bulletin and Review*, 25:2, 793–826.

Colletti, L. (1975), "Marxism and the Dialectic," *New Left Review*, 93, 3–29.

Drichoutis, Andreas C. and Nayga, Rodolfo M. (2020), "Economic Rationality under Cognitive Load," *Economic Journal*, 130:632, 2382–409.

Dryzek, John S. (1990), *Discursive Democracy*, Cambridge: Cambridge University Press.

Edgley, Roy (2006), "Dialectical Materialism," in Bottomore, T. (ed.), *A Dictionary of Marxist Thought*, Oxford, England: Blackwell, 142–43.

Engels, F. (1877), *Anti-Duhring*, Moscow, Russia: Foreign Languages Publishing House.

Felin, Teppo, Koenderink, Jan, and Krueger, Joachim I. (2017), "Rationality, Perception, and the All-Seeing Eye," *Psychonomic Bulletin and Review*, 24:4, 1040–59.

Foley, Duncan K. (2004), "Rationality and Ideology in Economics," *Social Research*, 71:2, Summer, 329–42.

Friedland, Roger and Robertson, A.F. (1990), "Beyond the Marketplace," in Friedland, Roger and Robertson, A.F. (eds.), *Beyond the Marketplace: Rethinking Economy and Society*, New York, NY: Aldine de Gruyter, Chapter 1, 3–49.

Geertz, Clifford (1973), "The Impact of the Concept of Culture on the Concept of Man," in *The Interpretation of Cultures: Selected Essays by Clifford Geertz*, New York, NY: Basic Books, Inc., Publishers, Chapter 2, pp. 33–54.

Gigerenzer, Gerd (2021), "Axiomatic Rationality and Ecological Rationality," *Synthese*, 198:4, 3547–64.

Gillespie, James (2023), "Agent-Centered Epistemic Rationality," *Synthese*, 201:3, 95–117.

Gorz, Andre (1989), *Critique of Economic Reason*, London: Verso.

Granovetter, Mark (1985), "Economic Action and Social Structure: The Problem of Embeddedness," *AJS*, 91:3, November, 481–510.

Grinin, Leonid and Grinin, Anton L. (2023), "Historical Materialism: Does the Concept Have a Future?" *Social Evolution and History*, 22:1, 22–36.

Habermas, Jurgen (1983), *The Theory of Communicative Action, Volume One: Reason and Rationalization of Society*, Boston, MA: Beacon Press.

Hahn, Ulrike (2022), "Collectives and Epistemic Rationality," *Topics in Cognitive Science*, 14:3, 602–20.

Halevy, Yoram and Mayraz, Guy (2022), "Identifying Rule-Based Rationality," *Review of Economics and Statistics*, 106:5, 1369–80.

Hertwig, Ralph, Leuker, Christina, Pachur, Thorsten, Spiliopoulos, Leonidas, and Pleskac, Timothy J. (2022), "Studies in Ecological Rationality," *Topics in Cognitive Science*, 14:3, 467–91.

Hogarth, Robin M. and Reder, Melvin W., eds. (1987), *Rational Choice: The Contrast Between Economics and Psychology*, Chicago, IL: University of Chicago Press.

Hollis, Martin and Sugden, Robert (1993), "Rationality in Action," *Mind*, 102:45, January, 1–35.

Horkheimer, Max (1947), *Eclipse of Reason*, New York, NY: Oxford University Press.

Horkheimer, Max and Adorno, Theodor W. (1944), *Dialectic of Enlightenment*, New York, NY: Seabury Press.

Hsu, Shi-Ling (2022), "Whither Rationality?," *Michigan Law Review*, 120:120.6, 1165–85.

Jones, Karen (2004), "Gender and Rationality," in Mele, Alfred R. and Rawlings, Piers (eds.), *The Oxford Handbook of Rationality*, Oxford, England: Oxford University Press, Chapter 16, pp. 301–19.

Jordan, Z.A. (1967), *The Evolution of Dialectical Materialism*, London: Macmillan.

Kravchenko, Alla and Morozov, Andrii (2021), "On Instrumental Rationality: Nihilistic and Totalitarian Potential," *Osvitnij Diskurs*, 31:2–3, 7–19.

Lash, Scott and Whimster, Sam, eds. (1987), *Max Weber, Rationality and Modernity*, London: Allen and Unwin.

Lenin, V.I. (1908), *Materialism and Empirico-Criticism*, Moscow: Foreign Languages Publishing House.

Lettow, Susanne (2017), "Turning the Turn: New Materialism, Historical Materialism, and Critical Theory," *Thesis Eleven*, 140:1, 106–12.

Losonc, Alpar (2020), "Self-Understanding of the Crisis in the Humanities against the 'Invasive' Instrumental Rationality," *Anafora*, 7:2, 341–57.

Lukojanov, Valery and Sherikhova, Ekaterina (2018), "Lukacs and Benjamin: Two Versions of Historical Materialism," *Logos*, 28:1, 143–54.

MacIntyre, Alasdair C. (1988), *Whose Justice? Whose Rationality?*, Notre Dame, IN: University of Notre Dame Press.

Mallard, Graham (2020), *Bounded Rationality*, Newcastle Upon Tyne: Agenda Publishing.

Marcuse, Herbert (1964), *One-Dimensional Man: Studies in the Ideology of Advanced Industrial Society*, Boston, MA: Beacon Press.

Marx, Karl (1873/1976), *Capital*, Volume One, Second Edition, Harmondsworth: Penguin.

Mirowski, Philip (1988), "The Philosophical Foundations of Institutionalist Economics," in Mirowski, Philip, *Against Mechanism: Protecting Economics from Science*, Totowa, NJ: Rowman and Littlefield, Publishers, Chapter 7, pp. 106–33.

Munroe, Wade (2021), "Reasoning, Rationality, and Representation," Synthese, 198:9, 8323–45.

Nieswandt, Katharina (2023), "Instrumental Rationality in the Social Sciences," *Philosophy of the Social Sciences*, 25:1, 1–18.

Noonan, Jeff (2021), "Historical Materialism as Mediation between the Physical and the Meaningful," *Philosophy and Social Criticism*, 47:9, 1043–59.

Novack, George Edward (1971), *An Introduction to the Logic of Marxism*, New York, NY: Pathfinder Press, Inc.

Nozick, Robert (1993), *The Nature of Rationality*, Princeton, NJ: Princeton University Press.

Ostapiuk, Aleksander (2019), "Human Now versus Human Over Time: When Instrumental Rationality and Utility Are Not Enough," *Panoeconomicus*, 66:5, 633–57.

Ozdemir, Esin (2021), "Rationality Revisited: Politicization through Planning Rationality against the Rationality of Power," *Planning Theory*, 20:4, 350–71.

Petracca, Enrico (2021), "Embodying Bounded Rationality: From Embodied Bounded Rationality to Embodied Rationality," *Frontiers in Psychology*, 12, 710607.

Pothos, Emmanuel M. and Pleskac, Timothy J. (2022), "Rethinking Rationality," *Topics in Cognitive Science*, 14:3, 451–66.

Raz, Joseph (2017), "Instrumental Rationality: A Reprise," *Journal of Ethics and Social Philosophy*, 1:1, 1–20.

Rojot, Jacques (2008), "Culture and Decision Making," in Hodgkinson, Gerard P. and Starbuck, William H. (eds.), *The Oxford Handbook of Organizational Decision Making*, Oxford: Oxford University Press, Chapter 7, pp. 134–54.

Rupert, Mark and Smith, Hazelle, eds. (2016), *Historical Materialism and Globalization*, New York, NY: Routledge.

Sent, Esther-Mirjam (2018), "Rationality and Bounded Rationality: You Can't Have One Without the Other," *European Journal of the History of Economic Thought*, 25:6, 1370–86.

Simon, Herbert Alexander (1982), *Models of Bounded Rationality*, 2 Vols, Cambridge, MA: MIT Press.

Singh, Keshav (2022), "New Work for a Theory of Instrumental Rationality," *Analysis*, 82:3, 537–51.

Sugden, Robert (1991), "Rational Choice: A Survey of Contributions from Economic and Philosophy," *Economic Journal*, 101:407, July, 751–85.

Thagard, Paul (2004), "Rationality and Science," in Mele, Alfred R. and Rawlings, Piers (eds.), *The Oxford Handbook of Rationality*, Oxford: Oxford University Press, Chapter 19, pp. 363–79.

Viale, Riccardo, Gallagher, Shaun, and Gallese, Vittorio (2023), "Editorial: Embodied Bounded Rationality," *Frontiers in Psychology*, 14:1235087.

Weber, Max (1968), *Economy and Society: An Outline of Interpretive Sociology*, Volume 1, New York, NY: Bedminster Press.

Weirich, Paul (2004), "Economic Rationality," in Mele, Alfred R. and Rawlings, Piers (eds.), *The Oxford Handbook of Rationality*, Oxford: Oxford University Press, Chapter 20, pp. 380–98.

Wetter, G.A. (1952), *Dialectical Materialism*, London: Routledge and Kegan Paul.

Winch, Peter (1958), *The Idea of Social Science*, New York, NY: Humanities Press.

Xu, Shuangshuang (2019), "Revisiting Bruner's Legacy from the Perspective of Historical Materialism," *Integrative Physiological and Behavioral Science*, 53:4, 590–601.

Zafirovski, Milan (2008), "Classical and Neo-Classical Conceptions of Rationality – Findings of an Exploratory Survey," *Journal of Socio-Economics*, 37:2, April, 789–820.

5

# Ethics

## A Multi-Paradigmatic View

Any explanation of ethics is based on a worldview. The premise of this book is that any worldview can be associated with one of the four broad paradigms: functionalist, interpretive, radical humanist, and radical structuralist. This chapter takes the case of ethics and discusses it from the four different viewpoints. It emphasizes that the four views expressed are equally scientific and informative; they look at the phenomenon from their certain paradigmatic viewpoint, and together they provide a more balanced understanding of the phenomenon under consideration. In this chapter, the first through the fourth sections present the four perspectives, and the fifth section concludes the chapter.

### Functionalist View

A normative ethical system is an ordered set of moral standards and rules of conduct that can be used in conjunction with factual knowledge to determine what a person, when confronted with alternatives, ought or ought not to do. Utilitarianism is one of the normative ethical systems that is most widely discussed and defended in contemporary moral philosophy. Its classical formulation was made by two British philosophers: Jeremy Bentham (1748–1832) and John Stuart Mill (1806–73).[1]

Utilitarianism is a teleological ethical system. The term teleological is derived from the Greek word telos, which means end or purpose. According to the teleological system, an action is morally right if it will have good consequences. This action can be taken by a person or by everyone. In either case, in the final analysis, it is the goodness or badness of the consequences of the action that makes it right or wrong.

In a teleological ethical system, in order to determine whether an action is right or wrong, the consequences of that action are subjected to a standard of value. If the consequences of someone's action, or of everyone's action, satisfy the standard of value, then the consequences are good and the action is right. If the consequences of the action fail to fulfill the standard, then the consequences are bad, and the action is wrong. In a teleological ethical system, the "consequences" of an action consist of all the effects of the action in the indefinite future. These consequences include everything that takes place as a result of the action. That is, they include everything that would have been different in the future if the action had not been taken. For instance, consider the assassination of Abraham Lincoln in 1865 by John Wilkes Booth. If this assassination changed the history of the United States during the Reconstruction following the Civil War, then that change is considered one of the consequences of Booth's action. If what happened as a result of Lincoln's murder is tested against a certain standard of value and found out that it is neither good nor bad, then this consequence of Booth's action has no effect on the rightness or wrongness of his action. If the result of the test comes out to be good or bad (depending on its degree), then it has its corresponding effect on the rightness or wrongness of his action.

In utilitarian ethics, the standard of value that is used to test the rightness or wrongness of an action is called "utility." This is the basic concept of utilitarian ethics, as its name indicates. An act is right if it is useful. More specifically, an act is right when it is useful in the sense that it leads to a desirable or good end, that is, an end with intrinsic value. An end has intrinsic value when that end has value in itself, and not as a means to some other end. This is clarified by the following examples. We value certain things because of their consequences or effects, but not because of their value in themselves. For instance, we go to the dentist because we have reason to believe that the dentist can help bring about healthy teeth, that is, a good ending. But very few people value the act of visiting the dentist as good in itself. In other words, we visit the dentist not for its own sake but for the sake of some other thing. This other thing may in turn be valued not as an end in itself but as a means to another end. Eventually, we reach a certain state of life that we want to have and enjoy just for its own sake. This end is intrinsically good, that is, it has intrinsic value to us. In contrast, visiting the dentist only has instrumental value to us. We value it as good because we use it as a means to some other end. Conversely, if we do not value the end as good, we do not value the means as good either. For example, if we do not mind experiencing problems with our teeth, then we do not value going to the dentist as good. In this way, the value of some things—such as visiting the dentist—is entirely derivative. The value of these things is derived from the value of other things. The other things—things that we desire for their own sake—have non-derivative value. Their value is not derived from the value of some other thing, and therefore, their value is intrinsic to them. In short, derivative value is instrumental value, and non-derivative value is intrinsic value. Of course, something might have both kinds of value. For instance, if we play tennis both for enjoyment and for exercise, then the game of tennis has both intrinsic and instrumental value to us. That is, the game of tennis is both intrinsically good and instrumentally good. Contrary to this, visiting the dentist is intrinsically bad but instrumentally good. One can think of the other two combinations as well. Something can be intrinsically good but instrumentally bad, for example, eating too much of our favorite but unhealthy dessert; and something can be both intrinsically and instrumentally bad, for example, having a painful illness that involves heavy medical expenses.

Utilitarian ethics is based on the principle that the right depends on the good. This means that in order to determine whether an act is morally right, first, we must determine its consequences, and then, determine whether those consequences are intrinsically good or intrinsically bad. The moral rightness of an act is not an intrinsic value in itself. On the contrary, an act is right if it is instrumentally good, that is, its rightness is due to its instrumental goodness.

Different utilitarians have proposed different standards of intrinsic value to test the goodness of the consequences of a right act. Some classical utilitarians, like Jeremy Bentham, have proposed "pleasure"; others, like John Stuart Mill, have proposed "happiness," and have noted that happiness is not merely the total sum of pleasures. A twentieth-century utilitarian, G. E. Moore (1873–1958), has proposed that the intrinsic goodness of a thing is a unique and indefinable property, which cannot be defined in terms of either pleasure or happiness. Thus, there are three types of utilitarianism. They are categorized according to how they view the end, to which morally right conduct is a means. They are called "hedonistic utilitarianism" (from the Greek word "hedone" that means pleasure); "eudaimonistic utilitarianism" (from the Greek word "eudaimonia" that means happiness or well-being); and "ideal utilitarianism" or "agathistic utilitarianism" (from the Greek word "agathos" that means good).

Hedonistic utilitarianism is based on the following fundamental norm: An act is right if it results in more pleasure (or prevents more pain); and an act is wrong if it results in pain (or prevents more pleasure). Eudaimonistic utilitarianism is based on the following fundamental norm: An act is right if it results in more happiness (or prevents more unhappiness); and an act is wrong if it results in unhappiness (or prevents more happiness). Agathistic utilitarianism is based on the following fundamental norm: An act is right if it results in more intrinsic good (or prevents more intrinsic evil); and an act is wrong if it results in intrinsic evil (or prevents more intrinsic good).

In general, many alternative answers come to mind in response to the question: pleasure/pain, or happiness/unhappiness, or intrinsic good/intrinsic evil for whom? One answer is: pleasure, happiness, or intrinsic good for the individual actor, that is, for the person taking the action. This answer is indeed provided by an ethical system called "ethical egoism." Another answer is: pleasure, happiness, or intrinsic good for the individual actor's family, friends, class, caste, tribe, nation, race, religion, or sex. This answer brings about an ethical system that gives the interests of some people a higher priority than the interests of others. Still another answer is: pleasure, happiness, or intrinsic good for everyone but the individual actor himself. This answer leads to the ethics of pure altruism or brotherly love. In this ethical system, the moral ideal encourages each individual to devote himself/herself to the welfare of others without regard to his/her own loss of welfare. The answer provided by utilitarians is: everyone's pleasure, happiness, or intrinsic good.

According to utilitarianism—whether hedonistic, eudaimonistic, or agathistic—the application of the standard of value must be impartial and universal. In calculating the value of consequences, every individual's pleasure, or happiness, or intrinsic good has to be counted exactly equally. Both the individual's own interests and everyone else's interests have to be accounted for, but neither of them has to be given higher weight. The individual must be strictly impartial when comparing his/her own pleasure, or happiness, or intrinsic good and someone else's. The individual must never favor himself/herself and his/her friends. For utilitarians, all human beings are equally entitled to the fulfillment of their interests.

In applying the principle of impartiality to determine the rightness or wrongness of a particular action, a typical utilitarian—setting apart the differences among hedonistic, eudaimonistic, and agathistic forms of utilitarianism—prescribes the following decision-making steps. First, we specify all possible alternative courses of action that we can choose from. Then, we use all available information and apply our best ability to calculate the consequences of each alternative action. In this step, our intention is to calculate the amount of pleasure (or happiness) and the amount of pain (or unhappiness) that result in the individual actor's own life and in the lives of all other people as a consequence of the individual's taking each alternative course of action. Then, we compare all consequences in order to determine the alternative course of action that leads to the greatest amount of pleasure (or happiness) and the least amount of pain (or unhappiness). This act that maximizes the intrinsic value and minimizes the intrinsic disvalue is the act we morally ought to do. To do any other alternative act is morally wrong.

In everyday life, it is not practical for us to stop and make such detailed calculations each time we need to choose from among alternative courses of action open to us. Indeed, if we force ourselves to do this, we might cause more unhappiness or less happiness in the world than if we make choices based on habits which we have developed from our past experience. Therefore, making an accurate calculation each time is wrong, according to utilitarianism. Instead, we must make our choice based on our common sense which we have developed from similar situations in the past. For instance, it is very clear to all of us that murdering someone will produce more unhappiness in the world than having respect for the person's life. It is not necessary for us to have murdered someone in the past to know this. It is only necessary for us to use our reason and imagination to foresee the consequences of such an act.

To utilitarians, no act in itself is morally wrong. This is because the wrongness of an act depends solely on its consequences. For instance, let us consider the act of murder and suppose that we are considering murdering a particular man in a particular set of circumstances (e.g., assassinating Hitler in 1935). If murdering the man results in less unhappiness in the world than if he remained alive, then it is not wrong to murder him. As a matter of fact, it is our duty to murder him. This is because, under such circumstances, if we do not do the act it results in more unhappiness (intrinsic disvalue) and less happiness (intrinsic value) than if we do the act. This might appear as a shocking and outrageous ethical prescription, but utilitarians argue that, after all, the act of murder is considered to be wrong because it causes so much pain and unhappiness both to the victim and to his/her family, friends, and relatives; and it nullifies the victim's right to the pursuit of happiness. The following example might shed some light on this argument. Suppose we live in a different world with a different kind of people in it. In this world, when people reach the age of thirty, suddenly, they physically and mentally deteriorate and lose their capability of enjoying their life thereafter. Further, suppose that there is a method of killing people at that age such that it gives them great pleasure until the final moment of death. Finally, suppose that their death at this age is considered by others as a happy event and is celebrated. In that world, the murder of people at the age of thirty is not something to be condemned. This is because there is more unhappiness in the world as a result of not ending their lives. In fact, based on similar reasoning, some people in our actual world advocate the painless killing of human beings under specific conditions. They suggest that a doctor be allowed to administer a drug that painlessly kills a person who has an incurable disease under the following conditions: first, the probability is zero for the discovery of a cure during the rest of the life of the person; second, the suffering of the person is intense and cannot be alleviated by medical means; and third, both the person himself/herself and his/her relatives ask for the administration of such a drug to him.

This example illustrates another aspect of utilitarian ethics. According to utilitarians, in some situations, it is right to do an act that brings about unhappiness. This is the case when the act brings about less unhappiness than any other possible alternative. In this situation, to do anything else—including "to do nothing," that is, to let matters take their own course—results in more unhappiness for people. These unfortunate situations may occur in cases of war, natural disasters, and incurable diseases.

With respect to the function of moral rules of conduct, utilitarianism is divided into two branches. One is called "act" or "unrestricted" utilitarianism; the other is called "rule" or "restricted" utilitarianism. The distinction between the two can be made in the following way: all utilitarians use the principle of utility as the ultimate test of the rightness or wrongness of human conduct. However, in applying this test, act-utilitarianism applies the utility principle directly to particular acts, but rule-utilitarianism applies it to rules of conduct to determine whether a particular act is right or wrong. In unrestricted or act-utilitarianism, based on the consequences of a particular act, we determine whether the act is right or wrong. It is act-utilitarianism that is presented in the foregoing paragraphs. Act-utilitarianism applies the principle of utility directly to each alternative act available in a situation of choice. Then, the right act is determined as the one that results in the greatest utility among all available alternative acts. All the other available alternative acts are wrong. This is because any of these alternatives does not maximize intrinsic value and does not minimize intrinsic disvalue in the world. A person's duty is always to do that act in his set of choices that has such consequences.

According to restricted or rule-utilitarianism, an act is right if it conforms to a valid rule of conduct, and an act is wrong if it violates such a rule. The test of utility determines the right rules of conduct. That is, the true normative ethical system that applies to all human beings consists of a set of rules such that, if all people adhere to these rules, the greatest intrinsic value and least intrinsic disvalue result for everyone than if they followed a different code of conduct. There are two kinds of rules: positive rules or requirements and negative rules or prohibitions. A positive rule specifies the characteristics of certain types of action that are required of everyone. It requires every person to do a certain kind of action where he/she has the choice of doing or not doing the act. For example, the rule "Keep your promises" states that when we promise someone to do something, and then we have the choice of keeping or breaking our promise, we must keep it. The right act is to do what the rule requires, and the wrong act is not to do what the rule requires. A negative rule requires everyone not to do a certain kind of act. It requires that an individual not perform a certain kind of behavior when he/she has the choice of doing or not doing it. For instance, the rule "Thou shalt not steal" states that we must not steal even when we have the choice to steal. When we act in accordance with a positive rule means we do what the rule requires us to do; and when we act in accordance with a negative rule means we refrain from doing what the rule prohibits. It is wrong to refrain from an act which is required by a positive rule, and it is wrong to perform an act which is prohibited by a negative rule. In this way, a "right" or "wrong" act can be defined as an action that conforms to or violates a rule of conduct that is binding upon us. The rules that bind us can be distinguished from among all the possible rules that can regulate our conduct. According to the rule-utilitarian, the rules that bind us are those rules that, when they are generally complied with, bring about more happiness or pleasure for everyone and less unhappiness or pain for everyone than results from the general compliance with any other set of rules.

Rule-utilitarianism overcomes certain difficulties that act-utilitarianism faces. For instance, suppose a man commits the "perfect" crime by murdering someone without leaving any evidence. Therefore, the murderer is never caught and is never punished. Compare this case with an exactly similar case, except that the murderer leaves some evidence; therefore, he/she is caught and is sentenced to life imprisonment. Ordinarily, we judge the two acts of murder as equally wrong, and whether a murderer is caught and punished does not change our judgment. But act-utilitarianism may state that the first act is not as wrong as the second. This might be based on the reasoning that the consequences of the first act involve less unhappiness compared to that of the second act since the murderer is not caught and does not suffer imprisonment. Alternatively, an act-utilitarian might state that the first case is worse than the second case because—even though the murderer is not caught and does not suffer punishment—he/she will suffer from guilt-conscience and live the rest of his/her life in fear of the police, and his/her avoidance of legal punishment may encourage him/her and others to commit more crimes with worse consequences than if he/she had been caught and imprisoned. Still alternatively, an act-utilitarian might state that the "perfect" murderer is a hardened, amoral person without a conscience, is fully confident that he/she will never be caught by the police, and has no intention to commit another murder because his only crime was based on personal revenge; therefore, the "perfect" crime is not as wrong as the second one. On the other hand, according to rule-utilitarian, both acts of murder are equally wrong since both violate the same rule of conduct: that we ought to respect the lives of others.

## Interpretive View

The Kantian approach to ethics has at its core Kant's famous thesis that moral obligations or oughts are "categorical imperatives." This thesis has four dimensions: normativity, universality, supremacy, and necessity. Normativity means that for any morally wrong act, there is a normative reason not to take that action. Universality emphasizes that this holds for all agents and all situations. Supremacy stresses that the reasons against wrongdoing always override or defeat any reasons to the contrary and therefore are invariably conclusive. Necessity states that all these three aspects hold necessarily, but not because of some special characteristics that moral agents have or lack.[2]

Kantian thesis consists of two components: the analytical or conceptual interpretation, and the normative interpretation. Moral obligations and moral responsibilities are conceptually tied together. Responsibilities are our demands to one another as free and equal moral persons. An appreciation of the Kantian thesis involves an adequate understanding of the concept of moral obligation and the necessary awareness of the distinctive kind of freedom, autonomy, that a Kantian must hold in order to vindicate the categoricity of moral reasons.

The conceptual thesis of Kantian ethics is that moral oughts are categorical imperatives. To understand this, we need to understand the various aspects of categorical imperatives.

Normativity: We usually judge that it is wrong for corporate officers to intentionally mislead potential investors by hiding losses. Normativity means that if this action is wrong, then there is a genuinely normative reason for corporate officers not to engage in it. But what is a "normative reason"?

There are three meanings associated with "reason for acting." A normative reason for acting favors or justifies an action in deliberation about what to do. This is in contrast to the explanatory sense in which "reason for action" provides explanation for an action. This type of reason for an action is not a normative reason. For instance, the fact that I forgot about a meeting yesterday explains why I missed it, and it constitutes a reason for my missing it. But obviously, it does not constitute a normative reason for my missing it.

An important type of explanatory reason—called "motivating reasons"—is an agent's reason for taking a particular action. This type of reason is what the agent counts in favor of an action and on the basis of which the agent takes an action. For instance, the fact that I forgot about the meeting is obviously not my reason for missing the meeting either. The fact that I forgot about it did not give me a reason for missing it. This is because I did not miss it intentionally.

Although there are differences among different types of reasons, there are important connections among them. An agent's reason must be a consideration that the agent himself/herself takes as a normative reason. In addition, there may be an important converse relationship as well. "Existence internalism" is the view that a necessary condition for a consideration to be a normative reason for an agent is that the consideration acts as the basis for the action of the agent, in some suitable sense. It must be possible for the consideration to be the agent's reason to motivate him/her under some suitable conditions. The putative normativity of moral oughts gives agents normative reasons for acting.

Universality: Universality means that normativity has a property of holding universally. Whenever an agent morally ought to do something, there are some normative reasons for him/her to do so. Universality makes explicit what was implicit in normativity. It is important to distinguish between universality and another aspect of Kantian ethics that says moral oughts are always backed by universal principles. That is, the universal principles are not necessary for universality to hold. Universality only requires that an agent who morally ought to do A has some normative reason to do A. Universality does not require that this reason necessarily be derived from some universal principle.

Supremacy: Normativity does not, by itself, mean that moral oughts provide conclusive reasons. Normativity and Universality say that whenever an agent morally ought to take some specific action, then there is some genuinely normative reason to do so. Supremacy adds that there are always conclusive reasons for agents to take actions that are moral oughts.

Supremacy states that moral reasons are always conclusive in relation to a moral obligation. It does not state that moral reasons always outweigh other reasons. It states that there can never be a reason for doing what is wrong. For instance, there is always a moral reason to donate to any worthy charity, but not donating is not always wrong. Of course, it is wrong not to donate at all or not to donate enough. Supremacy states that there is a conclusive normative reason for everyone to donate to the extent that is morally required. Supremacy does not state that the moral reasons for donating to any particular charity invariably outweigh (or do not outweigh) the reasons for not giving, if not donating to that charity would not be wrong.

Reasons provided by moral oughts are invariably supreme in the sense that they invariably override and defeat (i.e., reduce or undermine the force of) other reasons. Moral reasons reduce or eliminate the weight of other reasons. For instance, consider a torturer who enjoys himself when his/her victim squirms. The wrongness of torture or the wrongness of enjoying the pain of others not only outweighs any reason provided by the enjoyment but also silences it.

Necessity: Necessity means that moral oughts hold for all possible situations. Necessity means that moral oughts do not hold just for situations that human beings can be expected actually to face, given their psychology and circumstances. Necessity means that moral oughts hold for any situation any moral agent might face.

The necessity aspect of the Kantian thesis can be seen more clearly by comparing it with the normativity of Hobbesian view of morality. Hobbes and Kant are in agreement that moral oughts are invariably supremely binding as no agent ever finds any reason to violate them. Hobbes believes that even in the state of nature, covenants bind when there is no reasonable suspicion that the covenants are not honored and are voided by others. Hobbes argues that when I reasonably believe that the counterparty to my covenant will perform his/her part, then I have conclusive reason to perform mine as well. But, according to Hobbes, this is contingent on features of the human situation: the violence and insecurity of living in the state of nature, the need to have confederates for self-defense, and the role of covenants and the reputation for keeping them in confederacy and in establishing a sovereign. Under these conditions, it is in the best interest of everyone to gain the trust of others so that they can trust him/her in keeping the covenants. Otherwise, there would not be any reason for anyone to keep them.

Hobbes believes in supremacy but not necessity. This is because he believes that supremacy is contingent on the features of the human situation. Hobbes denies necessity because he believes that self-interest is the ultimate source of the normativity of moral reasons and is external to what constitutes moral ought. In contrast, for Kant, the source of the normativity of moral ought is internal to morality itself. According to Kant, regardless of contingent differences, for any moral agent there will always be conclusive moral reasons not to do what is wrong.

The analytical or conceptual aspect of the Kantian thesis is that moral oughts are categorical imperatives in all four respects. However, this is different from the normative aspect of the Kantian thesis, which holds that there actually are moral oughts in all these four respects. The conceptual thesis is closely related to the normative claim. There are true or valid moral oughts only when the normative claim is true.

Kant believes that a pure moral philosophy must be purged of everything that may be only empirical and that belongs to anthropology. Kant does not believe that human contingencies are never relevant to moral duties. He believes that even when contingencies are relevant to human moral duties, they are themselves the outcome of some deeper norm or principle that applies to human beings, as free and rational beings.

Kant believes that a law, if it is to hold morally and act as a ground of an obligation, must have the property of being an absolute necessity. That is, moral obligations are moral necessities; they state what we must do. Furthermore, moral laws hold not only for human beings but also for all other rational beings. Consequently, every human moral duty derives from a "law" that necessarily applies to all rational beings.

For instance, consider the command "thou shalt not lie." Rational beings are vulnerable to deception and rely on others for information. Therefore, it is wrong for rational beings to lie in any circumstance in which they interact with beings who have the kind of vulnerability and need for information that we do.

Kant states that the ultimate scope of moral duty is free and rational beings. For instance, if Star Trek's Vulcans actually exist, they would be equally bound by moral obligations as we are. Their specific moral duties might be different because their situation might be different in morally relevant ways. Nevertheless, both our morality and their morality would be equally driven by the same principles, from which the specific contents of our and their obligations would derive. Kant concludes that the most fundamental moral principles apply to any possible free and rational agent. Therefore, moral principles necessarily apply to rational agents and are knowable a priori.

Two of our characteristics, that is, being free and rational agents, make us not only subject to moral oughts but also to comply with them. In the Critique of Practical Reason, Kant argues that we become conscious of our freedom when we become aware of our being bound by moral law. For instance, suppose the prince demands a person, with the threat of immediate execution, to give false testimony against an honest man. Although the person himself might not be able to determine whether he/she would actually refuse this demand, he/she must certainly admit that he/she is able to do so since he/she realizes that he/she ought to. Therefore, the person recognizes that he/she can do something because he/she realizes that he/she ought to do it and becomes aware of the freedom within him. In other words, without moral law, freedom would have remained unknown to him/her.

This is correct, of course, because the person himself/herself believes that moral norms are supremely binding. Moral norms are fundamentally different from other norms in terms of the authority they represent themselves as having. For instance, a person who accepts norms of etiquette regards them as having some normative weight. But the person does not think that the norms of etiquette bind unconditionally, or that oughts of etiquette are invariably supreme. Accepting a conditional and restricted normativity for etiquette is not the same as accepting etiquette wholeheartedly. For morality, in contrast, a person who accepts moral obligations only under certain conditions, for certain purposes, or to the extent that they do not conflict with certain other considerations, has hardly fully accepted moral norms.

Kant explains that moral oughts, in contrast to more local and restricted norms, bind us as one free and rational being. Accordingly, we are necessarily subject to an ought (the moral ought) that presents itself as both unconditional and supreme. Therefore, we must comply with the moral oughts by exercising the capacities by virtue of which we are subject to them.

According to Kant, commitment to moral demands is based on the deliberative capacity of a free rational agent. An agent must have normative reasons for taking an action. Moreover, the normative reason for acting must be anchored in some norm that applies to all rational agents. For instance, if an action I take is based on the reason that it is in my interest, then it must be because rational agents should act in their own interest. Therefore, the deliberative standpoint guarantees the existence of all-encompassing norms.

It is a necessary truth that when an act violates moral norms, then there are conclusive "moral reasons" against taking such action. That is, against any wrongdoing, there are reasons from the perspective of these moral norms. It should be emphasized that this proposition is not itself normative. For instance, one can accept it and at the same time deny that deliberation needs to take any account of "moral reasons." In contrast, the Kantian thesis is considerably normatively strong. It claims that indeed there are always supreme and genuine normative reasons not to violate moral obligations.

In Kantian ethics, these ideas have a firm foundation in moral common sense and experience. We rarely view morality from a purely abstract and external perspective that violates what we regard as moral obligations with equanimity. We usually make some self-justifying or self-excusing statements to ourselves—such as "everybody does it"—or we usually make, based on our feelings, for example, guilt, some self-addressed statements—such as "I really shouldn't have done that."

One of the most fundamental questions of moral philosophy is: Are moral imperatives categorical or not? This question boils down to two other questions: one is conceptual or analytical, and the other is genuinely normative. The conceptual or analytical question is: Are moral imperatives categorical in any or all of the previously mentioned aspects? The question with respect to normativity is: Are moral oughts genuinely normative? Then, if, in fact, there is no valid normative reason not to do what is morally wrong (i.e., just because it is wrong), the claim that there are things one morally ought not to do will be false, invalid, or unsupported. Similarly, the question with respect to universality is: Are normative moral oughts applicable to all agents in all cases? The question with respect to supremacy is: Do normative moral oughts invariably provide conclusive reasons? The question with respect to necessity is: Do normative moral oughts provide such reasons necessarily or just because of contingent features of human agents and their normal context?

Suppose the answer to all these conceptual questions is yes. That is, from a conceptual perspective, moral oughts are categorical in all of the four respects. However, even with affirmative answers to all these questions, we cannot conclude that there are any categorical moral oughts in any respect. This is because if genuine moral oughts necessarily provide valid normative reasons that are conclusive for all agents in all situations, there might be no actual putative moral ought that provides these reasons ever, for anyone in any situation. Or they might provide them, but only for some agents in some situations. Or they might provide them for all, but are invariably not conclusive. Or they might always be conclusive for all agents, but only because of some contingent human characteristic—such as the capacity for human sympathy, which an agent might lack. The result of affirmative answers to all the analytical, conceptual questions is that there are oughts with these four aspects, but the question that remains is: Are any valid moral oughts at all? A skeptic can deny that we have a reason not to do what people consider as being morally wrong. That skeptic can accept the conceptual claims of categorical imperatives, but can also deny that there are any valid moral oughts. That is, such a skeptic would deny that what anyone considers to be morally wrong is really wrong. The skeptic might admit that there are certain acts that are "wrong" from the perspective of "moral" norms. But the skeptic denies that these norms really bind us as categorical imperatives suggest.

Kant claimed both that moral oughts are categorical imperatives in all four respects and that they actually exist. He argued that moral duty provides conclusive reason for moral acts that necessarily apply to any agent. He further argued that moral duties actually exist that invariably and necessarily provide conclusive reasons. Kant was cognizant that the latter normative thesis does not logically follow from the former conceptual one. In fact, the structure of his book—Groundwork of the Metaphysics of Morals—reflects this recognition. Kant proceeded analytically with the discussion of the generally received concept of morality and showed that the categorical imperative (CI) and "autonomy of the will" lie at the foundation of morality. Kant emphasizes respect for human dignity and places stress on always treating "humanity" or "rational nature" as an "end" and never as a "means only." The "autonomy of the will" refers to the property of the will such that it is a law to itself and is independent of any property of the objects of the agent's choice. Kant argues that moral duty means that the will is subject to a law, the CI, which is both the fundamental principle of morality (i.e., the source of moral duties) and the will's own law. It logically follows that moral duties bind the will independently of any contingent features. Therefore, moral oughts necessarily bind all wills.

## Radical Humanist View

The concrete moral life of an individual should be considered from the time that he/she is born into an existing ethical world and is confronted with social institutions in which he/she must perform his part and at the same time obtain his/her satisfaction and free activity. These institutions can awaken in the individual a distinct moral consciousness, a consciousness for active relations to other persons, a consciousness which exists in contemplation. An individual can participate in these institutions to realize his/her role in them, or can avoid them by living in isolation from them. Through these interactions, a moral character comes into being. The consideration of the concrete moral life of an individual has to deal with (1) the practical consciousness, that is, the formation and growth of ideals of conduct; (2) the moral struggle, that is, the process of realizing ideals; and (3) moral character, that is, the virtues.[3]

## 1. The Formation and Growth of Ideals of Conduct

The practical consciousness is usually referred to as conscience. It is the recognition of ends and relations of action. It is the relation between persons and deeds. Conscience involves three interrelated and unified elements: (1) the knowledge of specific forms of conduct, (2) the recognition of the authority or obligatory character of these forms, and (3) the emotional factors that are formed around this recognition.

The "customary or conventional conscience" refers to the strong impression that the existing moral world leaves on the immature mind. The existing moral world does this through its various institutions. It places moral demands on individuals and enforces them via its various powerful means, such as punishment, reward, blame, public opinion, and social leadership. These demands and expectations give rise to an individual's convictions regarding what he/she should or should not do. Such convictions are the outcome of the molding influence of social institutions, but not the individual's independent reflection. The morality of a society becomes consolidated into its proverbs, maxims, and law codes. It crystallizes in specific habitual ways of viewing matters and judging them. The morality of a society is instilled into the growing mind of an individual through the society's language, literature, association, and legal custom, such that they leave in the individual's mind a firm habit and attitude toward what things should be done and what things should not be done. This process is comparable to the process of the initial grasp of the knowledge of the physical world. Some more permanent features of the physical world—especially those that play important roles in the continued physical existence and well-being of individuals—leave strong impressions on the minds of individuals. Consciousness, without any reflections, mirrors some of the main features of the physical world. These more important features find their way into language, and then into the individual's mind, and give the individual's mind a specific orientation, which remains unconscious to the individual at this stage of moral development, that is, the customary or conventional conscience.

The "loyal conscience" is the next stage of moral development. Whereas initially the mind acts as a passive vessel and pours into itself the facts and features of the world, later in time it experiences, verifies, and appreciates their meaning and forms its moral relations. The individual practically recognizes that these social institutions provide him/her satisfactions, and that it is through the existing moral codes that he/she is protected. The individual identifies himself/herself, and his/her own life, not only with the social institutions in which he/she lives, but also with the social ideals with which he/she lives. The individual repels any attack on the existing social institutions and social ideals in the same way that he/she would repel any attack on himself/herself. If the "conventional conscience" does not grow into this stage, it becomes slavish. However, an individual's intelligence practically realizes, although without personal reflection, the importance of conventional morality and is free in its convictions and service. At this stage, the individual does not critically look at the institutions and codes that form individuals' character, and consequently, the individual does not consider whether those institutions and codes are what they should be. The individual does not recognize that the dictates of the existing institutions are similar to the coercions of a despot. In contrast, the individual views existing institutions as the expressions of his/her will, and therefore such institutions require loyalty.

The "independent or reflective conscience" is the third and last stage of moral development. In this stage, intelligence does not take current conventional institutions and codes as its own but reflects on them. It asks various questions. What is the essence of existing institutions, and what types of conduct does this essence require? Do the current rules suit the true needs of the current situation, or are they expressions of old relations? Do the current conventional institutions work as they should, or do they require some modifications? This relation in the ethical world is similar to the one in physical science as it pertains to the external world. Intelligence is not content with the theoretical impressions it has received from facts, either through direct contact or through language. It is not content until it values for itself the truths so impressed. It acts independently and interrogates nature. It generates its own ideas, theories, and hypotheses and observes facts with the hope that those can be verified. It questions what passes as truth and makes more adequate statements. On the practical side, intelligence may have a wider or a narrower scope. In its wider role, intelligence criticizes prevailing social institutions and ideals and aims to reform them—even those that are thought to be most fixed. This is what the great moral teachers of the world do. But a critical conscience does not necessarily require that its scope be so wide. A typical individual can reflect upon his/her immediate relationships in life to see whether they are what they should be. The individual can regulate his/her conduct by his/her own rules and based on his/her own examination of the situation, and not necessarily by customary rules. There is no difference in kind between such wider or narrower work of intelligence. This is because it is through the persistent exercise of reflective examination on the smaller scale that deeper criticism and transformation will be made possible efficiently. It is thoroughly misleading to think of conscience as a private possession, which can be exercised by each individual independently of existing historical forms and contemporary ideals. At the same time, conscience should not necessarily repeat the existing customs and opinions. Reflective conscience is based on moral consciousness, which is embodied in prevailing institutions, manners, and beliefs. Otherwise, it is arbitrary and meaningless. The existing morality is never entirely consistent. It implements ideals with respect to one group in society, but it does not do the same with respect to another group in the same society. It gives specific rights to aristocrats, but it denies them to the poor. It gives certain rights to men, but it refuses them to women. It exempts the rich from various obligations, but it imposes all those obligations upon the poor. Its institutions claim a common good, but in actuality, it is good only to a privileged few. It promises the implementation of certain goals, but its execution is only feeble or intermittent. These are examples of existing contradictions. Reflective intelligence interrogates the existing morality, extracts the ideals that it pretends to embody, and criticizes the existing morality based on the contradictions with its own ideals. It brings to the fore the inconsistencies, the incoherencies, the compromises, and the failures, based on the comparisons between the actual practice and its underlying theory. In this way, the proposed new ideals of the individual are not the products of his/her private opinions but are the outcomes of the ideals embodied in existing customs, ideas, and institutions.

The content of moral ideals is, by its very nature, progressive. In other words, the permanence of specific moral ideals shows moral stagnation. While truth-telling, charity, loyalty, and temperance might have always been considered moral ends, the content of these various ideals (e.g., what is meant by temperance) has been constantly changing by necessity. This is because the realization of moral ends changes the social situation such that in the new social situation, the old moral ends are no longer held, and new ones are adopted. The history of human social life begins with groups in which everything is massed, and the good is undifferentiated and common to all. Then, there is the division of labor and the corresponding freedom in functioning that leads to the evolution of individuality. The trend in history is marked by the appearance of progression in internal and distinguishing traits, with the outcome of peculiar gifts entrusted to each, and correspondingly, of the specific service demanded of each. At the same time, there has been an enlargement in moral ends, which has been called growth in "comprehensiveness." That is, historically, there has been a widening of social consciousness, that is, an expansion of the range of persons whose interests need to be considered when taking an action. There was a time when the community was limited to a man's immediate family group. Later, the community expanded to the clan, the city, the social class, and the nation. The last extension to the community of interests and ends is humanity itself. Although the growth in comprehensiveness is a growth in the number of persons with a common end, this quantitative growth affects the nature of the ends. For instance, when the community was small, bravery was defined as the willingness to fight for one's own community against other groups at a time of hostility. However, when these other groups merge into the moral community, courage changes its meaning to the resoluteness and integrity of purpose in defending humanity. In other words, when the formation of community is based on physical criterion—such as common blood, territory, and so on—the ideal of courage has an external and physical manifestation. However, when the formation of community is based on spiritual criterion—the recognition of the unity of destiny and cooperation toward an all-inclusive life—the ideal of courage becomes more internal and spiritual.

## 2. The Moral Struggle or the Realizing of Ideals

Goodness is struggle; and struggle is to take action to replace the experienced good with a possible ideal good. Morality is associated with aspiration and faith. The individual is required to be constantly willing to surrender past goods as the good, and take action toward new ends. This is not because past achievements are bad, but it is because past achievements have created a new situation that requires larger and more intricately related achievements. This willingness feeds on aspiration and faith. The old good has been seen, sensed, and experienced. The new ideal—the end that corresponds to the new situation—is felt as good because the individual has formed the conviction that to meet the obligation is itself a good. One can prove to a man that he ought to take a specific action because such an action is the one that fits the new situation, but one cannot prove to the man that the performance of that duty is good. However, faith in morality, duty, and goodness can assert this. When an individual takes a new action toward his/her moral end, he/she expresses his/her belief in the goodness of that action. This faith is not only intellectual, but it is also, more importantly, practical—engaging oneself in certain activity as opposed to remaining in passive possession.

Moral badness is in contrast to moral goodness, which involves taking action in new situations. In other words, moral badness means repeating former actions. Goodness is taking action and refusing to be content with past good deeds, and it rejects the view past good as exhausting the entire content of goodness. Goodness is the continued effort to be better. A man with a bad history and limited intellectual, aesthetic, and social activity, who takes action because he is dissatisfied with his past, is regarded as better than the man with a respectable past and a higher standard of life who is content with his past deeds and does not take any further action. This is because past deeds are passive enjoyments. The bad man does not love badness. All conduct, whether good or bad, is done for some satisfaction, that is, some good. The bad man chooses the satisfaction that is aimed at the continuation of old circumstances, without regard to the sufficiency of those choices in the context of new environments. Indeed, the bad man's choice is a good of having. The bad man does not appreciate any ideal or active good, that is, new good. The choice of the bad man may be good in itself, but it is bad because, when considered in the new context, his choice does not fulfill the present capacity or meet the present situation. In this way, bad is distinguished from good, which translates into action.

Badness has four characteristics: (1) "lawlessness" is the denial that there is law for conduct, that desires based on future acting have to replace the desires based on past having; (2) "selfishness" is the refusal to recognize that the conduct with a larger social range is superior to the conduct aimed at private and assured satisfaction; (3) "baseness" is the lack of distinction between the low, degraded, sensual self and the higher, spiritual self; and (4) "demoralization" is the loss of the principle that the moral end is always an activity.

Goodness is in struggle. Conscientiousness is a role played by intelligence in habitually staying alert and responsive to the nature of obligation, both in general and with respect to specific obligatory acts. Goodness is in progressive aspirational adjustments for future conduct.

Goodness has a self-sacrifice or self-renunciation dimension. This is because in an environment where there are constantly growing wants, their satisfaction must be given up for active goods. The self-sacrifice is made toward the surrender of private interests to the welfare of the whole. The smaller local life of the private self is forgone in order to realize the richer and fuller social life of the active self. Self-sacrifice is genuine and real. However, the individual does not self-sacrifice and forgo the smaller satisfaction in order to get a larger one. Moral conduct generates greater activity and a larger life. Based on his/her morality, the individual has formed the conviction that moral conduct will bring satisfaction; and that such conviction is not one of sense, but of faith. The individual forgoes a real satisfaction which is congruent to the actualized self. But the individual obtains an ideal satisfaction which is ethical.

Goodness is not separate from badness. Goodness can be regarded as being based on badness. In other words, good action is founded on an action that was once a good action, but this good action turns into a bad action if it persists even when circumstances change. The moral struggle is constituted by the tension between this "bad" and the good that suits the new circumstances. This good does not annihilate the previous good—the present bad—but the new good subordinates the old good, which will be assigned a new function. That is, badness is the material of good action.

Badness is only potential when avoided—that is, the bad is in contrast to the better. Badness becomes actual when adopted into character. Even in this case, goodness is dependent on evil. Badness is still the material of goodness. It can be used as an element in the construction of good action. The good man can learn from his bad acts. He recognizes their badness. He stops repeating such acts. He takes right actions, even though he previously had bad conduct. The recognition of the consequences of his own wrong acts, the change in his capacities, and the altered relations between him and other people, then he acts in such a way to suit the situation which his own bad act has helped to create. His conduct is then right, which is made to some extent by his previous wrong conduct.

An action can be judged in two ways. First, the action can be judged as right or virtuous when it fulfills duty. This judgment may be passed by anyone, whether by the individual or anyone else. This type of judgment involves the recognition of the moral character of the act. Virtue and duty are mutually interdependent. An action is a duty when it needs to be taken in a given situation; and the taking of the action which needs to be taken in a given situation is right or virtuous. Second, an individual's right act can convince others to grant him/her a reward. This is the case when the act furthers the needs of society, and therefore it is considered meritorious. Even though the individual decides and takes the right action, he/she cannot claim reward for his/her virtuous action. This is not the kind of judgment that the individual can pass with respect to his own act. This is because he/she took virtuous action as this is what he/she had to do morally. Furthermore, no act can be so virtuous to go beyond what is needed in a given situation. However, when others notice that the individual's action has been taken despite great temptation, with hard struggle, based on unusual qualification, or achievement of remarkable service, then it is not only right but also obligatory for others to show gratitude to the individual.

### 3. Realized Morality or Virtues

Virtue is goodness in an individual's character. The good character, in the context of moral struggle, chooses the right end in its endeavors to be better. But, if this process involves struggle, then morality is not yet naturally and spontaneously established in the character. A wholly good person obtains satisfaction with a view to the ideal good and is confident that contrary desires do not influence him/her. This type of person gains satisfaction only when he/she takes the right action. Every morally right action has this outcome, that is, moral realization generates satisfaction. Satisfaction becomes united with the right act. Duty and desire approach harmony. Interest and virtue tend to become unified.

Virtue lies in the attitude of the person toward duty, his/her obedience to right forms, his/her preparedness to undertake new duties, his/her enthusiasm in engaging in new relations. In their progression, moral codes qualitatively change from the dichotomy between "Do not" and "Do," to "Be." In this progression, virtues make increasingly less reference to specific acts but more to the spirit of conduct. It is futile to try to specify all possible special right acts. These are not the same for any two men, and they do not stay the same for a particular man.

Virtue involves the person's interest in anything except the act itself. The person's interest in taking a moral action is not in the wonderful moods, wonderful sentiments, ulterior gain, or private advantage that it brings, but in the act itself—in the real and concrete relations involved.

## Radical Structuralist View

Moral rules change as society changes. However, their change is neither sudden, nor in the same manner, nor to the same extent as that of social needs. The existing moral rules are promptly recognizable as rules of conduct because they have already turned into habits. When moral rules take root as habits, they can have a long-lasting life independent of the advances in technology, the development of the method of production, and the transformation of social needs.[4]

Morality, as a component of the complicated sociological superstructure, raises itself on the method of production. It can have, for some time, a life independent of its foundation. This should not encourage some people to introduce, in their analysis, the spirit as an independent driving power in the development of society. These people incorporate into their analysis the fact that the intellectual factors of society can temporarily work independently of their economic base. They argue that there is a reciprocal interaction between the economic factor and the spirit, and that both of them affect social development. They argue that in some periods the economic factor, in some periods the spiritual force, and still in other periods both of them together drive society forward. That is, they believe that the will and wishes of people can, at least at times, overpower the strength of hard economic necessity and change it.

Of course, there is a reciprocal interaction between the economic basis and its spiritual superstructure—such as morality, religion, art, and so on. Similarly to other components of the ideological superstructure, morality can enhance economic and social development. Indeed, this is the important social role that it plays. Social rules are generated based on their corresponding social needs. Therefore, they make social cooperation much easier when they are closely adapted to the society that generated them. In this way, morality feeds back on social life. But morality plays its important social role when it is dependent on its corresponding social needs, since it then meets the requirements of the social needs based on which it was generated.

The interaction between morality and society takes a totally different path when morality starts to follow a life independent of society; that is, when morality is no longer controlled by society. The further morality develops along this path, the more its development becomes purely logical and formal. The further morality is isolated from the influence of the surrounding world, the more it fails to create new conceptions. Then, it can only arrange the ones which have already been attained in the sense that their contradictions will disappear. By doing this, the thinking spirit eliminates contradictions, solves all problems related to the contradiction, and creates a unified conception. In this way, it can only secure the existing intellectual superstructure, but it cannot rise above it. Only new contradictions and new problems can lead to new developments. However, contradictions are not created by the human spirit internally; they are generated in it only by the effect of the outer world on it. When moral principles follow their life independent of society, they turn into barriers to social progress. This is because they ossify, become conservative, and form an obstacle to progress. Thus, morality, instead of becoming an indispensable social bond, can become an intolerable restraint on social life.

The contradictions between moral principles and their corresponding social needs can reach their height in a primitive classless society. Such contradictions become much more prominent in the presence of class antagonisms. In a classless society, moral principles are followed based on habit, and therefore moral contradictions can be resolved by the supervision of habit. From now on, with the appearance of classes in society, the creation and maintenance of particular moral principles become a matter of particular and powerful interest. In a class-divided society, not only weapons of force—of physical compulsion—are used to control the exploited classes, but also, they are used to enforce "morality," that is, to force exploited classes to abide by the moral principles that support and protect the interests of the ruling classes.

The classless society does not need such weapons. In a classless society, social instincts do not always result in the observance of moral codes by every individual. This is because different individuals are affected to different degrees by their social impulses, in the same way that different individuals are affected to different degrees by their other instincts, such as self-maintenance and reproduction. Social instincts do not always gain the upper hand. However, in a classless society, public opinion of society acts as a means of compulsion, of punishment, of warning. Public opinion does not create in people moral law and the feeling of duty. Conscience works in an individual in the absence of other people and in the absence of public opinion. Conscience can force an individual to defy public opinion in a class-divided society with its consequent contradictory moral codes.

In a classless society, public opinion acts as a strong force such that it secures public obedience to moral codes. Society is so strong that the individual is unable to defy society's unanimous voice. Society is so strong that it does not need any means of compulsion or punishment in order to control the course of social life. Similarly, in a class-divided society, the public opinion of the exploited class, or the public opinion of the exploited-class-formed political party, is more powerful than the compulsory weapons of the state. The exploited class prefers prison, poverty, and death to shame.

The public opinion of one class differs from that of the opposing class. Public opinion can certainly be used in a society to control individuals and force them to obey the existing laws, as long as there are no class antagonisms in society, and when the social instincts of the individual do not suffice. However, public opinion fails in the performance of its role when there is class against class in society instead of individual against society. Thus, in order to prevail, the ruling class resorts to other weapons of compulsion, such as its superior physical, economic, organizational, and intellectual capabilities. As its means of rule, the ruling class not only uses soldiers, police, and judges, but also men of religious ranks. It is to the religious organization that the ruling class assigns the special task of conserving the traditional morality. The connection between religion and morality has been made much easier by the new religions, which started to appear when primitive communism and gentile society were decaying. The new religions are totally opposite of the ancient nature religions, which have roots in the old classless period, and which have no knowledge of special religious castes. In the old religions, divinity and ethics are separate from each other. In contrast, the new religions are based on the philosophy that ethics and the belief in God are most intimately connected to each other, such that each supports the other. Since then, religion and ethics have been mutually interdependent and have been used as a weapon of rule by the ruling class. There is no doubt that the moral law is one of the results of the social nature of man. There is no doubt that the moral code of any time period is the result of the particular social needs of that time period. There is no doubt that neither of them is related to religion. But the moral code that must be maintained in the interests of the ruling class requires the support of the religion and the religious caste. Otherwise, it would soon break apart.

Economic development creates new social needs, and these new social needs demand new moral standards. The longer the old moral standards remain in force, the greater will be the contradiction between the ruling moral standards of society and the life and action of its members. But this contradiction appears differently in different classes. The conservative classes firmly hold to the old morality, because their existence is dependent on the old social conditions. However, they can do this only in theory, because in practice they cannot deny the new social conditions. This is the well-known contradiction between moral theory and moral practice. Many think of this as the natural law of morals, because, in their view, moral demands are desirable but unrealizable. Again, the contradiction between theory and practice in morality can take two forms. Classes and individuals who feel strong disregard the demands of traditional morality, while they recognize its necessity for others. Classes and individuals who feel weak disregard the moral codes only secretly, while they preach them publicly. Thus, the phase of the decaying classes leads either to cynicism or hypocrisy. Therefore, the conservative, that is, ruling classes, act immorally.

The growing contradiction between the developing social conditions and the stagnating morality of the conservatives—that is, the ruling classes—affects different classes differently. On the one hand, in the ruling class, it leads to growing immorality that crystalizes in the increase of hypocrisy and cynicism within the class. On the other hand, it leads to quite the opposite results in the rising, or exploited, class. This is because the interests of the exploited class are in direct antagonism to the social foundation that produced the ruling class and its morality. The exploited class not only sees no reason to accept it but also has every ground to oppose it. When the exploited class becomes more conscious of its antagonism to the ruling social order, then its moral indignation grows, and it confronts the old traditional morality with a new morality for the whole society. When uprising classes feel stronger, their moral ideals become bolder. In the process of class struggle, the power of the social instincts develops so that the enthusiasm of uprising classes for the new moral ideal also increases. Thus, the same social process that leads to the increasing immorality of conservatives or downgoing classes, also leads to ethical idealism in the rising classes. This ethical idealism, however, is not related to philosophical idealism. The uprising classes are indeed associated with philosophical materialism, which the declining classes oppose as soon as they become aware that reality has started to work against them and they feel they can only ask for help from supernatural powers, divine or ethical.

The content of the new moral ideal is not completely known. It is not the result of any scientific analysis of society, which is most often unknown to the actual authors of the ideal. But it is the result of a deep social need, a strong desire, and an energetic drive for an ideal to replace the existing one. The new ideal is the opposite of the existing one and replaces the existing hypocrisy.

As long as a class-divided society has existed, the ruling morality has always guarded the ruling class at times of sharp class antagonism. Thus, historically, the moral ideal of the uprising classes seems to have always been the same, the same as that of the French Revolution: Freedom, Equality, and Fraternity. It seems as if this is the ideal of every human being, independent of time and space. It seems as if this is the task of the human race. It seems as if the human race, from its beginning, has had to strive for the same moral ideal. It seems as if the evolution of man is considered as the gradual approach to this ideal.

But a close examination reveals that the similarities of the moral ideals of the different historical periods are only superficial and that there are substantial differences among their social aims. These differences reflect the differences in the social situation at the time.

For instance, Liberty and Equality meant something quite different to Christianity, the French Revolution, and social democracy according to how they viewed property and production. The purpose of primitive Christians when they demanded equality of property was its equal division for the purpose of consumption by all. And their understanding of freedom was the emancipation from all work, as the toilers of the field toiled and spun.

For the French Revolution, equality meant the equality of property rights. It declared private property to be sacred. And for the French Revolution, freedom was considered to be the freedom to apply property in economic life, which meant in the most profitable manner.

Social Democracy neither defends private property nor demands its division. But it demands the socialization of private property. For social democracy, equality means equal rights for all in the social products of labor. Freedom as meant by social democracy is not freedom to dispose of the means of production and to produce at will. But it is the minimization of the necessary labor by gathering capable workers and by applying labor-saving machinery and methods. Consequently, the necessary labor can be reduced to a minimum for all, and release time can be given to all. This release time assures freedom, for free artistic and scientific activity, for free enjoyment of life. Social freedom—which is different from political freedom—is obtained through the minimization of the period of necessary labor.

It is clear that the same moral ideals of freedom and equality translate into very different social ideals. The common pattern of moral ideals of different times and countries, despite their social differences, is based on the fact that the main outlines of class divisions and class rules in human society have always been the same. This is in contrast to the view that believes the common pattern of moral ideals is the result of a moral law that is independent of time and space and that is sent to human beings from a supernatural world.

A new moral ideal does not necessarily arise from class antagonism. Individuals within the conservative classes may develop loose social ties with their class and have no class consciousness. However, their strong social instincts and virtues make them realize the extent of hypocrisy and cynicism. Their intelligence clearly realizes the contradiction between the traditional moral code and the new social needs. These individuals will, at some point, come to support of the new moral ideal. The new moral ideal obtains social force only when it becomes a class ideal. Only the driving force behind the class struggle can enhance the new moral ideal. This is because it is only the class struggle—not the unitary endeavor of self-interested individuals—that has the strength to develop society farther in order to meet the requirements of the new, more advanced method of production. The new moral ideal can only be realized through the development of society.

Some people argue that moral ideals can never be reached. There is some merit in this argument if its foundation is understood. The moral ideal is a complex composition of wishes and endeavors. It is invoked by the opposition to the existing situation. It acts as the driving force of the class struggle, and combines and spurs the forces of the uprising classes in their struggle against the existing situation. It acts as a powerful lever in the overturning of the existing situation. However, the new social conditions that replace the old social conditions do not depend on the moral ideal but depend on the material conditions, the technical conditions, the natural milieu, the nature of the predecessors and the predecessor of the existing society, and so on.

Thus, a new society can considerably diverge from the moral ideal of those who overturned the old one. This divergence is all the more considerable when the moral ideal is less congruent with the objective knowledge of the material conditions. In this way, the moral ideal turns into an illusion after it performs its historical duty by acting as an impulse in the destruction of the old society.

It was noted above that in the conservative classes the contradiction that arises between moral theory and moral practice leads them to conclude that everybody demands morality, but nobody practices it. That is, morality is beyond human strength, but it is only within the capability of supernatural powers to carry it out. It was also noted above that in the revolutionary classes a contradiction arises between moral theory and moral practice, but this contradiction is of a different kind than the one experienced by the conservative classes. The contradiction between the moral ideal and the reality for the revolutionary classes is created by the social revolution. This contradiction leads the revolutionary classes, as well, to conclude that everybody strives for morality, but nobody obtains it; that is, human beings cannot attain it. Thus, some moralists argue that morality has a supernatural origin and that the animal character of human beings drives them to cling to the Earth such that they can only wishfully look at morality from a far distance, but they can never reach it.

In contrast, historical materialism brings morality from above down to Earth. The materialist conception of history completely removes the determining role of the moral ideal in the evolution of society. Instead, it bases social aims solely on the knowledge of the material foundations. It emphasizes the difference between the moral ideal and material conditions and that the confusion between the two has to be avoided. It notes that the revolutionary reality should not be expected to coincide with the social ideal. It stresses that illusions and disappointments have to be avoided. The extent to which these can be avoided in practice depends on the degree of understanding of the laws of development of society. Of course, the moral ideal influences society, but this influence needs to be reduced to its proper dimensions. The moral ideal has to be treated as a force or a weapon in social struggle and class war.

Social democracy, as an organization of the proletariat, has to use moral ideals in its class struggle. Its moral ideals are expressions against exploitation and class rule. But these ideals are separate from scientific socialism. This is because scientific socialism is the scientific examination of the laws of the development of society. Scientific socialism has to be well understood in order to know the necessary tendencies and aims of the proletariat class struggle.

## Conclusion

This chapter briefly discussed four views expressed with respect to ethics. The functionalist paradigm believes that an ethical system is an ordered set of standards that are determined based on factual information. The interpretive paradigm believes that moral obligations are categorical imperatives that are normative, universal, supreme, and necessary. The radical humanist paradigm believes that ethics is the moral struggle for the realization of ideals. The radical structuralist paradigm believes that moral principles support and protect the interests of the ruling classes.

Each paradigm is logically coherent—in terms of its underlying assumptions—and conceptualizes and studies the phenomenon in a certain way, generating distinctive kinds of insight and understanding. Therefore, different paradigms in combination provide a broader understanding of the phenomenon under consideration. An understanding of different paradigms leads to a better understanding of the multifaceted nature of the phenomenon.

## Notes

1 For this literature, see Anderson (1993); Donner (1991); Foot (1976); Moore and Shaw (2005); Pettit (1997, 1993); Smart and Bernard (1973); and West (2004). This section is based on Taylor (1984).
2 For this literature, see Barnsley (1972); Bauman (1993); Dreier (2006); Edwards (1982); Ladd (1973); Mackie (1977); Wong (1985); and Wyschogrod (1990). This section is based on Darwall (2006).
3 For this literature, see Alexander (1899); Andersen (1990); Baum (1996); Bracci and Christians (2002); Green (1884); Habermas (1990); and Nielsen (1990). This section is based on Dewey (1891, 1969).
4 For this literature, see Kamenka (1962, 1969); Lukes (1985); Nielsen (1989); Nielsen and Patten (1981); Selsam (1943); and Trotsky (1969). This section is based on Kautsky (1907, 2002).

## References

Alexander, Samuel (1899), *Moral Order and Progress: An Analysis of Ethical Conceptions*, London: Kegan Paul, Trench, Trubner, and Co. Ltd.

Andersen, Heine (1990), "Morality in Three Social Theories: Parsons, Analytical Marxism and Habermas," *Acta Sociologia*, 33:4, 321–39.

Anderson, Elizabeth (1993), *Value in Ethics and Economics*, Cambridge, MA: Harvard University Press.

Barnsley, John H. (1972), *Social Reality of Ethics: The Comparative Analysis of Moral Codes*, London: Routledge and Keagan Paul Ltd.

Baum, Gregory (1996), *Karl Polanyi on Ethics and Economics*, Montreal, Quebec: McGill-Queen's University Press.

Bauman, Zygmunt (1993), *Postmodern Ethics*, Oxford: Blackwell Publishers.

Bracci, Sharon L. and Christians, Clifford G., eds. (2002), *Moral Engagement in Public Life: Theorists for Contemporary Ethics*, New York, NY: Peter Lang Publishing, Inc.

Darwall, Stephen (2006), "Morality and Practical Reason: A Kantian Approach," in Copp, David (ed.), *The Oxford Handbook of Ethical Theory*, New York, NY: Oxford University Press, Chapter 11, pp. 282–320.

Dewey, John (1891, 1969), *Outlines of a Critical Theory of Ethics*, New York, NY: Greenwood Press Publishers.

Donner, Wendy (1991), *Liberal Self: John Stuart Mill's Moral and Political Philosophy*, Ithaca, NY: Cornell University Press.

Dreier, James (2006), "Moral Relativism and Moral Nihilism," in Copp, David (ed.), *The Oxford Handbook of Ethical Theory*, New York, New York: Oxford University Press, Chapter 9, pp. 240–64.

Edwards, James C. (1982), *Ethics without Philosophy: Wittgenstein and the Moral Life*, Tampa, FL: University Presses of Florida.

Foot, Philippa, ed. (1976), *Theories of Ethics*, London: Oxford University Press.

Green, Thomas Hill (1884), *Prolegomena to Ethics*, London: Claredon Press.

Habermas, Jurgen (1990), *Moral Consciousness and Communicative Action*, Cambridge, MA: MIT Press.

Kamenka, Eugene (1962), *The Ethical Foundations of Marxism*, New York, NY: Frederick A. Praeger Publisher.

Kamenka, Eugene (1969), *Marxism and Ethics*, London: Macmillan and Company Ltd.

Kautsky, Karl (1907, 2002), *Ethics and the Materialist Conception of History*, Chicago, IL: Charles H. Kerr and Company.

Ladd, John, ed. (1973), *Ethical Relativism*, Belmont, CA: Wadsworth Publishing Company.

Lukes, Steven (1985), *Marxism and Morality*, Oxford: Oxford University Press.

Mackie, J.L. (1977), *Ethics: Inventing Right and Wrong*, London: Penguin Books.

Moore, George Edward and Shaw, William H., ed. (2005), *Ethics: The Nature of Moral Philosophy*, New York, NY: Oxford University Press.

Nielsen, Kai (1989), *Marxism and the Moral Point of View: Morality, Ideology, and Historical Materialism*, Boulder, CO: Westview Press.

Nielsen, Kai and Patten, Steven C., eds. (1981), *Mars and Morality*, Guelph, Ontario: Canadian Association of Publishing in Philosophy.

Nielsen, Torben Hviid (1990), "Jurgen Habermas: Morality, Society and Ethics," *Acta Sociologica*, 33:2, 93–114.

Pettit, Philip (1993), *Consequentialism*, London: Dartmouth Press.

Pettit, Philip (1997), "Embracing Objectivity in Ethics," in Leiter, Brian (ed.), *Objectivity in Law and Morals*, Cambridge: Cambridge University Press, 234–86.

Selsam, Howard (1943), *Socialism and Ethics*, New York, NY: International Publishers Co., Inc.

Smart, J.J.C. and Bernard, Williams (1973), *Utilitarianism: For and Against*, Cambridge: Cambridge University Press.

Taylor, Paul (1984), "Utilitarianism," in Brodsky, Garry, Troyer, John, and Vance, David (eds.), *Contemporary Readings in Social and Political Ethics*, Buffalo, NY: Prometheus Books, pp. 17–35.

Trotsky, Leon (1969), *Their Morals and Ours: Marxist vs. Liberal Views on Morality*, fifth edition, New York, NY: Pathfinder Press, Inc.

West, Henry (2004), *Introduction to Mill's Utilitarian Ethics*, Cambridge: Cambridge University Press.

Wong, David (1985), *Moral Relativity*, Berkeley and Los Angeles, CA: University of California Press.

Wyschogrod, Edith (1990), *Saints and Postmodernism: Revisioning Moral Philosophy*, Chicago, IL: University of Chicago Press.

6

# Environmental Governance

## A Multi-Paradigmatic View

Any explanation of environmental governance is based on a worldview. The premise of this book is that any worldview can be associated with one of the four broad paradigms: functionalist, interpretive, radical humanist, and radical structuralist. This chapter takes the case of environmental governance and discusses it from the four different viewpoints. It emphasizes that the four views expressed are equally scientific and informative; they look at the phenomenon from their certain paradigmatic viewpoint; and together they provide a more balanced understanding of the phenomenon under consideration. In this chapter, the first through the fourth sections present the four perspectives, and the fifth section concludes the chapter.

## Functionalist View

Environmental policies typically identify a goal and devise means to achieve that goal. The means—the "instruments"—of environmental policy are composed of a relatively new set of economic-incentive or market-based policy instruments. These instruments can be placed in four categories: charge systems, tradable permits, market friction reductions, and government subsidy reductions. The charge systems consist of effluent charges, deposit-refund systems, user charges, insurance premium taxes, sales taxes, administrative charges, and tax differentiation. The tradable permit systems consist of credit programs and cap-and-trade systems. The market friction reductions consist of market creation, liability rules, and information programs. This extensive list of policy instruments should not be taken to mean that market-based instruments have come anywhere close to replacing the conventional, command-and-control approach to environmental protection.[1]

Market-based instruments regulate market signals in order to encourage desired behavior on the part of market participants. They are in contrast to explicit directives regarding pollution control levels or methods. These policy instruments are intended to "harness market forces." When these instruments are well-designed and properly implemented, they encourage firms (and/or individuals) to undertake pollution control projects that are in their own interests and that collectively meet policy goals.

Again, these are in contrast to conventional, "command-and-control" approaches to regulating the environment that exhibit relatively little flexibility in the means of achieving policy goals. Such regulations tend to require firms to equally share the burden of pollution control, regardless of the cost. Command-and-control regulations subject firms to such requirements by setting uniform standards, which are mostly technology- and performance-based standards. Technology-based standards specify the method, and sometimes the specific equipment, that firms must use in order to become compliant with a particular regulation. A performance-based standard sets a uniform control target for firms but allows some flexibility in the way the target is arrived at.

Requiring all firms to adhere to the same target can be expensive and, under certain circumstances, counterproductive. Standards might effectively reduce emissions of pollutants, but they typically impose relatively high costs in the process, as some firms are forced to undertake unduly expensive means of controlling pollution. The costs of controlling emissions may vary greatly among firms, and even among sources within the same firm, because the appropriate technology in one situation may not be appropriate (cost-effective) in another. Thus, control costs can vary enormously among firms due to a firm's production design, physical configuration, age of its assets, or other factors.

Furthermore, command-and-control regulations tend to discourage the development of technologies that might lead to higher levels of pollution control. There is almost no financial incentive for businesses to exceed the control targets, and both technology-based and performance-based standards discourage the adoption of new technologies. A business that adopts a new technology may be "rewarded" for reaching a higher standard of performance but not be given the opportunity to benefit financially from its investment, except to the extent that its competitors have difficulty in reaching the new standard.

Market-based instruments, when properly designed and implemented, lead to the realization of the desired level of pollution cleanup at the lowest overall cost to society. This is accomplished by providing incentives to those firms that can achieve the greatest reductions in pollution most cheaply. Rather than equalizing pollution levels across firms (which is the case with uniform emission standards), market-based instruments equalize the incremental costs that firms incur to reduce pollution—that is, they equalize their marginal costs. For the command-and-control approaches to achieve this cost-effective solution, they would have to set different standards for each pollution source, and, consequently, that policy makers would have to be able to obtain detailed information about the compliance costs each firm faces. But such information is not available to the government. In contrast, market-based instruments provide for an allocation of the pollution control burden among sources that is cost-effective and does not require the government to have all that information.

In contrast to command-and-control regulations, market-based instruments provide strong incentives for companies to adopt cheaper and more efficient pollution-control technologies. This is because, with market-based instruments, especially emission taxes, firms always find it in their interest to search for and adopt a sufficiently low-cost method (technology or process) to clean up a bit more.

As noted before, market-based instruments can be placed in four major categories: pollution charges; tradable permits; market friction reductions; and government subsidy reductions.

## Pollution Charge Systems

*Pollution charge systems* consist of effluent charges, deposit-refund systems, user charges, insurance premium taxes, sales taxes, administrative charges, and tax differentiation.

*Effluent charges* are imposed as a fee or tax on the amount of pollution that a firm or entity generates. Therefore, the firm finds it worthwhile to reduce emissions to the point where its marginal abatement cost is equal to the tax rate. The charge systems have the challenge of identifying the appropriate tax rate, which should be set equal to the marginal benefits of cleanup at the efficient level of cleanup. However, policy makers typically think in terms of a desired level of cleanup, and they do not know in advance how firms will respond to a specified level of taxation. Selected effluent charges are as follows: carbon monoxide (CO);

carbon dioxide ($CO_2$); sulfur dioxide ($SO_2$); nitrogen oxides ($NO_x$); combined industrial air pollutants; biological oxygen demand (BOD) load; total suspended solids (TSS); combined industrial water emissions; nitrogen and phosphorous; and landfill, incinerator, and hazardous waste discharges.

*The deposit-refund system* requires consumers to pay a surcharge when purchasing potentially polluting products and receive a refund when returning the product to an approved center, either for recycling or for disposal.

Policies aimed at reflecting the social costs of waste disposal (such as waste-end fees) tend to increase the cost of legal disposal and therefore lead to unintended incentives for improper (i.e., illegal) disposal. For waste that might have significant negative consequences for health or ecology, ex post cleanup is not an attractive option. For such waste, it is important to prevent its improper disposal. One alternative might be a front-end tax on waste precursors. This is because such a tax would entice manufacturers to find safer substitutes and to recover and recycle taxed materials. However, there may be no substitutes available at reasonable costs, and after waste is generated, there are no incentives to affect the choice of disposal method.

This dilemma might be resolved with a combination of a front-end charge (i.e., a deposit) and a refund for turning in the substance under consideration for recycling or proper disposal. The principle of economic efficiency requires that the size of the deposit be set equal to the marginal social cost of the product being disposed of illegally (at the efficient level of return), minus the real welfare costs of the program's operation, where these costs are assumed to be proportional to the quantity of returns. As the product is exchanged in the production and consumption process (i.e., from wholesalers and distributors to consumers), at the point of each exchange, the purchaser of the product pays a deposit to the seller of the product.

Deposit-refund systems are most appropriate when the consequences of improper disposal are overwhelming. More specifically, they are most appropriate where: (1) the goal is to reduce illegal disposal, rather than reducing the waste stream or increasing recycling and (2) the legal cleanup costs and illegal (i.e., post-littering) cleanup costs are significantly different. For these reasons, deposit-refund systems are among the best policy options to deal with the disposal of hazardous waste, such as lead in motor vehicle batteries. Under this system, manufacturers collect deposits when they sell batteries to distributors, retailers, or original equipment manufacturers. Similarly, retailers collect deposits when they sell batteries to consumers. Consumers collect their deposits when they return their used batteries to redemption centers. Redemption centers collect their deposits when they return the used batteries to the manufacturers. These deposit-refund systems are largely self-enforcing, since participants have incentives to collect deposits on new batteries and obtain refunds on used ones.

*User charges* typically require direct users of a specific environmental service to pay for its provision. Thus, user charges may be defined as those charges designed to finance environmentally related services. This is in contrast to effluent charges, which are defined as those charges intended to influence behavior. In many cases, the distinction between user charges and effluent charges is clear. However, such distinction is somewhat blurred when those charges are directly related to pollutant emission levels, are set too low to influence behavior, and are earmarked for the provision of closely related environmental services.

*Insurance premium taxes* are levied on products in order to fund insurance pools against potential environmental risks created by the production or use of taxed products. For instance, taxes on petroleum products are pooled to meet unrecovered claims from oil spills.

*Sales taxes* and value-added taxes are levied on diverse goods and services to protect the environment. Frequently, these taxes are levied on motor fuels, other energy products, new automobiles, pesticides, fertilizers, chlorinated solvents, volatile organic compounds, lubricating oils, non-refillable containers, ozone-depleting substances, and new tires. These products can be placed in four categories: motor fuels; ozone-depleting chemicals; agricultural inputs; and product taxes. Motor fuel taxes are used to contribute to general funds. Tax rates are typically differentiated for leaded and unleaded gasoline, diesel fuel, light heating fuels, and heavy fuel oil, as these taxes have environmental functions. Ozone-depleting chemicals are also taxed, such as the "gas guzzler tax" on new cars, and the excise tax on chlorofluorocarbon (CFC). Agricultural inputs, such as fertilizers and pesticides, are taxed and the proceeds are used to finance environmental programs. Product taxes are levied on fuel-inefficient vehicles (to discourage the production and purchase of fuel-inefficient vehicles) and on disposable products as diverse as cameras, light bulbs, razors, disposable (beverage) containers, and packaging. The tax proceeds are earmarked for general environmental purposes.

*Administrative charges* raise revenues to partly cover the administrative costs of environmental programs. These charges are not intended to change behavior.

These charges are variously collected through discharge permits, permit fees, registration charges, licensing charges, and license processing fees.

*Tax Differentiation* refers to credits, tax cuts, and subsidies to promote environmentally desirable behavior. These implicitly serve as taxes on environmentally undesirable behavior. For example, in order to discourage fossil fuel energy generation and use, tax credits can be given to electricity produced from wind and biomass fuels or investments made in solar and geothermal energy generation. As for another example, employers can provide implicit subsidies to employees for commuting expenses such as free van pools and tax-free mass transit passes. Likewise, governments can provide subsidies to households for their energy-conserving investments by deducting such investments from individual income taxes. Similarly, tax differentiation can be used to reduce vehicle-related emissions by providing the incentive to switch from leaded to unleaded gasoline. Furthermore, differentiated taxes and fees on vehicles can be assessed according to cylinder capacity, age, fuel efficiency, and other environmentally relevant grounds. Moreover, differentiated import levies can be applied to promote smaller, more fuel-efficient cars.

## Tradable Permits

*Tradable permits* can achieve the cost-minimizing allocation of the control burden as can be achieved under a charge system, but it avoids the need to know in advance how firms will respond. A tradable permit system sets an allowable overall level of pollution and allocates it among firms in the form of permits. Firms with emission levels below their allotted level can either sell their surplus permits to other firms or use them to balance excess emissions in other divisions of their operations. Tradable permits take one of the following two basic types: credit programs and cap-and-trade systems.

Under credit programs, a firm earns credits when it reduces emissions below the required level; these credits can enable the same firm or another firm to balance and meet its control target. For example, "emissions trading" can be used to improve local air quality through the control of volatile organic compounds (VOCs), CO, SO2, particulates, and $NO_x$. Firms that reduce emissions below the level required by law receive "credits" which can be used against higher emissions elsewhere. Firms can take advantage of the concept of "netting" to trade emissions reduction credits among divisions within the firm, as long as total combined emissions do not exceed an overall firm limit. The netting program can go further and allow firms to trade emission credits. This allows firms that are not in compliance with ambient standards to offset their high emissions through agreements with other firms. Furthermore, under the "banking" program, firms can save earned emission credits either for future use or for sale to other firms.

Under a cap-and-trade system, an allowable overall level of pollution is set and then allocated among firms in the form of permits, which can be freely exchanged among firms. Theoretically, the allocation can be made through free distribution or through sale (e.g., auction) by the government. Examples include CFC trading, $SO_2$ trading, NOx trading, VOC trading, and TSP (total suspended particulates) trading.

## Market Friction Reductions

*Market friction reductions* can also play the role of market-based policy instruments. That is, substantial gains can be made in environmental protection when existing frictions in market activity are reduced. Three prominent types of market friction reductions are as follows:

1. *Market creation for inputs/outputs related to environmental quality*, examples are: (a) measures that facilitate the voluntary exchange of water rights and consequently promote the more efficient allocation of scarce water supplies; and (b) specific policies that facilitate the restructuring of the generation and transmission of electricity. The first example involves the shortage of water in southern California and how it was dealt with by opening such market to the suppliers in neighboring states of Colorado and New Mexico. The second example involves the substitution of monopoly system in the generation and distribution of electricity in the United States by a competitive system.
2. *Liability rules* that encourage firms to be cognizant of the potential environmental damages consequent to their decisions. For instance, when the national law sets retroactive liability for companies responsible for environmentally damaging a site, then the government can collect cleanup costs from waste producers, waste transporters, handlers, and current and past owners and operators of the site. More specifically, the national law can make firms liable for cleanup costs, natural resource damages, and third-

party damages caused by oil spills into surface waters. Similarly, the national law can make firms liable for cleanup costs for spills of hazardous materials.

3. *Information programs*, such as requiring companies to provide a label on each of their products showing its degree of energy-efficiency. This is based on the idea that well-functioning markets partly depend on the existence of well-informed producers and consumers. Therefore, information-enhancing programs can help foster market-oriented solutions to environmental problems.

### Government Subsidy Reductions

*Government subsidy reductions* are the mirror image of taxes and can provide incentives to mitigate environmental problems. However, many subsidies are neither economically efficient nor environmentally sound. Although subsidies have the potential to advance environmental quality, they have important and well-known disadvantages compared to taxes. Although such subsidies are not typically used in developed market economies, they are more commonly used in transition and, to a lesser degree, in developing economies. However, most transition economies neither select efficient projects nor calculate efficient subsidies.

## Interpretive View

A theoretical framework can be formed to help in the understanding of a cultural group's definition of and relationship with nature and the environment. The framework is based on a social constructionist perspective that reflects on the sociology of knowledge—specifically social constructionist—combined with phenomenology and symbolic interactionism. The human act of conferring meaning on nature and the environment creates a symbolic environment which is defined as a "landscape." This landscape is a reflection of the self-definition of the people within a particular cultural context. The physical environment is transformed into a landscape according to the people's definitions of themselves, and the landscape is reconstructed when people's definitions of themselves is changed.[2]

Any river or rock is more than just one river or rock. When a real estate developer looks across an open field and sees comfortable suburban ranch homes, a farmer sees rows of waving wheat, and a hunter sees a five-point buck grazing in preparation for the coming winter. The same physical entity, that is, the open field, carries multiple symbolic meanings to different people. The symbolic meanings emanate from the values by which people define themselves. The real estate developer, the farmer, and the hunter define who these three groups of people are, and the physical entity of the open field—that is, the natural environment—is symbolically transformed with reference to these self-definitions. These symbolic meanings and definitions are not physical phenomena, but they are sociocultural phenomena, and they transform the natural environment into a symbolic landscape.

"Landscapes" are the symbolic environments that are created by humans when they confer meaning to nature and the environment. They are created when humans give the environment definition and form from a particular point of view and through a special lens of values and beliefs. These landscapes reflect humans' self-definitions, which are grounded in their culture. The transformation of the physical environment into landscapes is made through cultural symbols, and these landscapes reflect humans' definitions of themselves.

Our understanding of nature and our relationships with the environment are cultural expressions that define who we were, who we are, and who we aspire to be in this place and in this space. Landscapes are a reflection of our cultural identities. They are about us, not the natural environment. In identifying and understanding the mutual effects of humans and the natural environment, it is crucial that these consequences are viewed from various cultures that create landscapes, for example, the landscape created by the real estate developer, the farmer, and the hunter. Any given physical place has the potential to lead to multiple landscapes, each of which emanates from the cultures of those who deal with that place. Every river or rock is more than just one river or just one rock.

Cultural groups transform the natural environment into landscapes through the use of their different symbols that assign different meanings to a given physical object or condition. These symbols and meanings are sociocultural; they are socially constructed, and they are the outcome of ongoing negotiations within a cultural context. There is no doubt that humans reside in a natural world that is out there, but this world is meaningless. Things do not inherently have meanings. Rather, the symbols and meanings that form landscapes reflect the culture of people and their values, that is, what they define to be proper and improper relationships among themselves and between themselves and the physical environment.

It is through sociocultural phenomena that we transform the physical environment into landscapes, which are the reflections of how we define ourselves. Accordingly, when events or technological innovations challenge the meanings of these landscapes, we enter a process of negotiating new symbols and meanings and, in the meantime, change our conceptions of ourselves. The focus of social science inquiry ought to be these self-definitions, negotiations over landscapes, and subsequent social actions. This is because there are no natural meanings inherent in the world that is out there. The following contemporary examples from different parts of the world illustrate how landscapes are the reflections of sociocultural symbols and meanings, which define the meaning of being human in a particular culture.

In India, the World Bank was financing a major development project along the 800-mile course of the Narmada River consisting of the construction of 2 super dams; 30 large dams; 150 medium-sized dams; and 3,000 smaller dams, dikes, and irrigation projects. The Narmada is the holiest river among the holy rivers for people who have faith in the Hindu religion. The river is sacred, well-known, and highly admired for its great healing power. Over the centuries, thousands of Hindus have joined healing pilgrimage and walked the 1,600 miles of Narmada's banks. The discussion of the World Bank project typically centered on the costs of the lakes created by the dams—as they flooded thousands of acres of highly productive farmland—versus the benefits from the new jobs—that would be created by the installation of the new sources of hydroelectric power. However, there was an alternative way of framing the effect of the World Bank project and the human-environment relationship along the Narmada River. This frame would focus on the landscape which was created by Hindu people and reflected their definitions of themselves. That is, how would the damming of the river into a series of pools affect the healing powers of the Narmada River?

In the southwest of the United States, the US Department of Energy was conducting studies to see whether a geologic formation called tuff at Yucca Mountain, Nevada, could suitably be used for a high-level radioactive waste repository. Tuff was known to be a form of compressed volcanic ash. As part of these studies, engineers were developing canisters that could safely hold the waste for about 300 years, and thereafter, the canisters would disintegrate, and the tuff was expected to form a natural shell around the waste to safeguard the environment for another 10,000 years. Almost all the scientific debate centered on either technical questions about the geologic stability of the site or whether tuff would act as an effective natural barrier to the radioactive waste.

However, Southern Paiute elders had a totally different perspective on the repository. Their perspective reflected on the landscape emanating from their beliefs and their definitions of themselves. Rocks were spiritually powerful elements of the natural environment for Southern Paiute people. They believed that different rocks could heal, bring luck, or cause problems. "Yellow cake" constituted a spiritually powerful paint, which was made from fine radioactive rock dust, and was used only after taking culturally approved precautions. The place where yellow cake was accumulated was also a spiritually powerful place, and Southern Paiute people were taught to avoid spending too much time there. Some Southern Paiute elders interpreted the case of the radioactive repository in fundamentally different ways than the scientists and engineers associated with the repository program. They interpreted it in ways that were consistent with their landscape and definition of themselves. For them, the problems of high-level radioactive waste emanate from the angry spirit of the rock because it was mined without appropriate cultural precautions and because it was put to uses that the spirit did not approve of. Southern Paiute elders asked: Can engineered and natural materials that are used to prevent the escape of radioactive waste ever stop the angry spirit of the rock?

The abovementioned examples about the landscape suggest that the views of people about nature and the environment emanate from various symbols through which cultural groups transform nature and the world that is out there into meaningful subjective phenomena. These subjective phenomena are reflections of how people define themselves within their group or culture. The process of change involves the process of negotiating new self-definitions, but such negotiations take place within the context of existing landscapes that frame the directions that the new self-definitions may take.

To understand human relationships with the natural environment, it is necessary to describe the subjective symbols and meanings through which a group of people socially construct the landscape. Natural phenomena are sociocultural phenomena as they are constructed by social interactions among members of a culture and when they negotiate the meanings of nature and the environment. The origin of natural resources is not to be found on Earth, but in society. Unlike nature, human society survives on myth, rhetoric, faith, and persuasion, which filter and sort the meanings of man and nature. Different social and cultural contexts create various conceptions of nature; and nature then becomes indistinguishable from that context. Each culture constructs its own world from among the infinite variety of nature. Nature is socialized, reorganized, and made part of a material manifestation of social structure. The natural environment is transformed into culturally meaningful phenomena, and then such natural environment is viewed from the perspective of these same cultural definitions. In essence, through culturally meaningful symbols, a sociocultural group constructs a landscape from nature and the environment and then reifies it. Humans are constantly involved in taking natural phenomena, transforming them into cultural objects, and reinterpreting them with cultural ideas.

Through the processes of negotiation, shared, taken for granted, and reified symbols and meanings emerge that define both social and natural phenomena and the situations in which they are located. It is these intersubjective definitions of the situation, rather than the situations per se, that constitute the reality for the cultural group. The group of people continues to reconstruct and redefine its realities—past, present, and future—through ongoing social interactions in the form of negotiations over meanings that reinforce and change the symbols, meanings, and definitions of the situation.

Although symbols and their meanings change over time, they have a persistent character that gives them long-term continuity. Historically, human societies have experienced natural and social calamities—earthquakes, volcanic eruptions, hurricanes, wars, riots—but there has always been a core of continuity, survival, and reconstruction evident. The prevalence of the systems of symbols makes this core possible. Therefore, understanding systems of symbols is an essential prerequisite for understanding of the relationships between human societies, nature, and the environment.

A landscape persists and sustains a core understanding of human-natural environment relations among a group of people despite technological, economic, and other changes. There is an explanation for the tenacity of significant symbols and values. The relatively observable worldview of a culture is founded on a structure of beliefs that is shared in a community. The system of values is formed by shared convictions of what is proper. This structure of beliefs, which is comprehensive, is so taken for granted by the individual that it is regarded as obvious by the individual and is indistinguishable from the individual's self-definition. The most tenacious and significant symbols are embedded in the structure of beliefs.

The structure of beliefs underlies the superficial manifestations of the structure of beliefs. These manifestations change relatively easily. New technologies or other externally introduced changes may be taken as such superficial manifestations.

People may voluntarily incorporate them into their lives in such a way that they enhance or, at least, do not contradict their self-definitions and taken-for-granted relationships with each other and their landscapes. People embody their belief structure when they engage with a new situation that requires definition. Their belief structure provides a context within which negotiations with respect to the meaning of the new situation occur. Thus, the more durable traditional symbols and beliefs form an interpretive framework—a familiar context—within which people can construct the meanings of new technologies and other changes.

Cultural groups use symbols to define the natural environment according to their ongoing, everyday, taken-for-granted worlds. Within their world, they organize both their relationships with each other and their relationships with the environment. People transform the natural environment through symbols and concepts that organize their relationships in the social world.

Sociocultural groups socially construct the natural environment and reify it. Reification implies that people are capable of ignoring their own authorship of the human world. Instead of regarding human meanings as world-producing, they are regarded as the products of the "nature of things." In this way, the symbolic social constructions—including the landscape—become part of the world taken for granted. Members of the group act based on the intuitive knowledge that their relationships to the natural environment can be no other way. These reified elements inform ideas and the realities that are naturally and indissolubly bound up together.

The landscapes that cultural groups socially construct are reflections of themselves. In this process, they mesh the social, cultural, and natural environments, which become part of the shared symbols and beliefs of the members of the groups. In this way, the natural environment and the changes associated with it carry different meanings depending on the specific social and cultural symbols affiliated with it. When a cultural group's definition of itself—that is, the essence of what it means to be human—is renegotiated, so does its definition and conception of the environment.

Human beings live in a world of meaningful objects. They socially produce their world by fabricating its meanings through their process of social interaction. In this way, different groups develop their different worlds. These worlds change when the objects that constitute them change in meaning. In order to identify and understand the life of a cultural group, it becomes necessary to identify and understand their world of objects in terms of the meanings these objects carry for the members of the group.

Note that the previous paragraph did not state that groups' worlds change as their objects change. This type of statement belongs to the camps of ecological or materialist determinism. Rather, it stated the primacy of meaning over material and located the origin of meaning in the negotiations of social interaction. The definition of "object" is expanded by the sociological idea of landscape to include nature and the environment. Accordingly, sociocultural outcomes are not the result of an environmental change per se, but are the result of the meanings of that change that are negotiated among groups of people.

An interpretive framework for understanding people's relationships with each other and the environment links people's changing conceptions of nature and the environment with people's changing conceptions of themselves. A combination of perspectives on the constructionist sociology of knowledge, phenomenology, and symbolic interaction provides a framework for the understanding of the symbolic transformation of the environment into cultural reflections of people. From the constructionist sociology of knowledge perspective, people construct social reality, and people create the meanings of things within this reality. At the same time, people regard this reality and the meanings of things as empirical facts; that is, these phenomena are reified. From a phenomenological perspective, people create and maintain a shared reality, which is an ordered, meaningful field of action and interaction and forms the arena for the interplay of commonsense knowledge, anonymity, and social relationships in everyday life, which is taken for granted by the same people. From a symbolic interaction framework, people share symbols and meanings by which they define everyday life situations, and they negotiate the meanings as a change in context occurs.

These perspectives together suggest that people perceive and categorize whatever they encounter in life—the social and natural environment—in terms of their intersubjective, taken-for-granted symbols and meanings and accordingly define the situations in which they are located. Their definitions of the situations constitute their reality. As the context changes—for example, as environmental change occurs—there is no inherent meaning in the change per se. In response to change, however, people negotiate the meaning of contextual or environmental change as a reflection of their changing definitions of themselves. In this way, nature and the environment are socially and culturally constructed through these social processes and are transformed into landscapes through social interaction and negotiation.

The sociological framework of landscape, developed above, can be applied to more effective management of project development and community responses to environmental change. The framework emphasizes that (1) the environment has different meanings to different people, (2) these meanings are symbolic reflections of how different people define themselves, and (3) changes in the environment can challenge this cultural expression and require people to renegotiate the meanings of both themselves and their relationships to the environment.

## Radical Humanist View

Today, any credible political economic vision must address ecological problems. Ecological problems are so widespread and serious that the environment can no longer be treated as just another problem. Ecological problems can be used to test actual and proposed political and economic arrangements, and processes of institutional reconstruction, whether they are incremental or revolutionary. It is notable that current, dominant institutions in the Western world fail this test, and that their consequent contradiction and confusion have created a space for discursive democracy, as an alternative, to show the promise of effectively meeting the ecological challenge. The currently dominant arrangements in the Western world may be characterized in terms of a nexus of capitalism, liberal democracy, and the administrative state.[3]

Each of these three institutions is thoroughly inept in dealing with ecology. In addition, any combination of them only compounds their errors. Furthermore, their only redeeming feature is the possibility that they create for their own transformation. The collision of the institutional status quo with environmental imperatives makes certain kinds of political and economic structures both possible and attractive. One such structure is discursive democracy.

Capitalism: Recently, capitalism has been showing an environmentally friendly face. It is intellectually supported by those who argue that the market is the best mechanism for satisfying what individuals want—including their environmental wants. In the environmental political economy, all neoconservative regulatory reformers, new resource economists, and cornucopian free marketeers propagate the virtues of privatization and decentralization.

The ecological rationality of capitalism (whether monopolistic or market) is questionable. This can be summarized as follows:

First, capitalism needs economic growth. The absence of economic growth causes reduced investment that leads to general economic decline. As a consequence, capitalism confronts distributional inequality, unemployment, and political instability. For this reason, governments in capitalist market systems are primarily concerned with the promotion of growth.

With ecological limits, growth has to cease at some point. The counterargument of the proponents of the market system is that our world is infinite because the market price mechanism ensures that substitutes are found for any scarce resource. However, this desirable outcome may be obtained in particular cases; for example, substitutes were easily located when whale oil ran out in the nineteenth century. Most importantly, there is no substitute for the assimilative capacity of the biosphere. This constraint cannot be avoided even if a source of unlimited cheap energy could be found to convert degraded nature into useful nature. This is because when such energy is massively used, it has to be dissipated somewhere in the biosphere, threatening warming beyond tolerable bounds. On this planet, there is only a finite supply of low entropy, which capitalism can degrade. Currently, there are no indicators of the entropic level or the overall state of the biosphere. When based on the possibility of substitution, evidence regarding the condition of particular resources or environmental "sinks" becomes misleading.

The only escape for capitalism might seem to be a shift to growth in economic activities that do not involve the consumption of materials or environmental services. To the extent that the capitalist system becomes informational—that is, centered around the production, exchange, and dissemination of information rather than those of material goods—its growth might seem to have no ecologically deleterious effects. However, societies that have moved into the information age have not stopped material growth. These societies have continued the growth in the level of their material consumption, even if actual production has increasingly been transferred to other societies. Their local environment might have improved as a result of this shift, but at the global level, the environment has deteriorated.

Secondly, capitalism gives less weight to the future. In capitalism, interest rates are positive, according to which market actors discount expected future costs and benefits at the prevailing interest rate. When interest rates are higher, people and the capitalist system become more short-sighted and give long-term results less weight. Capitalism is inconceivable without interest rates because capital would be free then.

Thirdly, markets, as decentralized systems based on the logic of self-interest, have no mechanisms for dealing with common properties and public goods. In the capitalist market system, actors act based on private profit and consequently are not concerned about damage to third parties who are not directly involved in transactions. Such actors are even less concerned about environmental resources, which do not carry a price tag. The market system leads to the tragedy of the commons, which is the result of the behavior of instrumentally rational actors motivated by private material self-interest in an unregulated social environment that eventually ruins resources held in common. Self-interest behavior is not only required for the operation of capitalist market systems, but also necessary for actors wishing to survive and prosper in these systems.

Solutions to problems posed by public goods and common property are sought and implemented within the basic structure of the capitalist market system. Examples include rearrangement of property rights to give each actor a private stake in a former common, regulation of access to resources, and the control of harmful practices such as pollution. But all such regulatory solutions require governmental action. In addition, solutions to the problems of ozone depletion and global warming have been sought within the political arena. That is, capitalism passes to the government the environmental problems which it creates but cannot solve. However, governments in mixed capitalist political economic systems may not be able to respond to such problems effectively. The reasons for this are discussed next.

Liberal Democracy: Liberal democracy as a system of governance can be regarded as involving competition for elective office, opportunity for the exertion of popular pressure upon government through free political association, a series of individual rights—secured through constitutional limitations—for protection against government, and a politics of the strategic pursuit of private interests. Liberal democracies have made more progress in dealing with environmental problems than any other political system. This has been accomplished mainly through the mechanisms of interest group politics. Environmentalists have joined the politics of interest groups and have been able to finalize a series of environmental legislation. Liberal democracy resolves ecological problems more effectively than the market system. The market system coexists with liberal democracy, and it passes on to liberal democracy the environmental problems that it generates but cannot solve. However, the failures of liberal democracy to properly deal with energy problems in the 1970s, issues related to nuclear waste, and the chronic impasse on old growth forests in the Western United States demonstrate that there are limits to the problem-solving ability of liberal democracy. These limits are five-fold.

First, in liberal-democratic systems, the distribution of power is skewed. Business is given a privileged position because of: (1) the financial resources it owns, (2) the government's dependency on business cooperation in implementing its policies, and (3) the government's pro-business policy, otherwise the business pursues an investment strike with the consequent economic downturn. Being in a privileged position, the business, of course, promotes and supports policies that favor its own profits, rather than ecological values. Waves of popular support for environmental values are typically counteracted and broken when they threaten the privileged position of business. Such environmental initiatives fail wholesale when business mobilizes a public relations campaign declaring that these initiatives take away people's jobs.

Second, when liberal democracies identify an environmental problem, they disaggregate it based on the particular interests of affected parties. These disaggregated particular interests most often do not combine to form a general ecological interest, even if some of the disaggregated components are environmentally inspired. Third, in liberal democracy, tangible rewards are given to identifiable interests. This may be functional in terms of the distribution of the costs and benefits of government activity, but it is barely useful in relation to large-scale, non-reducible ecological problems. Fourth, the time horizon in liberal democracy, as in the market system, is rather short. Short-term problems are located at the center of attention, and any problem that extends beyond the next election is often ignored. Even when projects with anticipated long-range benefits are funded—for example, fusion research—the funding is provided not as a result of foresight, but to appease the particular constituencies who benefit from this funding in the near future. Fifth, liberal democracy, as the market system, needs economic growth. In the absence of growth, distributional inequities become more apparent. This undesirability of economic downturn shows that liberal democracies follow the market's growth imperative.

The Administrative State: Currently, mainstream politics consists of a combination of liberal democracy and the administrative state. Whereas administration follows an instrumental rationalistic logic, liberal democracy follows a political and interactive logic. Administration's ecological rationality embodies common purpose, neutral expertise, the capability to make sense of complex problems, and the will and authority to effect solutions to these problems. However, administrative systems suffer from the following three problems.

The first problem is that in response to problems, these systems are highly constrained. The common purpose is often undermined because subordinates do not necessarily comply with the goals set at the apex of the hierarchy. In addition, bureaucratic organizations are only capable of performing a limited range of routines, which are inadequate to deal with complex and variable environmental problems. Large, centralized organizations only provide large, centralized solutions to problems. Moreover, in a hierarchical organization, failure or misinterpretation at any point in the chain of command can be devastating. A growing political science literature demonstrates that successful implementation by bureaucratic organizations is the exception rather than the rule, both in environmental matters and otherwise.

The second problem is that administrative rationality cannot properly deal with complex problems. This is because the administrative division of labor leads to the disaggregation of the environmental problem, which means that aspects of complex problems are artificially separated from one another. This results in a situation where solutions from the perspective of one sub-unit involve placing a problem elsewhere. This displacement can take place across space—for instance, when a toxic waste dump is cleaned up by transferring its contents to another dump. Problems can be displaced across media—for example, a sub-unit solves its air pollution problem by mandating the capture of the pollutant in a toxic sludge. Displacement can occur over time—for instance, when long-lived nuclear wastes are placed in a hole in the ground. Disaggregation of problems also undermines the claim to *neutral* expertise. This is because different administrative units typically consist of different types of specialists who are committed to different goals and values.

The third problem is that hierarchical systems obstruct the free flow of information, which is essential to the effective solution of non-routine problems. A typical effective problem-solving community is decentralized, so that good argument rather than hierarchical authority prevails. Hierarchy may be adequate for dealing with routine tasks but is not adequate for dealing with complex and variable problems.

The will and authority to impose solutions on the part of the administration are the only claims left from the ecological rationality of the administrative state. The above arguments suggest that the imposition of such solutions rarely contributes to the amelioration of the environmental crisis.

Discursive Democracy: The real possibilities for change are sensibly located in vulnerable areas of the political economy. Such possibilities exist either where there is strong opposition to dominant structures and their imperatives, or where contradictions and confusion in dominant structures make them vulnerable to action undertaken toward some alternative institutional order. Circumstances in which both of these opportunities exist are most promising. In fact, where one of them exists, it is likely that the other one exists as well.

Capitalism and the Keynesian welfare state have had negative effects on gender, expertise, ecology, age, and even life itself. Each negative effect contributes to the constitution of subjects in different ways. Since subjectivity is plural, radical politics must be plural as well. That is, there must be a "radical and plural democracy" consisting of various, self-defining struggles. Such a plurality can be in association with an autonomous public sphere or spheres. The public sphere may be defined as the space for people to enter into discourse with mutual respect, openness, scrutiny of their relationships with each other, the creation of true public opinion, and, most importantly, confrontation with state power. Of course, it is not necessarily the case that social movements embody these virtues. However, green, feminist, direct action, and peace groups—among others—support discursive and consensual decision-making. They do this consciously in contrast to the hierarchical political style of the institutions they oppose. The public sphere operates on criteria—those of open communication, or what is called communicative rationality—that transcend the boundaries of struggles and discourses. Communicative rationality respects reflectively held positions of people and forms a procedural standard for political interaction that does not dictate any substantive way of life.

The public sphere is central to the reconstruction of the political economy based on ecological rationality. There are discernable signs that such a process is underway. Indeed, public spheres are emerging and expanding with respect to the types of struggles noted above. This process is hastened by the contradiction and confusion in liberal democracy and the administrative state. It was noted earlier that liberal democracy and the administrative state are incapable of properly dealing with ecological problems, and the same may be equally true in cases where these institutions have to deal with issues of concern to other social movements. The perceived incapability of liberal democracy and the administrative state is a contributing factor in leading social movements to the public sphere as an alternative venue for political action. Public spheres are a necessity, rather than a choice, to those who are excluded by the mainstream institutions.

When states are not able to export or displace ecological problems, environmental conservation becomes firmly established as an additional imperative. This establishment only adds to the contradictions of the Keynesian state, because this is in conflict with capital accumulation. The deleterious effects of economic growth on the environment become very clear. In corridors of power, those who intend to veto environmental proposals but claim to represent citizens rather than corporations or bureaucracies tend to seek legitimacy through concessions to a more participatory model of democracy. For instance, in the UK, central government cannot build nuclear power stations without first holding elaborate public inquiries at which all parties are allowed to express their ideas and positions. Canada, the United States, and some other countries have experienced enormous growth in environmental and social impact assessment, participatory models of planning, right-to-know legislation, public hearings, public inquiries, regulatory negotiation, and environmental mediation.

These phenomena may be called discursive designs; or more accurately, *incipient* discursive designs, because they are imperfect representations—occasionally gross violations—of the ideals of free discourse. They do not constitute *autonomous* public spheres, because they are associated with the state. Nonetheless, they suggest that in order for a policy decision to be legitimate, it is now required to be based not only on expertise and the backing of constitutional authority but also on informed participation by affected parties.

There is a complex relationship between discursive and liberal democracy. Liberal democracy has a continued quest for legitimation that can modify it to discursive democracy. But, at the same time, liberal democracy strictly limits the extent to which incipient discursive designs can change public policy, which is subject to the capital accumulation imperatives. Within such limits, the public sphere can flourish in its discursive challenge to the liberal-democratic state. Although liberal democracy and discursive democracy can have simple confrontations, in a more ambiguous terrain they may intersect. In this terrain, the liberal-democratic state might subvert and take over discursive forms. It is also possible that discursive democracy might erode the strategic, private interest-driven character of liberal democracy.

In short, democratization needs to take place at all possible levels: in the autonomous public spheres, such as those created by new social movements; in discursive exercises at the boundaries of the state where legitimacy is sought by the state; and in the state, for example, in the form of impact assessment.

## Radical Structuralist View

At this juncture, the confrontation of reality with reason leads one to wonder: Is the planet facing a major ecological collapse? Is civilization on the edge of the abyss? Is the survival of the human species itself in doubt? The raising of these questions is both rational and necessary because scientific research consistently shows that if current trends continue for a century, there will be a total collapse of the Earth and its inhabitants. The continuation of current trends for about a decade will lead to ecological tipping points—associated with the rapid disintegration of ice sheets in West Antarctica and Greenland, the disappearance of Arctic Sea ice, the thawing of frozen tundra, and vanishing glaciers in the Himalayas and elsewhere—that will change the climate and the ecosystems such that countless human beings and innumerable species will be endangered. Accordingly, it is now widely recognized that there is a need for an ecological revolution—that is, a massive and sudden change in the relation of humanity to the Earth.[4]

Ecological revolutions can be defined as major transformations in relations between humans and nonhuman nature. In a society, they arise from changes, tensions, and contradictions that develop between its mode of production and ecology, and between its modes of production and reproduction. Currently, society is confronted with a major transformation in its mode of production and its ecological regime due to the contemporary crisis of the Earth.

The literature on ecological revolution can be divided into two main approaches. The first approach can be called an eco-industrial revolution because it aims at a new industrial revolution that seeks to create the basis for sustainable capitalist development almost entirely by technological means, such as more efficient energy systems. The proponents of this green industrial revolution call it "ecological modernization," through which the rich countries lead the way in developing ecological innovations as new market opportunities. Such technological innovations—for example, increased energy efficiency—face no major barriers. In this approach, only technology changes, but nothing in the social organization of society changes. In this approach, there is no change in either the commitment to the unlimited accumulation of capital or to the order that gives primacy to artificially generated private wants over individual and social needs. The vision is one of vastly expanding commodity production and sales opportunities in a competitive and nationalist race for economic growth and dominance. It maintains the main "possessive-individualist" assumptions of the current social order.

The second approach is a more radical, eco-social revolution. It takes advantage of advancements in technology where necessary, but emphasizes the need to transform both the human relation to nature and the existing social relations of production. These can only be achieved through a process of sustainable human development. It requires a decisive break with the logic of the dominant social order and a move toward egalitarian and communal forms of production, distribution, exchange, and consumption. It reverses the further widening of the rift in the human/nature metabolism that characterizes the contemporary world economy. It aims at returning to more organic, sustainable social-ecological relations. These changes require a revolution in culture, economy, and society.

The ultimate goal of this approach is to construct a new system of production that replaces the capitalist system of production, which is responsible for the current destructive phase of historical civilization. This approach recognizes that such a replacement necessarily involves radical changes in technology, but it places the emphasis on changing the wider social relations of production. This is because it is the social relations of production, not technology as such, that are the problem. The problem is one of technics and human development, where the latter represents the sustainable development of human beings and their broader social relations.

This approach is more social, as opposed to being merely industrial, and constitutes the only genuine approach to an ecological revolution. It is futile to attempt to solve our problems merely by technological, industrial, or "free market" means, because they are divorced from fundamental social relations. At the crux of the current ecological problem is capitalism, which is a civilizational project that has reached a dead end. Although capitalism represents a great advance over earlier forms of production, the capital accumulation system includes the externalization of social costs onto the poor and the emergence of less-developed countries, which have increasingly become a hindrance to human development and even to the survival of humanity, along with most other species.

The debate between these two opposing approaches to ecological revolution is not about technology or non-technology, industrialism or non-industrialism. Rather, it is a dispute over whether capitalism can accommodate the necessary ecological changes or if capitalism is a system that, for a combination of material reasons (economic, social, and environmental), has reached its limits. At this time, a genuine ecological and social revolution is not only necessary but also possible. This is because "all the productive forces" for which the existing mode of production is "sufficient," and that are compatible with sustainability, have been developed. What is required now is a revolutionary shift in the social relations of production and society as a whole.

For the first approach, the problem goes no deeper than the narrow conception of technological characteristics. It sees increased efficiency as a free lunch that allows unending exponential growth of the economy without expanding the exploitation of the Earth. For the second approach, capitalism is chiefly at fault for the rapidly accelerating planetary catastrophe. Capitalism as a world economy is divided into classes and is driven by competition. Its logic does not accept any boundaries on its own expansion and its exploitation of the environment. In contrast, the planet Earth is limited. This is an absolute contradiction embodied in the capitalist system.

The first approach denies any lasting conflict between the capitalist economic and social order on one hand and ecology on the other hand. It promises unending technological breakthroughs connected to the market. It presents technology as a magical answer that defies both social sciences (our knowledge of capitalism as a social system), and natural sciences (i.e., physics and ecological science). It believes that ecological and social problems can be solved by improvements in technology. It denies that these major tasks can be accomplished quite rapidly by moving away from the narrow and restrictive goals of the accumulation of capital, the proliferation of economic waste, and the promotion of possessive individualism. It leads one to believe that improved engineering can solve all problems without altering social structure or human behavior.

The first approach supports strategies that perpetually guide society along the growth of a planetary risk economy, rather than changing direction in order to completely avoid the precipice. It equates sustainable development with engineering—that is, improved technology—with the maximum exploitation of the Earth (and human beings) that can currently be achieved without exceeding the absolute ecological limits of the planet. It views the accumulation of capital as an enterprise based on risk, which is extended to ever more risky endeavors with respect to the future of the biosphere, leading to a global risk society.

The first approach—that is, the green industrial revolution—considers only those changes that can take place within the boundaries of capitalism. It seldom questions either the capitalist engine itself or its inherent destructiveness. Its worries are largely limited to the quantity and quality (cleanliness) of its fuel, its efficiency as a motor, and the emissions that it releases. The narrow, technocratic nature of these concerns is not meant so much to do with their efficacy in solving the problem as to establish legitimacy for the existing system of production by ensuring that all wider, non-technocratic solutions remain off limits forever.

More sophisticated versions of the green industrial revolution strategy have been represented by a school of environmental sociologists under the title "ecological modernization." Its chief claim is that the sustainability of capitalism is possible. Therefore, ecological revolution requires the modernization of the existing system, as opposed to a radical transformation of the existing mode of production. It contends that the capitalist economy can "dematerialize" by reducing the inputs of energy and raw materials that it utilizes in production.

While it is true that the efficiency in the use of energy and raw materials has continually risen along with the advances made in the technology of production, the overall results have not been reductions in the consumption of energy and raw materials. This is because, under a capitalist economy, efficiency gains result in further capital accumulation and economic expansion such that the increase in scale typically overwhelms gains in efficiency (a phenomenon known as the "Jevons Paradox"). Furthermore, what are claimed as environmental gains are often nothing but the shifting of the problems elsewhere—from rich to poor regions and countries. Thus, ecological modernization has not been able to prevent the rapid overall rise in ecological destruction.

Purely technological approaches to ecological revolution are too narrow in their concept of technology. They focus only on very limited technological solutions that allow capital accumulation and economic expansion to proceed unaltered, unrestricted by the limits of planet Earth. They focus on advances in technology that increase the efficiency in the use of energy and raw materials. The main purpose of their modernizing technology is to perpetuate the existing treadmill of production rather than to solve ecological problems. Therefore, technological innovations that emerge in the efficient use of energy and raw materials are quickly undermined by the very desirable economic expansion which they had enabled. This feeds the insatiable appetite of capital for growth on planet Earth, and consequently, new technologies that are intended to overcome these contradictions run up against the challenge of transcending physics itself (the entropy law).

The first approach ignores the much wider universe of technologies. Many technologies that are neither new nor high-tech are currently available to meet social needs and ecological restoration. But the existing political economy does not allow their usage because it confines the technology and its usage to certain restrictive parameters. The current use of machines is one of the relations of our existing economic system, but how the machinery is used is totally distinct from the machinery itself. For instance, powder can be used to wound a man or to dress his wounds. How and why existing technologies are used or not used within human production and consumption is as important as making such decisions with respect to new technologies. The answers to these questions depend to a very large extent on the socio-economic relations of production. For example, solar power has been available for many years, but its use has been restricted by the fact that it is in many cases less profitable than less ecologically sound alternatives.

Currently, the most serious industrial and technological danger for climate change is coal-fired plants. In the United States, this technology emits more carbon dioxide into the atmosphere than the entire US transportation system. Some of the proponents of the green revolution propose the use of coal-sequestration technology, which is still being developed. They present the so-called "clean coal" as the magic answer. This technology involves de-carbonization of the power grid primarily through carbon sequestration and "clean coal." The strategy of accomplishing this technology would probably not take place in the United States prior to the second half of the twenty-first century at best. In addition, it might not be regarded as practical under the existing system of economic relations, where the externalization of environmental costs is the norm. With a focus on climate—and a disregard for economics—the best thing to do is to close down coal plants all across the country as soon as possible. In addition, even if coal-sequestration technology were feasible on the required scale, it involves heavy environmental costs associated with coal mining and coal use, plus the long-term risk of leakages of sequestered carbon. The more radical ecological group recommends: (1) the immediate closure of coal-fired plants and their substitution by solar, wind, and other forms of renewable power and (2) alterations on the demand-side through a transformation of social priorities. The vested interests view this recommendation as completely undesirable. Thus, a serious shift in favor of such genuine environmental alternatives is completely incompatible with the views of the proponents of the green industrial revolution. Such proponents have as their first principle the promotion of the needs of the powers that be, and in their green technological revolution, they see no alternative to Big Coal (except perhaps Big Nuclear power). Technocratic choices, frequently based on futuristic notions, are often more about the requirements of the profit system than about the environmental efficacy of the technology itself. The social embeddedness of present-day science and technology is devastating. The point is not whether or not we should use science and technology to solve our problems—because we know we must—but the point is whether or not we should radically change their direction, which is currently narrowly determined and circumscribed by the self-serving and self-perpetuating needs of profit maximization.

Currently, there is excessive technological optimism in society. In the modern economic system of monopoly-finance capital, technology is seen first and foremost as a means to accumulate wealth. Therefore, it is disproportionately directed at reducing labor costs and maximizing the surplus. The system becomes increasingly energy-intensive, as opposed to labor-intensive, without regard to its impact on the environment, employment, and human welfare. In this system of production, economic efficiency is viewed as efficiency in generating profits rather than sustaining people and the Earth. In this economic system, rational accounting is impossible because costs are socialized—that is, imposed on the environment and the majority of human beings—in order to maximize private gain. Waste generation within the production process becomes "rational" as long as it increases markets and hence the sales of commodities. If nature and human beings are not incorporated into the market, then they are valueless. To the extent that nature and human beings are incorporated into the prevailing economic system, their values lie solely in their abstract existence as commodities. The quid pro quo that is claimed to exist in this mode of production—that is, the equal exchange and the mutual benefit of all—is denied everywhere outside of its abstract justification. In capitalism, a substantial portion of costs of production are unpaid because these costs remain unaccounted for in entrepreneurial outlays. Instead, such costs are shifted to and ultimately borne by third parties or by the community as a whole.

When society's goal is the treadmill of accumulation, everything is geared toward growth, and growth is primarily growth in profits and wealth for a relative few. This explains why economics is the dominant social science, why economics and economists have the highest command in addressing ecological problems, and why they constitute the main source of skepticism against those who attempt to promote egalitarian, ecological ends. There is no doubt that the development of green technologies is needed. But such a policy vision does not recognize that real and rapid ecological change can only be achieved by altering the economic and social order and that the whole population needs to reshape the whole society. Many of the technologies that are advocated by futuristic technocrats are not in existence. Moreover, available solutions such as conservation and alterations in the organization of production and consumption (e.g., the substitution of mass transit for the private automobile or limiting the role of marketing in the promotion of wasteful consumption) are not decided upon. This is because these types of solutions interfere with the accumulation system.

The primary difference between a genuine ecological revolution and a green industrial revolution is the social agency. The green industrial revolution is based on a top-down attempt at a technological shift. This hierarchy is led by ecologically modernizing elites, and there is no popular uprising that would challenge the economic, social, cultural, and environmental norms of capitalist society. The goal of the vested interests is to keep social change in relation to any challenge—including the environmental challenge—contained within the limits acceptable to the system, without regard for the consequent risk to the entire planet. For this purpose, involvement in social change is restricted only to technocrats.

In contrast, a genuine ecological revolution involves the transformation of the relations between the mode of production and the ecology. It is engaged with a wider social, not merely industrial, revolution, as it emanates from the great mass of the people. As is the case with a social revolution, it would question every aspect of society down to its roots. It would reestablish economics as a political economy, and in line with today's necessity, transform ecological economics to ecological political economy. An eco-social revolution leads to the rise of a new political economy, which is founded on the interdependence of social, political, and economic realms, and is connected to the encompassing social and natural ecologies. Ecological and socialist revolutions are necessary and sufficient conditions for each other. A genuine ecological revolution destroys the metabolism of capitalism and replaces it with a communal metabolism encompassing all of humanity and the Earth.

## Conclusion

This chapter briefly discussed four views expressed with respect to environmental governance. The functionalist paradigm believes that environmental governance should be made through the use of market mechanisms and advancement in technology. The interpretive paradigm believes that environmental problems and environmental governance are socially constructed and managed. The radical humanist paradigm believes that environmental governance is best made through discursive democracy. The radical structuralist paradigm believes that environmental governance is best made through socialism.

Each paradigm is logically coherent—in terms of its underlying assumptions—and conceptualizes and studies the phenomenon in a certain way, generating distinctive kinds of insight and understanding. Therefore, different paradigms in combination provide a broader understanding of the phenomenon under consideration. An understanding of different paradigms leads to a better understanding of the multifaceted nature of the phenomenon.

## Notes

1 For this literature, see Andersen and Sprenger (2000); Anderson and Leal (1991); Baumol and Oates (1988); Catton and Dunlap (1978); Dunlap (1997, 2002); Dunlap and Catton (1994); Edwards (2005); Huber (1982, 1985); Mol (1995, 1996, 1997); Mol and Sonnenfeld (2000); Mol and Spaargaren (1993, 2000); Montgomery (1972); Pearce and Barbier (2000); Pearce, Markandya, Barbier (1989); Pearce and Turner (1990); Spaargaren (2000); Spaargaren and Mol (1992); Spaargaren, Mol, and Buttel (2000); Tietenberg (1995); and Weidner (2002). This section is based on Stavins (2003).

2 For this literature, see Burningham and Cooper (1999); Capek (1993); Eder (1996); Fischer and Hajer (1999); Hajer (1995); Hannigan (2006); Hansen (1993); Irwin (1995); Jasanoff (1992); Jasper (1990); Mazur and Lee (1993); Rayner (1991); Shove (1994); Solesbury (1976); Taylor and Buttel (1992); Thompson (1991); Ungar (1992); Waterton and Wynne (1996); Williams (1998); Wynne (1994, 1996); and Yearley (1992, 1996, 1997, 2002). This section is based on Greider and Garkovich (1994).

3 For this literature, see Beck (1999); Beder (1997); Buttel (1998, 2000); Buttel and Taylor (1992); Deleage (1994); Dickens (1992, 1996); Dryzek (1987, 1992, 1996, 2005); Eckersley (1992); Goldblatt (1996); Gorz (1980); Martell (1994); McLaughlin (1990); Murphy (1994); O'Connor (1994, 1988, 1998); Pepper (1984); Redclift (1984, 1987); Scott (1991); Sklair (1994); Sonnenfeld (1998, 2000); Sonnenfeld and Mol (2002); Stretton (1976); Vogel (1996); and Wehling (2002). This section is based on Dryzek (1992).

4 For this literature, see Barbosa (1993, 1996); Barham, Bunker, and O'Hearn (1994); Bartley and Bergensen (1997); Benton (1989, 1996, 2007); Bunker (1985, 1989); Burkett (1997, 1999, 2006); Bunker and Ciccantell (1995); Burns, Davis,

and Kick (1997); Chase-Dunn and Hall (1997); Chew (1995, 1997); Covello and Frey (1990); Foster (1994, 1997, 1999, 2000, 2002); Foster, Clark, and York (2010); Gould, Schnaiberg, and Weinberg (1996); Moore (2000, 2003a, 2003b, 2003c, 2008); Panitch and Leys (2007); Parsons (1977); Roberts (1994, 1996a, 1996b); Roberts and Grimes (2002); Sanderson (1995); Schnaiberg (1980); Schnaiberg and Gould (1994); Smith (1994); and Sweezy (2004). This section is based on Foster (2009).

# References

Andersen, M.S. and Sprenger, R.U. (2000), *Market-Based Instruments for Environmental Management*, Northampton, MA: Edward Elgar.

Anderson, T.L. and Leal, D.R. (1991), *Free Market Environmentalism*, Boulder, CO: Westview Press.

Barbosa, Luis (1993), "The World-System and the Destruction of the Brazilian Rain Forest," *Review*, 16, 215–40.

Barbosa, Luis (1996), "The People of the Forest against International Capitalism: Systemic and Anti-Systemic Forces in the Battle for the Preservation of the Brazilian Amazon Rainforest," *Sociological Perspectives*, 39, 317–31.

Barham, Bradford, Bunker, Stephen G., and O'Hearn, Denis (1994), *States, Firms, and Raw Materials: The World Economy and Ecology of Aluminum*, Madison, WI: University of Wisconsin Press.

Bartley, Tim and Bergensen, Albert (1997), "World-System Studies of the Environment," *Journal of World-Systems Research*, 3:3, Fall, 369–80.

Baumol, W.J. and Oates, W.E. (1988), *The Theory of Environmental Policy*, Second Edition, Cambridge: Cambridge University Press.

Beck, U. (1999), *World Risk Society*, Cambridge: Polity Press.

Beder, Sharon (1997), *Global Spin: The Corporate Assault on Environmentalism*, Totnes: Green Books Ltd.

Benton, Ted (1989), "Marxism and Natural Limits," *New Left Review*, 178, 51–86.

Benton, Ted (1996), *The Greening of Marxism*, New York, NY: Guilford Press.

Benton, Ted (2007), "Greening the Left? From Marx to World-System Theory," in Pretty, Jules, Ball, Andrew S., Benton, Ted, Guivant, Julia S., Lee, David R., Orr, David, Pfeffer, Max J., and Ward, Hugh (eds.), *The Sage Handbook of Environment and Society*, Thousand Oaks, CA: Sage Publications Inc, pp. 91–106.

Bunker, Stephen G. (1985), *Underdeveloping the Amazon: Extraction, Unequal Exchange, and the Failure of the Modern Sate*, Urbana, IL: University of Illinois Press.

Bunker, Stephen G. (1989), "The Eternal Conquest," *NACLA Report on the Americas*, 23, 27–36.

Bunker, Stephen G. and Ciccantell, Paul S. (1995), "Restructuring Space, Time, and Competitive Advantage in the Capitalist World-Economy: Japan and Raw Materials Transport after World War II," in Smith, David A. and Borocz, Jozsef (eds.), *A New World Order? Global Transformations in the Late Twentieth Century*, Westport, CT: Greenwood Press, Chapter 7, pp. 109–29.

Burkett, Paul (1997), "Nature in Marx Reconsidered," *Organization and Environment*, 10:2, 164–83.

Burkett, Paul (1999), *Marx and Nature: A Red and Green Perspective*, New York, NY: St. Martin's Press.

Burkett, Paul (2006), *Marxism and Ecological Economics: Towards a Red and Green Political Economy*, Leiden: Koninklijke Brill NV.

Burningham, Kate and Cooper, Geoff (1999), "Being Constructive: Social Construction and the Environment," *Sociology*, 33, 297–316.

Burns, Thomas J., Davis, Byron L., and Kick, Edward L. (1997), "Position in the World-System and National Emissions of Greenhouse Gases," *Journal of World-Systems Research*, 3:3, Fall, 436–66.

Buttel, Frederick H. (1998), "Some Observations on States, World Orders, and the Politics of Sustainability," *Organization and Environment*, 11:3, September, 261–8.

Buttel, Frederick H. (2000), "Ecological Modernization as Social Theory," *Geoforum*, 31, 57–65.

Buttel, Frederick H. and Taylor, Peter (1992), "Environmental Sociology and Global Environmental Change: A Critical Assessment," *Society and Natural Resources*, 5:3, 211–30.

Capek, S. (1993), "The 'Environmental Justice' Frame: A Conceptual Discussion and an Application," *Social Problems*, 40, 5–24.

Catton, W.R., Jr., and Dunlap, R.E.(1978), "Environmental Sociology: A New Paradigm," *American Sociologist*, 13, 41–9.

Chase-Dunn, Christopher K. and Hall, Thomas D. (1997), "Ecological Degradation and the Evolution of World-Systems," *Journal of World-Systems Research*, 3:3, Fall, 403–31.

Chew, Sing C. (1995), "Environmental Transformations: Accumulation, Ecological Crisis, and Social Movements," in Smith, David A. and Borocz, Jozsef (eds.), *A New World Order? Global Transformations in the Late Twentieth Century*, Westport, CT: Greenwood Press, Chapter 12, pp. 201–15.

Chew, Sing C. (1997), "For Nature: Deep Greening World-Systems Analysis for the 21st Century," *Journal of World-Systems Research*, 3:3, Fall, 381–402.

Covello, Vincent T. and Frey, Scott R. (1990), "Technology-Based Environmental Health Risks in Developing Nations," *Technological Forecasting and Social Change*, 37, 159–79.

Deleage, Jean-Paul (1994), "Eco-Marxist Critique of Political Economy," in O'Connor, Martin (ed.), *Is Capitalism Sustainable?*, New York, NY: Guilford Press, pp. 37–52.

Dickens, Peter (1992), *Society and Nature*, Philadelphia, Pennsylvania: Temple University Press.

Dickens, Peter (1996), *Reconstructing Nature: Alienation, Emancipation and the Division of Labor*, London: Routledge.

Dryzek, John S. (1987), *Rational Ecology: Environment and Political Economy*, Oxford: Basil, Blackwell.

Dryzek, John S. (1992), "Ecology and Discursive Democracy: Beyond Liberal Capitalism and the Administrative State," *Capitalism, Nature, Socialism*, 3:2, June, 18–42.

Dryzek, John S. (1996), "Foundations for Environmental Political Economy: The Search for Homo Ecologicus," *New Political Economy*, 1:1, 27–40.

Dryzek, John S. (2005), *The Politics of the Earth: Environmental Discourses*, Oxford: Oxford University Press.

Dunlap, R.E. (1997), "The Evolution of Environmental Sociology: A Brief History and Assessment of the American Experience," in Redclift, M. and Woodgate, G. (eds.), *The International Handbook of Environmental Sociology*, Cheltenham: Edward Elgar, pp. 21–39.

Dunlap, R.E. (2002), "Paradigms, Theories, and Environmental Sociology," in Dunlap, Riley E., Buttel, Frederick H., Kickens, Peter, and Gijswijt, August (eds.), *Sociological Theory and the Environment: Classical Foundations, Contemporary Insights*, Lanhma, MD: Rowman and Littlefield Publishers, pp. 329–50.

Dunlap, R.E. and Catton, W.R., Jr., (1994), "Struggling with Exemptionalism: The Rise, Decline, and Revitalization of Environmental Sociology," *American Sociologist*, 25, 5–30.

Eckersley, Robyn (1992), *Environmentalism and Political Theory*, New York, NY: State University of New York Press.

Eder, K. (1996), *The Social Construction of Nature: A Sociology of Ecological Enlightenment*, London: Sage Publications.

Edwards, Andres R. (2005), *The Sustainability Revolution*, Gabriola Island, British Columbia: New Society Publishers.

Fischer, F. and Hajer, M. (1999), *Living with Nature: Environmental Politics as Cultural Discourse*, Oxford: Oxford University Press.

Foster, John Bellamy (1994), *The Vulnerable Planet: A Short Economic History of the Environment*, New York, N: Monthly Review Press.

Foster, John Bellamy (1997), "The Crisis of the Earth," *Organization and Environment*, 10:3, 278–95.

Foster, John Bellamy (1999), "Marx's Theory of Metabolic Rift: Classical Foundations for and Environmental Sociology," *American Journal of Sociology*, 105:2, September, 366–405.

Foster, John Bellamy (2000), *Marx's Ecology: Materialism and Nature*, New York, NY: Monthly Review Press.

Foster, John Bellamy (2002), *Ecology against Capitalism*, New York, NY: Monthly Review Press.

Foster, John Bellamy (2009), *The Ecological Revolution: Making Peace with the Planet*, New York, NY: Monthly Review Press.

Foster, John Bellamy, Clark, Brett, and York, Richard (2010), *The Ecological Rift: Capitalism's War on the Earth*, New York, NY: Monthly Review Press.

Goldblatt, David (1996), *Social Theory and the Environment*, Boulder, CO: Westview Press.

Gorz, Andre (1980), *Ecology as Politics*, Boston, MA: South End Press.

Gould, K.A., Schnaiberg, A., and Weinberg, A.S. (1996), *Environmental Struggles*, New York, NY: Cambridge University Press.

Greider, Thomas and Garkovich, Lorraine (1994), "Landscapes: The Social Construction of Nature and the Environment," *Rural Sociology*, 59:1, 1–24.

Hajer, M. (1995), *The Politics of Environmental Discourse: Ecological Modernization and the Policy Process*, Oxford: Oxford University Press.

Hannigan, John (2006), *Environmental Sociology*, New York, NY: Routledge.

Hansen, A. (1993), *The Mass Media and Environmental Issues*, Leicester: Leicester University Press.

Huber, Joseph (1982), *The Lost Innocence of Ecology: New Technologies and Superindustrial Development*, Frankfurt and Main, Germany: Fischer.

Huber, Joseph (1985), *The Rainbow Society: Ecology and Social Policy*, Frankfurt and Main, Germany: Fischer.

Irwin, Alan (1995), *Citizen Science: A Study of People, Expertise and Sustainable Development*, London: Routledge.

Jasanoff, Sheila (1992), "Science, Politics, and the Renegotiation of Expertise at EPA," *Osiris*, 7, 1–23.

Jasper, J.M. (1990), *Energy and the State in the United States, Sweden, and France*, Princeton, NJ: Princeton University Press.

Martell, L. (1994), *Ecology and Society*, Amhurst, MA: University of Massachusetts Press.

Mazur, Allan and Lee, Jinling (1993), "Sounding the Global Alarm: Environmental Issues in the U.S. National News," *Social Studies of Science*, 23:4, November, 681–720.

McLaughlin, Andrew (1990), "Ecology, Capitalism, and Socialism," *Socialism and Democracy*, 10, 69–102.

Mol, Arthur P.J. (1995), *The Refinement of Production*, Utrecht, the Netherlands: Van Arkel.

Mol, Arthur P.J. (1996), "Ecological Modernization and Institutional Reflexivity: Environmental Reform in the Late Modern Age," *Environmental Politics*, 5:2, summer, 302–23.

Mol, Arthur P.J. (1997), "Ecological Modernization: Industrial Transformation and Environmental Reform," in Redcliff, M. and Woodgate, G. (eds.), *The International Handbook of Environmental Sociology*, London: Edward Elgar, pp. 138–49.

Mol, Arthur P.J. and Sonnenfeld, David A. (2000), *Ecological Modernization around the World: Perspectives and Critical Debates*, Portland, Oregon: Frank Cass Publishers.

Mol, Arthur P.J. and Spaargaren, Gert (1993), "Environment, Modernity and the Risk Society: The Apocalyptic Horizon of Environmental Reform," *International Sociology*, 8, 431–59.

Mol, Arthur P.J. and Spaargaren, Gert (2000), "Ecological Modernization Theory in Debate: A Review," *Environmental Politics*, 9:1, 17–49.

Montgomery, D. (1972), "Markets in Licenses and Efficient Pollution Control Programs," *Journal of Economic Theory*, 5, 395–418.

Moore, Jason W. (2000), "Environmental Crisis and the Metabolic Rift in World-Historical Perspective," *Organization and Environment*, 13:2, June, 123–57.

Moore, Jason W.(2003a), "Nature and the Transition from Feudalism to Capitalism," *Review*, 26:2, January, 97–172.

Moore, Jason, W. (2003b), "'The Modern World-System' as Environmental History? Ecology and the Rise of Capitalism," *Theory and Society*, 32:3, June, 307–77.

Moore, Jason W. (2003c), "Capitalism as World-Ecology: Braudel and Marx on Environmental History," *Organization and Environment*, 16:4, December, 431–58.

Moore, Jason W. (2008), "Ecological Crises and the Agrarian Question in World-Historical Perspective," *Monthly Review*, 60:6, November, 54–62.

Murphy, Raymond (1994), *Rationality and Nature: A Sociological Inquiry into a Changing Relationship*, San Francisco, CA: Westview Press.

O'Connor, James (1994), "Is Sustainable Capitalism Possible?," in O'Connor, James (ed.), *Is Capitalism Sustainable?* New York, NY: Guilford Press, pp. 152–75.

O'Connor, James (1988), "Capitalism, Nature, Socialism: A Theoretical Introduction," *Capitalism, Nature, Socialism*, 1:1, 11–38.

O'Connor, James (1998), *Natural Causes: Essays in Ecological Marxism*, New York, NY: Guilford Press.

Panitch, Leo and Leys, Colin (2007), *Coming to Terms with Nature: Socialist Register 2007*, New York, NY: Monthly Review Press.

Parsons, Howard L., ed. (1977), *Marx and Engels on Ecology*, Westport, CT: Greenwood Press.

Pearce, David W. and Barbier, Edward (2000), *Blueprint for a Sustainable Economy*, London: Earthscan Publications Ltd.

Pearce, David W., Markandya, Anil, and Barbier, Edward B. (1989), *Blueprint for a Green Economy*, London: Earthscan Publications Ltd.

Pearce, David W. and Turner, R. Kerry (1990), *Economics of Natural Resources and the Environment*, Baltimore, MD: Johns Hopkins University Press.

Pepper, D. (1984), *The Roots of Modern Environmentalism*, London: Croom Helm.

Rayner, Steve (1991), "A Cultural Perspective on the Structure and Implication of Global Environmental Agreements," *Evaluation Review*, 15, 75–102.

Redclift, Michael (1984), *Development and the Environmental Crisis: Red or Green Alternatives*, London: Methuen.

Redclift, Michael (1987), *Sustainable Development: Exploring the Contradictions*, London: Methuen.

Roberts, J. Timmons (1994), "Economic Crisis and Environmental Policy [Brazil]," *Hemispher*, May, 26–30.

Roberts, J. Timmons (1996a), "Global Restructuring and the Environment in Latin America," in Korzeniewicz, Roberto P. and Smith, William C. (eds.), *Latin America and the World Economy*, Westport, CT: Greenwood, pp. 187–210.

Roberts, J. Timmons (1996b), "Reducing Participation in Environmental Treaties: A World-System Analysis," *Social Inquiry*, 66, 38–57.

Roberts, J. Timmons and Grimes, Peter E. (2002), "World-System Theory and the Environment: Toward a New Synthesis," in Dunlap, Riley E., Buttel, Frederick H., Kickens, Peter, and Gijswijt, August (eds.), *Sociological Theory and the Environment: Classical Foundations, Contemporary Insights*, Lanhma, MD: Rowman and Littlefield Publishers, Chapter 8, pp. 167–94.

Sanderson, Stephen K. (1995), *Social Transformations: A General Theory of Historical Development*, London: Basil Blackwell.

Schnaiberg, Allan (1980), *The Environment: From Surplus to Scarcity*, New York, NY: Oxford University Press.

Schnaiberg, Allan and Gould, Kenneth Alan (1994), *Environment and Society: The Enduring Conflict*, New York, NY: St. Martin's Press.

Scott, A. (1991), *Ideology and the New Social Movements*, London: Unwin Hyman.

Shove, E. (1994), "Sustaining Developments in Environmental Sociology," in Redclift, M. and Benton, T. (eds.), *Social Theory and the Global Environment*, London: Routledge, pp. 256–66.

Sklair, Leslie (1994), "Global Sociology and Global Environmental Change," in Redclift, Michael and Benton, Ted (eds.), *Social Theory and the Global Environment*, London: Routledge, pp. 205–27.

Smith, David A. (1994), "Uneven Development and the Environment: Toward a World-System Perspective," *Humboldt Journal of Social Relations*, 20, 151–75.

Solesbury, William (1976), "The Environmental Agenda: An Illustration of How Situations May Become Political Issues and Issues May Demand Responses from Government: Or How They May Not," *Public Administration*, 54:4, Winter, 379–97.

Sonnenfeld, David A. (1998), "From Brown to Green? Late Industrialization, Social Conflict, and Adoption of Environmental Technologies in Thailand's Pulp and Paper Industry," *Organization and Environment*, 11, 59–87.

Sonnenfeld, David A. (2000), "Contradictions of Ecological Modernization: Pulp and Paper Manufacturing in South-East Asia," *Environmental Politics*, 9:1, 235–56.

Sonnenfeld, David A. and Mol, Arthur P.J. (2002) "Globalization and the Transformation of Environmental Governance," *American Behavioral Scientist*, 45:9, May, 1318–39.

Spaargaren, Gert (2000), "Ecological Modernization Theory and the Changing Discourse on Environment and Modernity," in Spaargaren, Gert, Mol, Arthur P.J., and Buttel, Frederick (eds.), *Environment and Global Modernity*, London: Sage Publications Ltd., Chapter 3, pp. 41–71.

Spaargaren, Gert and Mol, Arthur P.J. (1992), "Sociology, Environment, and Modernity: Ecological Modernization as a Theory of Social Change," *Society and Natural Resources*, 5, 323–44.

Spaargaren, Gert, Mol, Arthur P.J., and Buttel, Frederick (2000), "Introduction: Globalization, Modernity, and the Environment," in Spaargaren, Gert, Mol, Arthur P.J., and Buttel, Frederick (eds.), *Environment and Global Modernity*, London: Sage Publications Ltd., Chapter 1, pp. 1–15.

Stavins, Robert N. (2003), "Experience with Market-Based Environmental Policy Instruments," in Maler, Karl-Goran and Vincent, Jeffrey R. (eds.), *The Handbook of Environmental Economics*, Vol. 3, Amsterdam: North-Holland/Elsevier Science, pp. 355–435.

Stretton, Hugh (1976), *Capitalism, Socialism and the Environment*, Cambridge: Cambridge University Press.

Sweezy, Paul M. (2004), "Capitalism and the Environment," *Monthly Review*, 56:5, June, 86–93.

Taylor, P.J. and Buttel, F.H. (1992), "How Do We Know We Have Global Environmental Problems? Science and the Globalization of Environmental Discourse," *Geoforum*, 23, 405–16.

Thompson, M. (1991), "Plural Rationalities: The Rudiments of a Practical Science of the Inchoate," in Hansen, J. (ed.), *Environmental Concerns: An Interdisciplinary Exercise*, London: Elsevier Applied Science, pp. 243–56.

Tietenberg, T. (1995), "Tradable Permits for Pollution Control When Emission Location Matters: What Have We Learned?" *Environmental and Resource Economics*, 5, 95–113.

Ungar, S. (1992), "The Rise and (Relative) Decline of Global Warming as a Social Problem," *Sociological Quarterly*, 33, 485–501.

Vogel, Steven (1996), *Against Nature: The Concept of Nature in Critical Theory*, New York, Ny: State University of New York Press.

Waterton, Claire and Wynne, Brian (1996), "Building the European Union: Science and the Cultural Dimensions of Environmental Policy," *Journal of European Public Policy*, 3, 421–40.

Wehling, Peter (2002), "Dynamic Constellations of the Individual, Society, and Nature: Critical Theory and Environmental Sociology," in Dunlap, Riley E., Buttel, Frederick H., Kickens, Peter, and Gijswijt, August (eds.), *Sociological Theory and the*

*Environment: Classical Foundations, Contemporary Insights*, Lanhma, MD: Rowman and Littlefield Publishers, Chapter 7, pp. 144–66.

Weidner, Helmut (2002), "Capacity Building for Ecological Modernization: Lessons from Cross-National Research," *American Behavioral Scientist*, 45:9, May, 1340–68.

Williams, J. (1998), "Knowledge, Consequences, and Experience: The Social Construction of Environmental Problems," *Social Inquiry*, 68:4, 476–97.

Wynne, Brian (1994), "Scientific Knowledge and the Global Environment," in Redclift, Michael and Benton, Ted, (eds.), *Social Theory and the Global Environment*, London: Routledge, pp. 169–89.

Wynne, Brian (1996), "May the Sheep Safely Graze? A Reflexive View of the Expert-Lay Knowledge Divide," in Lash, S., Szerszynski, B., and Wynne, B. (eds.), *Risk, Environment, and Modernity*, London: Sage Publications, pp. 43–83.

Yearley, Steven (1992), *The Green Case: A Sociology of Environmental Issues, Arguments and Politics*, London: Routledge.

Yearley, Steven (1996), *Sociology, Environmentalism, Globalization: Reinventing the Globe*, London: Sage Publications.

Yearley, Steven (1997), "Science and the Environment," in Redclift, M. and Woodgate, G. (eds.), *The Environmental Handbook of Environmental Sociology*, Northampton, MA: Edward, Elgar, pp. 227–36.

Yearley, Steven (2002), "The Social Construction of Environmental Problems: A Theoretical Review and some Not-Very-Herculean Labors," in Dunlap, Riley E., Buttel, Frederick H., Kickens, Peter, and Gijswijt, August (eds.), *Sociological Theory and the Environment: Classical Foundations, Contemporary Insights*, Lanhma, MD: Rowman and Littlefield Publishers, Chapter 12, pp. 274–85.

7

# Schools of Thought in Economics

## A Multi-Paradigmatic View

Any explanation of an economic phenomenon is based on a worldview. The premise of this book is that any worldview can be associated with one of the four broad paradigms: functionalist, interpretive, radical humanist, and radical structuralist. This chapter takes the major extant schools of thought in economics—neoclassical economics, new institutional economics, behavioral economics, Austrian economics, post-Keynesian economics, institutional economics, social economics, radical economics, and Marxist economics—and locates each of them on the map of the four paradigms, as in Figure 7.1. It emphasizes that these schools of thought in economics are equally scientific and informative; they look at economic phenomena from their certain paradigmatic viewpoint; and together they provide a more balanced understanding of the economic phenomenon under consideration. In this chapter, the first through the ninth sections present nine major extant schools of thought in economics, and the tenth section concludes the chapter.

### Neoclassical Economics

Neoclassical economics is an economic school of thought whose principal tenets have characterized and dominated economics since the end of the nineteenth century. During this long period, many other schools of economic thought—such as Austrians, Keynesians, behavioralists, institutionalists, and Marxists—have emerged in response to the changing times or as a reaction against the dominant neoclassical paradigm. These schools of economic

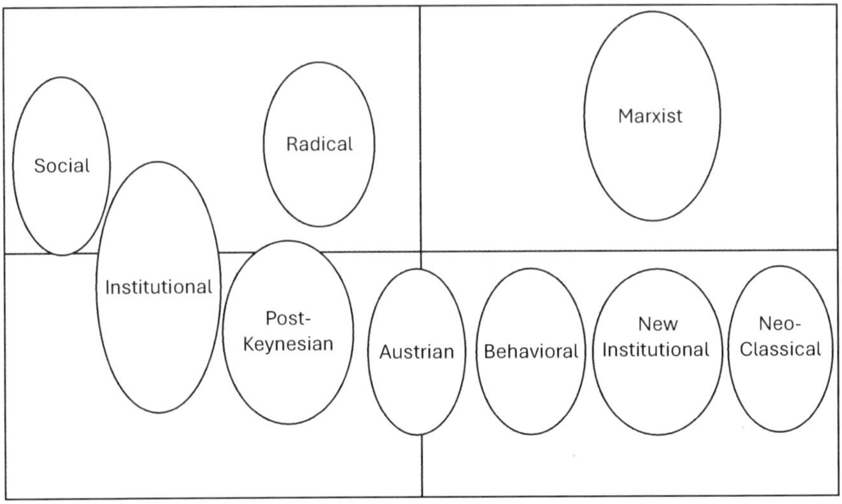


**Figure 7.1** Major extant schools of thought in economics.

thought have challenged the orthodoxy of the neoclassical system. Among them, Keynesians most spectacularly challenged the orthodoxy in the post–Second World War era. However, none of them has succeeded in replacing neoclassical microeconomic theory as the cornerstone of economics. The professional journals consistently publish papers that are written in the tradition of neoclassical microeconomic analysis, and macroeconomic analysts have increasingly paid attention to the microfoundations of their subject since the late 1960s.[1]

Neoclassical economics is founded on the simple proposition that economic agents act as constrained maximizers. People know what they want, whether they are consumers, producers, managers, shareholders, regulators, bureaucrats, politicians, voters, husbands and wives, teachers and students, thieves, archbishops, or any other group of people. However, they cannot have all that they want. This is because they face constraints. Therefore, economic agents need to choose from among alternative possible courses of action. For instance, parents cannot spend all their time at work and be able to play with their children; consumers cannot buy all the goods and services they could possibly enjoy; philanthropists cannot contribute significant amounts to every charitable organization; and as President Lincoln has stated, politicians cannot fool all the people all of the time; neoclassical microeconomics states, it is not possible to please all the people all of the time.

Although individuals' objectives cannot be observed, and their willingness to forgo some of one goal for more of some other goal depends on their subjective preference, their responses to changes in the constraints that they face can be predicted through the maximizing assumption. Such constraints are assumed to be objectively observable; for example, a given budget and a given set of market prices, a given amount of available time, a given endowment of resources or human skills, a given technological environment, and so on. When such constraints are changed, as a result, prices or opportunity costs associated with various goals change; therefore a qualitative response in behavior can be predicted.

For instance, a tax levied on a commodity increases its price in terms of the alternatives forgone when a unit of it is consumed; an increase in the wage rate increases the cost of forgone leisure; a technological invention that increases the productivity of resources used in a particular activity lowers the opportunity cost of production in that particular activity. As a result of these changes, people modify their behavior until the maximizing condition is reestablished, such that the use of an extra unit of the constraining resource yields the same subjective payoff no matter to which desired goal it is devoted.

The consistent and repeated applications of these principles form the distinguishing characteristics of neoclassical microeconomics, through which it has gained its strength. Such principles have been criticized by other economic schools of thought. Behaviorists question neoclassicals' confidence in the purely computational capabilities of individuals. Austrians question the implication of neoclassicals' objectivity of economic constraints. Institutionalists and Marxists question the thoroughgoing individualist premises of neoclassicals. Despite these philosophical objections, the vitality of neoclassical microeconomics and its extension to areas of inquiry far beyond economics, confirm its continued influence and supremacy.

Neoclassical economics is founded on constrained maximization, and therefore it can treat the subject in a highly mathematical and formal way. The place of mathematics in microeconomics is clearly seen in the general equilibrium theory, which is one of the greatest intellectual achievements in microeconomics. General equilibrium theory gains its importance because it deals with the question of whether decisions made by various individuals are compatible with constraints that characterize the entire system. Its analysis established the necessary and sufficient conditions required for the existence and stability of a general equilibrium, which illustrates the intellectual coherence of neoclassical microeconomics.

Neoclassical economics is fairly broad and diversified, as it encompasses both micro- and macroeconomics as well as axiomatic general equilibrium theory and applied partial equilibrium analysis. Nonetheless, distinct and fundamental characteristics of neoclassical economics are identifiable, consisting of either a methodological stance or a conception of what economics should be. These conceptions are the rules to which neoclassical economics adhere.

Neoclassical economics can be associated with a few presuppositions, some of which are methodological and others are technical. These presuppositions are instrumentalism, individualism, substantive rationality, and scarcity, which are applied, in the context of private property rights and market economy, to both the orthodox microeconomic and macroeconomic research programs.

1. Instrumentalism: Instrumentalism is the dominant epistemology in neoclassical economics. Econometrics is a typical application of instrumentalism and is a major tool of most neoclassical economists. The empirical work done by neoclassical economists are the predictions of the more abstract neoclassical theories. Neoclassical theories are abstract, non-descriptive, and non-realistic.

Neoclassical theorists select axioms, not for their close approximation to reality, but for their ability to allow the existence and uniqueness of equilibrium. Neoclassical economists describe the world as it should be rather than as it is. Neoclassical economists rely on general equilibrium theory as the basis for their scientific inquiry, and therefore, they are forced to start from unrealistic and non-descriptive hypotheses that support their inquiry.

Meanwhile, neoclassical economists want to follow the tradition of positive science. They want to emulate natural sciences. They, therefore, must rely on empirical work in their attempt to either verify or falsify their hypotheses. Neoclassical economists start from highly unrealistic hypotheses, and therefore, they need to test the consequences, that is, the predictions, of their theoretical models.

Neoclassical economists have made great efforts to frame several realistic characteristics within a multitude of their neoclassical models. Such realistic characteristics have been added as auxiliary secondary hypotheses to the basic neoclassical hypotheses. In their applied work, neoclassical economists attempt to verify or falsify hypotheses, but it is the auxiliary hypotheses that are subjected to verification or falsification, not the basic hypotheses—for instance, decreasing returns and profit maximization. Neoclassical economists augment their unrealistic basic model with realistic auxiliary hypotheses, the prediction of which serves as the means to rank the validity of the auxiliary hypotheses. They believe that it is possible to arrive at a model that adequately describes the real world by adding auxiliary realistic characteristics to its unrealistic foundations.

2. Individualism: Neoclassical economists attach great importance to their microfoundations. Despite the fact that many large-scale macroeconomic models have been built without much concern for theory, neoclassical economists require sound microfoundations for such models. This is because of neoclassical economists' individualist philosophy. More specifically, individualism, based on exogenously given tastes and preferences of individuals, constitutes a central methodological characteristic of neoclassical theory.

The individual is at the core of neoclassical economics, in which the wants and the preferences of individuals are sacred. Individuals are set in the forefront of neoclassical theory. Institutions, firms, and banks are treated as a front for the preferences of individuals. Individuals are regarded as being different in terms of their distinctive preferences, but they are all treated as equal in terms of their impact on the economy. Classes of individuals are treated as unimportant. Institutions are regarded as the veil of an aggregation of individual preferences. Otherwise, they are regarded as market imperfections that threaten to disrupt the ideal individualistic world.

This philosophical view crucially influences the neoclassical theory of value. Since the preferences of individuals are at the core of neoclassical theories, they affect prices. Consequently, the neoclassical theory of value becomes subjective because no one knows the preferences of all individuals for all goods.

As a result of atomistic individualism, voluntary exchange gains its importance in neoclassical theory, and any existing social constraint takes its form as the aggregate decision of individuals. As will be noted below, the concept of voluntary exchange between atomistic individuals is quite coherent with the following two essentials of neoclassical economics.

3. Substantive rationality: This and the following presupposition of neoclassical economics are at the level of economic technicalities, and both are based on the proper allocation of existing resources. The principle of rationality

assumes that individuals make the best of any job. The principle of rationality is very powerful and is a requirement for any theory in the social sciences. The neoclassical program, similar to many other programs, is based on the principle of rationality.

However, the neoclassical program is founded on a particular kind of rationality principle. Indeed, it is intertwined with constrained maximization. Neoclassical economics is concerned, as was noted earlier and will be noted later, with the constrained optimization of scarce resources. Other research programs are perhaps concerned with different subjects of constrained maximization.

Substantive rationality is the particular type of rationality that forms the third essential of neoclassical economics. The main characteristic of substantive rationality is that it assumes individuals are capable of substantial information processing and computational performance. Substantial rationality of neoclassical economics assumes that its rational economic man is able to predict all future events, properly use probability distributions of all possible alternatives, or properly form expectations by integrating all available knowledge and information. The environmental context in which the economic agent makes decisions is always assumed to be such that the individual's substantive rationality can always be properly put into use. For instance, uncertain situations in the Knight/Keynes/Shackle sense are transformed into risky situations with known probability distributions, which assume that events are of a recurrent nature.

Substantive rationality's various versions are used in various neoclassical theories and models. The selection of a specific version of substantive rationality depends on the goal of the specific theory. For instance, rationality may be defined axiomatically to help resolve the problems that arise in abstract neoclassical economics (e.g., existence or uniqueness of equilibrium) or to make tractable the mathematical formulations (e.g., expected utility). Sometimes, some limits may be placed on the available information in order to allow for some realism or some economic policy results.

But, in all various cases, the basic principle of substantive rationality remains in place in neoclassical economics. In all various cases, the computational abilities of the individual and the probabilistic riskiness of the environment remain in place. Neoclassical economists have modeled many realistic decision problems by elevating the computational and knowledge capabilities of the economic agents, but in doing so they have deviated from individuals' observed behavior. Substantive rationality fits very well with instrumentalism, because it allows for all possible events to be known and for their consequences to be assessed, even though this seems to be perfectly unrealistic, provided some predictions can be made.

4. Scarcity: Neoclassical economists define economics as the science of the optimal allocation of scarce resources. Consequently, the theme of scarcity prevails throughout neoclassical economics. In neoclassical economies, everything of significance is scarce, and everything has an opportunity cost. Every decision involves some form of arbitrage, that is, sacrifice. Prices are indicators of the extent of scarcity. As early as the first course in economics, students of economics are exposed to the definition of economics as the optimal allocation of scarce resources, which in turn, exposes students to the neoclassical research program. However, this definition of economics does not necessarily apply to economics as a whole, that is, to all schools of thought in economics.

Scarcity is clearly visible in pure exchange models, where there is no production. In pure exchange models, endowments in goods are fixed. In models with production, goods can be produced, but in such models, the endowments in productive resources are fixed. In neoclassical classical economics textbooks, the analysis starts with exchange, on which production is superimposed in the form of indirect exchange. But, in general, pure exchange models are the degenerate version of the more complete neoclassical production model. Interestingly, the structures and the main results of both models are the same. This has been accomplished through the careful addition of the supplementary hypotheses, which can be found in the various sophisticated production models, to safeguard all the main conditions and results of the pure exchange model. In neoclassical economics, production is a form of indirect exchange, which takes place between individual consumer agents who own resources, which transit through the same individual agents, who are called producers. These producers act as arbitrageurs who attempt to benefit from existing scarcities.

Scarcity is at the foundation of neoclassical economics. It is maintained by setting a variety of conditions: full employment, a fixed stock of money, and so on. Scarcity underlies the supply and demand analysis. It gives rise to prices. It governs the economy. It explains why neoclassical economists attach so much importance to the allocation of resources and use the techniques of constrained optimization. Scarce resources imply full employment, and therefore, all questions are about the proper use of existing resources rather than about unemployment and the creation of new resources.

A summary of the core of neoclassical economics is as follows:

1. economic agents have given endowments in goods or in productive services;
2. there exists a production set;
3. agents have ordered preferences;
4. agents are rational; they optimize subject to constraints;
5. agents act independently;
6. agents have proper information;
7. there are mechanisms assuring the coordination of decisions;
8. there is substitution when agents make choices among goods;
9. there is substitution when techniques of production are chosen;
10. there is a law of marginal diminishing returns;
11. each agent maximizes utility (or firms profits);
12. there exists a market for each input and output;
13. equilibrium results from the confrontation of demand with supply;
14. prices are the main adjustment or explanatory variable;
15. without imperfections or rigidities, the equilibrium would be optimal;
16. if information is imperfect, probability statements can still be made;
17. search for the existence of an equilibrium;
18. search for the uniqueness, stability, and optimality of equilibrium;
19. set conditions that are sufficient for the previous rules to be realized;
20. complete the model with the required conditions;
21. understand the real world from the completed general equilibrium model;
22. introduce some realism by omitting or replacing some of the conditions previously identified.

## New Institutional Economics

New institutional economics pays close attention to the role that institutions play in the operation of economic systems. Its new and insightful literature has emerged through the consolidation of empirical and theoretical studies in such specialties as industrial organization, labor economics, economic history, comparative economic systems, and so on. It is concerned with organizational issues, and it is interested in ever extending the range of applications of the neoclassical theory that incorporates the effect of property rights and transaction costs on economic incentives and economic behavior. Its analytic approach, although different from that of neoclassical economics, is not deliberately adopted in order to set up a new and distinct type of doctrine to counter the conventional theory. Its intention, rather, is to incorporate greater institutional detail into economic models because the standard neoclassical analysis is overly abstract and incapable of dealing effectively with many problems of interest to theorists and policymakers. It is convinced that conventional microeconomics fails in current economic situations because transaction costs are greater than zero and property rights to resources are different from those of classical capitalism. It has no disagreement with the use of deductive theory, which is fundamentally rejected by the earlier historical-descriptive institutionalists. Its theorists' writings are quite diverse in style and content, but they remain committed to the tenets of orthodox marginalism and appreciate its essential usefulness. Its emphasis is on the extension of the scope of standard microeconomic theory by taking into account some previously neglected characteristics of the economic system.[2]

Although the traditional analysis did not completely abstract from institutional structure, its treatment of institutions was superficial. Although it recognized the existence of political, legal, monetary, and other systems, either it regarded these systems as neutral in their effect on economic events and consequently it ignored them, or it took these systems as given and specified them in so perfunctory a way that meant institutional influence was not of much importance. The new institutional economics seeks to demonstrate the important economic impact of institutions. It attempts to illustrate not only that any distinct organizational structure affects incentives and behavior, but also that institutions are themselves legitimate objects of economic analysis. It uses theory to analyze institutions, to explain their operation, and to make it an integral part of the economic model. Its writers attempt to expand the applicability of neoclassical doctrine and, consequently, change the way economic activity is interpreted.

The new institutional economics systematically examines, among other things, the relationship between property rights and institutions. Property rights refer to the sanctioned behavioral relations among men with respect to the use of objects. Property rights assign specific norms of behavior with respect to things that each person, in his interactions with other persons, must observe or bear the cost for nonobservance. This means that property rights have economic value and must be enforced in the context of society. In general, property rights are determined and enforced by a governance structure or order—that is, a system of norms combined with the instruments that enforce this order. The enforcement of the order may be based on purely internal mechanisms or on the expectations of specific external consequences. The new institutional economics deals with the latter. In other words, it is concerned with enforcement based on sanctions that are established either by law or by custom.

An institution is a system of norms applicable to a particular set of activities. An institution consists of informal constraints, formal rules, and the way they are enforced. Institutions play a crucial role in economic development because they regulate, at least partly, the social behavior of individual citizens. There are different theories explaining how institutions arise. At one extreme, institutions are conceived as arising "spontaneously" based on the self-interest of decision-makers; that is, decision-makers organize themselves, which is referred to as "evolutionary rationalism." At the other extreme, institutions are thought of as being organized by a central authority, which is referred to as "legal centralism" or "constructivist rationalism." The new institutional economics advocates the hypothesis of spontaneously developing institutional structure. Both hypotheses are interested in the economic analysis of institutions and recognize that the aim of the creation of institutions is an organizational structure that will, in some sense, optimize the social behavior of people.

New institutional economics deals with both the institution of property and the system of norms that governs the acquisition or transfer of property rights. The acquisition or transfer of rights can take place through various activities, such as inheritance or gifts, purchase agreements, order from a central authority, tortuous acts, and so on. The distinction of these activities has practical importance as it specifies whether the analysis should be undertaken within the theory of the firm, public choice theory, the economic analysis of law, or some other specialty. Furthermore, it is important to differentiate between institutions in relation to law (e.g., the German civil code) and institutions in relation to rights (e.g., a concrete claim arising out of a labor contract).

New institutional economics transcends the idealized "frictionless" world of neoclassical theory by paying serious attention to the role that transaction costs play in the economy. Real resources are required in order to create, utilize, and guarantee an institution. It is costly to put the social and economic mechanism into operation. For instance, the concept of transaction costs when applied to private property rights, suggests that resources have to be used to obtain and process information about alternatives; to negotiate, monitor, and enforce contracts; and so on. Where there are transaction costs, there is a diversion of certain productive resources from the production of regular commodities to the implementation of transactions. Thus, ceteris paribus, a system that involves transaction costs has a smaller "factor endowment" than an otherwise comparable system that involves zero transaction costs.

The new institutional economics generally follows the methodology of contemporary neoclassical marginalist theory. However, for institutional analysis, it introduces several crucial changes into the orthodox theory of production and exchange, as follows.

1. Methodological individualism: An entirely new view is provided with respect to the role of individual decision-makers within an organization. That is, "society," "the state," "the people," "the firm," or "parties" are no longer conceived as collective entities that behave as if they were individual actors. The organization or collectivity per se is no longer the center of attention. Instead, the analysis of such social units is based on the positions and actions of their individual members.
2. Utility maximization: Individuals are viewed as actors who seek their own interests and maximize their utilities subject to the constraints set by the existing organizational structure. In contrast to the neoclassical practice, there is no dichotomy between the theory of consumer choice and the theory of the firm, as the utility maximization hypothesis is extended to all individual choices. That is, an individual—whether he is the manager of a government bureau or a capitalist entrepreneur—makes his own choices and pursues his own goals within the limits set by the system in which he is operating.
3. Bounded rationality: In the analysis of the real world of institutions, it is necessary to note that individuals have only limited ability to acquire and process information. The term "bounded rationality" is used to show that decision-makers are not hyper-rational. Limited rationality means that not all economic exchanges can be organized by contract and market. An individual who is "bounded rational" attempts to maximize his utility but finds out that it is costly to do so and that he is unable to anticipate all contingencies. This means that, with bounded rationality (and non-zero transaction costs), it is impossible to deal with complexity in all contractually relevant respects.

4. Opportunistic behavior: while bounded rationality leads to incomplete contracts, there can be general reliance on incomplete contracts if individuals were wholly trustworthy. However, some individuals (either principals or agents) may take dishonest actions, such as disguising preferences, distorting data, deliberately confusing issues, and so on. When there is self-seeking with guile, and when it is very costly to distinguish ex ante opportunistic from non-opportunistic actors, comprehensive contracting breaks down.

The new institutional economics notes that, in the absence of bounded rationality and opportunistic behavior, all problems of economic contracting would be trivial, and the need to study economic institutions would be nonexistent. However, when the actual decision-making involves difficulties and when operations are conducted in an environment of costly transactions and asymmetrical information, institutions become very important. Non-market forms of organization would be created in order to minimize the constraining effects of bounded rationality and maximize transaction safeguards against the hazards of opportunism.

Property Rights: In the standard model of competitive capitalism, there is a legal order that provides for private property rights and freedom of contract, which are recognized as crucial. The importance of property rights becomes more evident when they are considered in connection with the concept of an "economic good." A "good" refers to anything that provides utility or satisfaction to a person. An individual must "possess" the good in order to derive satisfaction from it. However, the "owner" may not be able to derive satisfaction from his good because of the existence of many competing individuals. Such ability depends on the extent to which guarantees are provided by social norms. Factors of production are also considered as goods; that is, they are goods that are in an "earlier stage" of consumption. A factor of production is customarily thought of as a physical entity that a firm acquires and uses (e.g., an acre of land or a ton of fertilizer) instead of being thought of as a right to perform certain physical actions. The firm owns and uses the land as a factor of production, but, in fact, what the firm possesses is the right to perform a circumscribed list of actions.

An asset or a commodity can be characterized not only by its physical properties but also by the set of legal restrictions that govern the use and exchange of it. Two houses that are physically identical constitute two different commodities if the property rights associated with them are different, and consequently, their market values are different.

Property-rights assignments affect the allocation of resources through exchange. In an exchange of a good, an owner can only transfer to others those rights in the good that he himself possesses. The volume of exchange and the terms of trade are influenced by the prevailing property-rights structure in society, that is, the particular rights that can be transferred legally. There are many categories of property rights, of which the right of ownership is the best known. Currently, the right of ownership in an asset consists of three components: (1) the right to use the asset (usus); (2) the right to obtain returns from the asset (usus fructus); and (3) the right to change the form, substance, and location of the asset (abusus). This last component—which means the right to experience the changes in the value of an asset—is the most fundamental component of the right of ownership. It implies that the owner of an asset (e.g., a house) is legally free to transfer to others all rights (e.g., to sell a house) or some rights (e.g., to rent a house) in the asset at a mutually agreed-upon price. This flexibility in the transfer of rights provides the owner with the opportunity to operate with an infinite planning horizon and, therefore, to participate in the efficient inter-temporal allocation of resources.

Although the right of ownership is an exclusive right, it is limited by those restrictions that are set by the law (or custom). The imposition of restrictive measures attenuates private property rights in an asset, limits the economic options available to the asset owner, and a corresponding reduction in the value of the asset.

A particular structure of property rights in an economy affects the allocation and utilization of economic goods (resources) in a specific and predictable way. Property rights that are associated with a good affect the value of that good. Individuals tend to maximize their utility not only as consumers but also as members of organizations (private firms, government bureaus, universities, etc.), as a consequence, any change in the system of property rights will have a specific and predictable effect on the allocation of resources, the composition of output, the distribution of income, and so on.

The property-rights approach was developed as a reaction to the extreme simplifications of the abstract general equilibrium models that were popular among neoclassical scholars during the postwar period. It introduced a method of analysis that could be uniformly applied to various organizational structures. It formulates an optimization model that incorporates the institutional features of the system that is under consideration, which consists of: (1) a criterion function, or objective function, that specifies the decision maker's preferences with respect to the decision variables and (2) the set of options (penalties and rewards) that is attainable by the decision maker. Then, the formal problem involves the maximization of the criterion function subject to the constraints imposed by the opportunity set.

New institutional economists have applied the model and have been able to generate valuable insights into the behavior of diverse organizations such as the modern corporation, the regulated firm, the nonprofit firm, the cooperative, the government bureau, the trade union, the codetermined firm, the socialist firm, etc. Property-rights models can deal with the role of incentives not only under circumstances of norm-abiding behavior but also under conditions of asymmetric information that may lead to hidden actions and opportunistic behavior.

Transaction Costs: The existence of positive transaction costs implies that the enforcement of rights is costly. To consider this matter and other friction-related problems, it is necessary to learn about transaction costs.

Historically, new institutional economists variously defined transaction costs as the cost of using the market as the cost of using the price mechanism, or as the cost of exchanging ownership titles. Currently, transaction costs are broadly defined as the costs that are associated with: (1) the creation or change of an institution or organization and (2) the use of an institution or organization.

The costs associated with institutions and the "rules of the game" increase with society's development and complexity ("civilization"). There are three basic duties/expenditures of the sovereign: (1) defense, (2) legal system, and (3) public works and public institutions. In addition, there are costs associated with running the government. These translate into the costs incurred for guaranteeing property rights and supplying public goods. These first-type transaction costs are mostly ignored in mainstream economic theory.

The second type of transaction cost has received greater attention in the mainstream literature because these costs are more directly related to firms or markets than to constitutional questions or governmental infrastructure. That is, there are transaction costs associated with the use of markets, as well as when entrepreneurs exercise the right to give orders within a firm.

Market transaction costs consist of the following components: (1) search and information costs, (2) bargaining and decision costs, and (3) policing and enforcement costs. Equivalently, they can be stated as follows: (1) the cost of preparing contracts, (2) the cost of concluding contracts, and (3) the cost of monitoring and enforcing the performance of a contract.

There are transaction costs associated with the manager's right to give orders within the firm. The firm concludes written or unwritten contracts with its employees, who are the owners of productive factors. The contracts indicate their tasks, their work conditions, and their division of labor within the firm and its organizational structure. The ultimate right to give orders is normally assigned to those people who own firm-specific resources and who have the ability to take risks and analyze the firm's conditions.

Indeed, the concept of transaction costs plays a crucial role in any adequate analysis of how a capitalist market economy actually functions. The characteristics of the institutional structure (and property rights) of an economy strongly affect the level of transaction costs by affecting the rewards accrued to self-interested individuals. Given the cost of production and organizational knowledge, individuals, in maximizing their utility, tend to choose an organizational structure (i.e., an institution) that minimizes transaction costs. In other words, decision-makers tend to choose that organizational form that economizes the sum of transaction cost and production cost, that is, they economize both the transaction costs and neoclassical production costs.

## Behavioral Economics

Behavioral economics is intended to increase the explanatory power of economics by providing it with more realistic psychological foundations. It is based on the conviction that increasing the realism of the psychological underpinnings of economic analysis results in new theoretical insights, improved predictions, and better policies. It attempts to modify the neoclassical approach to economics, which is based on utility maximization, equilibrium, and efficiency. It recognizes that the neoclassical approach to economics is useful because its theoretical framework can be applied to almost any form of economic (and even non-economic) phenomena and that it makes refutable predictions and suggests new theories.[3]

Behavioral economics modifies some of the assumptions made in standard economic theory in the direction of greater psychological realism. Such modifications are often not radical because they change those assumptions that are not central to the standard economic approach. For instance, the core of the neoclassical theory does not require that people disregard fairness, that they weigh risky outcomes in a linear fashion, or that they discount the future exponentially at a constant rate. Other behavioral economics assumptions acknowledge human limits on computational power, willpower, and self-interest. These assumptions can be regarded as "procedurally rational" (a la Herbert Simon) because they incorporate functional heuristics for solving problems that are often so complex that even modern computer algorithms cannot exactly solve them.

Some of the neoclassical economists believe that theories should be judged based on the following three criteria: congruence with reality, generality, and tractability. Theories in behavioral economics can be judged in the same way. Behavioral economists share the modernist view that the ultimate test of a theory is how accurately it identifies the actual causes of behavior. A theory's accurate predictions provide support for the degree to which the theory has pinned down the right causes. Furthermore, more realistic assumptions are very helpful.

Theories in behavioral economics also attempt to be general. For this purpose, they add only one or two parameters to the standard model such that with specific values for the parameters, the behavioral model reduces to the standard one. Then, the behavioral model can be tested against the standard model through the estimation of the values of the parameters. After such tests are successfully performed, the behavioral model can be applied as generally as the standard one.

Although adding behavioral assumptions often makes the models less tractable, many research papers have shown that it can be done. Moreover, even though behavioral models often add parameters to the standard models, they, in some cases, have been even more precise than the standard ones that assume more rationality in the context of dynamics and strategic interactions. For instance, in dynamic models, rational expectation models often conclude with multiple paths for inflation and asset prices, while adaptive expectation models often conclude with one path. Similarly, in game theory, in those games where the mutual consistency requirement of Nash often leads to multiple equilibria, models based on cognitive algorithms often generate precise predictions.

The realism, generality, and tractability of behavioral economics can be shown through the concept of "loss-aversion." Loss-aversion refers to the idea that people have a stronger aversion to losses relative to a reference point than the desire for gains of equivalent magnitude. Many experiments have demonstrated that loss-aversion is more realistic than the standard continuous, concave utility function over wealth. Loss-aversion has identified the instances in which predictions of standard theories have been wrong, for example, the equity premium puzzle in finance and asymmetry in price elasticities. Loss-aversion can also be generalized by parameterizing it as the ratio of the marginal disutility of a loss relative to the marginal utility of a gain at the reference point (i.e., the ratio of the derivatives at zero). Consequently, the standard model can be represented as its special case in which this "loss-aversion coefficient" is 1. The tractability of loss-aversion has been shown in several applications, though they have not been easy.

The methods used in behavioral economics are the same as those used in other areas of economics. Initially, behavioral economics heavily used experimental methods. More recently, however, behavioral economics has not only been using experimentation but also has used the full range of methods employed in other areas of economics.

Behavioral economics has heavily drawn on one of the subfields of psychology called "behavioral decision research," which typically classifies research into two categories: judgment and choice. Judgment research focuses on the processes that people use in order to estimate probabilities. Choice research focuses on the processes that people use in order to select among actions, taking into account any relevant judgments that they may have already made.

Probability judgment is central to economic life. Economics models probability judgment based on two standard principles: statistical sampling and Bayes's rule for updating probabilities to incorporate new evidence. Bayes's rule has several features that are cognitively unrealistic. First, Bayesian updating requires a prior, which it does not specify where the prior comes from. Second, Bayesian updating involves a separation between previously judged probabilities and the evaluations of new evidence. But this separability is violated by many cognitive mechanisms that use the previous information to interpret the new evidence. Third, subjective expected utility involves separability between probability judgments of states and utilities associated with those states. Fourth, Bayesian updating considers the order of arrival of information to be inconsequential. But order effects are important due to the strength of recent information in working memory and of increased "rehearsal" of older memories.

Cognitive psychologists have noted that people use heuristic mechanisms that result in judgments that sometimes violate either sampling principles or Bayes's rule. For instance, people may judge the probabilities of future events based on the ease with which those events can be imagined or can be retrieved from memory. This is called "availability heuristic" and leads to several biases. One is called "hindsight bias," according to which it is easier for people to imagine events that actually did occur than the events that did not occur, and consequently people often overestimate the probability they previously attached to events that later occurred. Another bias is called the "curse of knowledge," according to which people who know a lot find it hard to imagine how little others know.

Another heuristic that people use to make probability judgments is called "representativeness." People judge conditional probabilities—for example, P(hypothesis/data) or P(class/example)—based on the degree to which the data represents the hypothesis or the example represents the class. Representativeness, as with most other heuristics, is a shortcut that provides reasonable judgments with minimal cognitive effort in many cases but sometimes is misleading and is undisciplined by normative principles. People judge prototypical exemplars of a class to be more likely than they truly are (unless the prototype's extremity is part of the prototype). For instance, when judging whether a certain student described in a profile is a psychology major or a computer science major, people tend to focus on the extent to which the profile matches the stereotype of a psychology or computer science major. Many studies show that this practice of feature-matching leads people to under weigh the "base rate"—in the example just discussed, the "base rate" refers to the overall frequency of the two majors.

Representativeness also leads to the so-called "the law of small numbers." People tend to think that small samples represent the properties of the statistical process that generated them. This is in contrast to "the law of large numbers," which guarantees that a large sample of independent draws represents the process that generated them. One of the manifestations of the law of small numbers is the so-called "gambler's fallacy," according to which people expect a tail after a coin landed heads three times in a sequence.

Choice research of behavioral economics is related to the preference theory of neoclassical economics, which incorporates several strong and testable assumptions as follows: (1) that preferences are "reference independent," that is, preferences are not affected by the individual's transient asset position; (2) that preferences are invariant with respect to superficial variations in the descriptions of options; and (3) that elicited preferences are not influenced by the precise way in which preferences are measured as long as the method used is "incentive compatible," that is, the method provides incentives for individuals to reveal their "true" preferences. Behavioral economists note that all of these assumptions have been significantly violated.

For instance, numerous experiments of "framing effects" illustrate that the way that choices are presented to an individual often determines the preferences that are "revealed" by the individual. The classic example of a framing effect is the "Asian disease" that threatens the lives of 600 citizens. People are asked to choose between two options. In the "positive frame," the two choices are: (A) saving 200 lives for sure, or (B) a one-third chance of saving all 600 with a two-third chance of saving no one. In the "negative frame," the two choices are: (C) 400 people dying for sure, or (D) a two-thirds chance of 600 dying and a one-third chance of no one dying. In terms of lives lost or at risk, A is equivalent to C and B is equivalent to D. Nevertheless, most people choose A over B but D over C.

The standard theory is also violated by what is called an "anchoring effect." Experimentally, this effect has been demonstrated initially in the context of judgment and then in the context of choice. In the experiment with respect to judgment, subjects were shown a number on a wheel of fortune that had a range of 0 to 100, and then they were asked whether the number of African nations in the United Nations was greater than or less than this number. Subsequently, they were asked about the true value. Although the number from the wheel of fortune was random, subjects' answers were strongly influenced by the number obtained from the spin of the wheel. That is, subjects seemed to "anchor" on the number obtained from the spin of the wheel and then adjusted their answers for what they thought or knew, but adjusted insufficiently. In another experiment, which was with respect to choice, subjects were shown a number that had been chosen at random, and subjects were asked whether their certainty equivalent for a gamble was greater than or smaller than this number. Subsequently, the subjects were asked to specify their actual certainty equivalent for the gamble. Again, the stated values were correlated significantly with the random number.

The method of eliciting preferences can dramatically affect preferences thus revealed, even producing "preference reversals," that is, A is preferred to B under one method of elicitation, but B is preferred to A under a different method of elicitation. The best-known experiment contrasts the choice people make between two bets versus the price people are willing to pay for the two bets when the bets are offered to them separately. More specifically, bet A offers a high probability of a small payoff, and bet B offers a small probability of a high payoff. People often choose the more conservative bet A over bet B but are ready to pay a higher price for the riskier bet B than for bet A. Another form of preference reversal occurs in marketing experiments where joint and separate evaluations of pairs of goods are elicited. People often price or evaluate item A higher than item B when the two items are evaluated independently, but people often price or evaluate item B higher than item A when the two items are evaluated concurrently.

The set of choices also affects people's preferences with respect to each choice. This is called "Context effects." Experiments have shown that people are generally attracted to options that dominate other options. Furthermore, they are drawn disproportionately to "compromise" alternatives whose attribute values lie between those of other alternatives.

All of the above findings suggest that preferences are not as defined by standard economics. Preferences are often ill-defined, highly malleable, and context-dependent. Nonetheless, people make economic decisions; that is, they choose a brand of toothpaste, a car, a job, or how to invest. Behavioral economics refers to the process by which people make choices based on such preferences as "constructing preferences."

Next, the discussion focuses on major topic areas of behavioral economics: reference-dependence/loss-aversion and decision-making under risk/uncertainty.

Reference-dependence is in contrast to classical consumer theory's assumption that an individual's preferences over various commodities are invariant with respect to the individual's current endowment or consumption. Specifically, people often prefer not to lose commodities from their consumption bundle than to gain other commodities. In an experimental study, the subjects in one group were endowed with a mug, while the subjects in another group were endowed with a pen. Both groups were allowed to exchange their goods for the other. Under the assumption of preference-independence, the fractions of subjects exchanging their mug for a pen, and the fraction exchanging their pen for a mug should approximately add up to one. However, in the experiment, only 22 percent of the subjects made the exchange. This implies that people have a strong preference for the good in their endowment; that is, people prefer not to lose what they own. Loss-aversion has already been used to explain the following phenomena: (1) asymmetries in demand elasticities after price increases and decreases; (2) the tendency for New York City cab drivers to quit early after reaching a daily income target, producing surprising upward-sloping labor supply curves; and (3) the large gap between stock and bond returns, that is, the "equity premium."

Decision-making under risk/uncertainty in standard economics is based on the expected-utility (EU) hypothesis that considers the utility of a risky distribution of outcomes as a probability-weighted average of the utilities of outcomes. This is a normatively appealing hypothesis because it logically follows from seemingly reasonable axioms, for example, the independence (or "cancellation") axiom. According to the independence axiom, when people compare two gambles, they should cancel events that have the same outcome with the same probability, that is, their choice should be independent of all those equally likely common outcomes. Another feature of the EU hypothesis is that it simplifies matters because an individual's taste with respect to risky financial outcomes can be fully represented by the shape of the individual's utility function for money.

Many experimental studies in behavioral economics document the failures of expected-utility hypothesis' predictions in simple situations where subjects can earn substantial sums of money from their choices. Such studies have also offered new theories to account for the evidence. Some of these new theories change the weighting of probabilities but preserve a "betweenness" property that states: if A is preferred to B, then any probabilistic gamble between them is preferred to B but dis-preferred to A, that is, in terms of preferences, the gambles lie "between" A and B. Other new theories treat probability weights as "rank dependent." That is, first, outcomes are ranked; then their probabilities are weighted according to the rank of outcomes within the gamble under consideration. One way to do this mathematically is to nonlinearly transform the cumulative probabilities of outcomes and weigh the utilities of outcomes by the differences of those weighted cumulative probabilities. The best-known such theory is the cumulative prospect theory.

The above-mentioned experimental research has arrived at three clear conclusions. (1) That the two new classes of theories take more general functional forms than expected utility, and that the rank-dependent theories fit the data better than the betweenness class theories. (2) That the statistical evidence against the EU is so overwhelming that it is no longer necessary to perform tests of EU against alternative theories. (3) That EU fits worst when comparing two gambles that have different sets of possible outcomes (or "support").

Prospect theory has a more accurate explanatory power than EU because it properly accounts for the psychophysics of judgment and choice. It has two main components: a probability weighting function and a "value function," which replaces the utility function of the EU. The weighting function *w(p)* combines two elements: (1) the level of probability weight is a way of expressing preference toward risk (if an individual does not like to gamble, he/she places low weight on any chance of winning anything); and (2) the curvature in *w(p)* shows the degree to which people are sensitive to differences in probabilities. If people are more sensitive in the neighborhoods of possibility and certainty—that is, changes in probability near zero and one—than to intermediate values, then their *w(p)* curve will overweight low probabilities and underweight high ones. The value function is based on the insight that the utility of an outcome depends not on the absolute value of the resultant wealth, but on whether the outcome is a gain or a loss. Prospect theory also incorporates the ideas that risk preferences are reflections at the reference point and that preferences show "loss-aversion."

## Austrian Economics

The Austrian school of economics was founded in 1871 when Carl Menger's *Principles of Economics* was published. Carl Menger, William Stanley Jevons, and Leon Walras brought about the marginalist revolution in economic analysis. Menger dedicated *Principles of Economics* to one of his German colleagues, William Roscher, who was one of the leading figures in the German historical school that dominated economic thought in German-speaking countries. In *Principles of Economics,* Menger argued that economic analysis is universally applicable and that the appropriate point of reference in economic analysis is man and his choices. These choices, according to Menger, are determined by the subjective preferences of the individual and the margin on which his decisions are made. The logic of choice, Menger believed, acts as the foundation for the development of a universally valid economic theory.[4]

The historical school, in contrast, believed that economics does not lend itself to generating universal principles and that scientific research in economics instead should focus on detailed historical examination. The German historical school thought that the English classical economists mistakenly believed in economic laws that transcend time and national boundaries. Menger's *Principles of Economics*, through marginal analysis, introduced new universal laws, which were aligned with the views of classical political economists. Roscher's students, especially Gustav Schmoller, in response to Menger's defense of "theory," gave the work of Menger and his followers, that is, Eugen Bohm-Bawerk and Friedrich Wieser, the derogatory title of "Austrian school," who held faculty positions at the University of Vienna. The title has remained in effect since then.

Since the 1930s, the University of Vienna, or any other Austrian university, has produced no leading figure in the Austrian school of economics. This is because, in the 1930s and 1940s, the Austrian school moved to Britain and the United States. More specifically, the scholars associated with the Austrian approach to economic science held positions primarily at the London School of Economics (1931–50), New York University (1944–), Auburn University (1983–), and George Mason University (1981–). Many of the ideas of the leading mid-twentieth-century Austrian economists, such as Ludwig von Mises and F. A. Hayek, are rooted in the ideas of nineteenth-century classical economists, such as Adam Smith and David Hume, or early twentieth-century figures, such as Knut Wicksell, as well as Menger, Bohm-Bawerk, and Friedrich von Wieser. Contemporary Austrian school economists reflect a more diverse mix of intellectual traditions in economic science, as they have been influenced by modern figures in economics, such as Armen Alchian, James Buchanan, Ronald Coase, Harold Demsetz, Axel Leijonhufvud, Douglass North, Mancur Olson, Vernon Smith, Gordon Tullock, Leland Yeager, and Oliver Williamson, as well as Israel Kirzner and Murray Rothbard. This diversity raises the possibility for someone to argue that the label "Austrian" does not possess any substantive meaning. But one could also sensibly argue that a unique Austrian school of economics operates within the economic profession today. The following concentrates on the main propositions about economics in which Austrian economists believe. Propositions 1–3 fall under the heading of *The Science of Economics*, Propositions 4–7 fall under the heading of *Microeconomics*, and Propositions 8–10 fall under the heading of *Macroeconomics*.

*Proposition 1: Only individuals choose.* All economic analysis starts with man, with his purposes and plans. Only individuals make choices, and in contrast, collective entities do not make choices. Economic analysis has two main tasks. The primary task of economic analysis is to explain economic phenomena by basing it on individual purposes and plans. The secondary task of economic analysis is to follow up on the unintended consequences of individual choices.

*Proposition 2: The study of the market order is fundamentally about exchange behavior and the institutions within which exchanges take place.* The market economy and its price system are best understood when they are regarded as a "catallaxy," and thus, the studies of the market order fall in the domain of the science of "catallactics." These terms are derived from the Greek word "katallaxy," meaning exchange and bringing strangers into friendship through exchange. Catallactics requires the focus of the analysis to be placed on the exchange relationships that emerge in the market, the bargaining that characterizes the exchange process, and the institutions that constitute the context in which exchange takes place.

*Proposition 3: The "facts" of the social sciences are what people believe and think.* In contrast to the physical sciences, the human sciences start with the purposes and plans of individuals. Whereas the elimination of purposes and plans in the natural sciences overcame the problem of anthropomorphism and led to scientific advances; in the human sciences, the elimination of purposes and plans purges the science of human action of its subject matter. In the human sciences, the "facts" of the world are constituted by what the actors think and believe. The meaning that human beings place on things, practices, places, and people determines their orientation in making decisions. The goal of the sciences of human action is intelligibility, understanding, and explanation, not prediction. The human sciences can achieve this goal because human scientists are human beings who study humans, that is, human scientists possess knowledge from within, but the natural sciences cannot pursue a goal of intelligibility because they rely on knowledge from without. Human scientists can understand the purposes and plans of other human actors because human scientists themselves are human actors. The essential difference between the sciences of human action and the physical sciences can be brought to the fore through the classic thought experiment regarding a Martian observing the "data" at Grand Central Train Station in New York City. The Martian may observe that when the little hand on the clock points to eight, there is a bustle of movement as bodies exit these boxes, and that when the little hand points to five, there is a bustle of movement as bodies enter the boxes. The Martian may even develop a prediction about the direction of the little hand on the clock and the movement of bodies and boxes. But, unless the Martian has an understanding of human beings' purposes and plans (i.e., commuting to and from work), his "scientific" understanding with respect to Grand Central Station data would be limited. The sciences of human action are qualitatively different from the natural sciences, and human sciences are impoverished when they are forced into the philosophic/scientific mold of the natural sciences.

*Proposition 4: Utility and costs are subjective.* All economic phenomena take effect only after they have gone through the human mind. Since the 1870s, liberal economists have come to believe that value is subjective. However, following Alfred Marshall, many liberal economists believe that costs are determined by objective conditions. Marshall used the metaphor of a pair of scissors and emphasized that in the same way that both blades of a pair of scissors cut a piece of paper, the subjective value and objective costs determine price. But Marshall ignored the fact that costs are also subjective because they are themselves determined by the value of alternative uses of scarce resources. That is indeed both blades of the scissors cut the paper, but the blade of supply, as well, is determined by individuals' subjective valuations. In deciding among many courses of action, an individual must choose. That is, the individual must pursue one path among many paths. The pervasiveness and importance of alternatives in choices leads to one of the defining concepts of the economic way of thinking: opportunity costs. That is, the cost of any action is the value of the highest-valued alternative forgone in taking that action. By definition, the forgone action is never taken. But, at the time of decision-making, one weighs the expected benefits of an action against the expected benefits of alternative actions.

*Proposition 5: The price system economizes on the information that people need to process in making their decisions.* Prices summarize the prevailing terms of exchange in the market. The price system signals relevant information to market participants and helps them to realize mutual gains from exchange. For instance, when the price system informs people that the price of tin has risen, people do not need to know whether the increase in the price of tin was caused by an increase in the demand for tin or a decrease in the supply of tin. In either case, the increase in the price of tin leads them to economize on its use. In general, a change in underlying conditions leads to a change in market prices, which, in turn, leads to a quick adjustment by people.

*Proposition 6: Private property in the means of production is a necessary condition for rational economic calculation.* Liberal economists and social thinkers have long believed that private ownership acts as a powerful incentive for the efficient allocation of scarce resources. In contrast, socialist economists and social thinkers have believed that socialism transcends these incentive problems by changing human nature. But, even if socialism changes human nature, as assumed by socialists, socialism will fail because economic planners cannot rationally calculate the alternative uses of resources. This is because without private ownership in the means of production, there will be no market for the means of production, there will be no money prices for the means of production, there will be no money prices to reflect the relative scarcities of the means of production, and therefore, economic planners will not be able to rationally calculate the alternative uses of the means of production.

*Proposition 7: The competitive market is a process of entrepreneurial Discovery.* Many economists consider "competition" as a state of affairs. But "competition" requires an activity. If competition were a state of affairs, there would be no role for entrepreneurs. But competition is an activity in which the entrepreneur has a huge role to play. The entrepreneur, as the agent of change, engages and pulls markets in new directions. The entrepreneur is on the lookout for unrecognized opportunities for mutual gain. By recognizing and engaging in opportunities, the entrepreneur earns a profit. The entrepreneur's discovery of opportunities and gains from exchange results in mutual learning and moves the market system to a more efficient allocation of resources. An entrepreneur's discovery guarantees that a free market moves closer to the most efficient use of resources. In addition, the lure of profit continually provides entrepreneurs with the incentive to seek innovations that increase productive capacity. The entrepreneur recognizes imperfections and turns them into profit opportunities. Entrepreneurship has three main characteristics: serendipity (discovery), search (conscious deliberation), and seizing the opportunity for profit. The price system and the market economy act as learning devices that provide relevant information to individuals in order to discover mutual gains and use scarce resources efficiently.

*Proposition 8: Money is not neutral.* Money is defined as the medium of exchange that is commonly accepted by people. In general, government policy distorts the monetary unit, and as a consequence, exchange will be distorted as well. The goal of monetary policy should be the minimization of these distortions. When an increase in money supply is not offset by a corresponding increase in money demand, the result will be an increase in prices. But all prices do not adjust instantaneously throughout the economy. Some prices adjust faster than others, which results in changes in relative prices. These changes affect the pattern of exchange and production. Thus, by its very nature, money cannot be neutral. The importance of this proposition can be seen more clearly when considering the costs of inflation. The quantity theory of money correctly stated that printing money does not increase wealth. This is because when the government doubles the money supply, money holders' ability to buy more goods is prevented because of the doubling of prices. The quantity theory of money was an important advance in economic thinking. However, a mechanical application of the quantity theory of money leads to an underestimation of the costs of inflationary monetary policy. To see this, consider the situation in which the government doubles the money supply, and as a consequence, prices simply double. Then, economic actors can anticipate this price adjustment by closely following money supply figures and can adjust their behavior accordingly. In this way, the cost of inflation is minimal. But inflation has several socially destructive characteristics. First, even if inflation is fully anticipated, it breaches the basic trust between the government and its citizens because the government has used inflation to confiscate people's wealth. Second, unanticipated inflation redistributes wealth because debtors gain at the expense of creditors. Third, when the money is added somewhere in the system—for example, through the government's purchase of bonds—and because people cannot perfectly anticipate inflation and that some prices (e.g., the price of bonds) adjust before other prices, inflation distorts the pattern of exchange and production. Money is used for almost all transactions in a modern economy. Therefore, monetary distortions affect all those transactions. The conclusion is that the goal of monetary policy should be to minimize these monetary distortions, precisely because money is not neutral. In search of solutions to this elusive goal, Austrian economists generated some of their most innovative work that resulted in the development in the 1970s and 1980s of the literature on free banking.

*Proposition 9: The capital structure consists of heterogeneous goods that have multi-specific uses that must be aligned.* Car companies are designing cars that will be produced in a decade. A great challenge to them is the proper allocation of resources to meet that goal. Production is always made for meeting an uncertain future demand, and the production process requires investment in each stage of production, ranging from the starting stage (mining iron ore) to the ending stage (the car dealership). In general, the values of all producer goods at every stage of production are determined by the value that consumers place on the product produced by the producer goods. The production plan involves the sequencing of various investment goods into a capital structure in order to produce the final goods in the most efficient manner. Capital goods are not homogeneous, and the same type of capital goods cannot be used to produce all the final products that consumers desire. When a mistake is made, the capital goods cannot be reallocated quickly and with minimal cost toward producing the most-desired final product. Capital goods are heterogeneous and multi-specific. That is, an auto plant can make cars but not computer chips. The proper sequencing of capital goods for the production of various consumer goods is based on price signals together with the careful economic calculations of investors. If the price system is distorted, investors will improperly sequence their capital goods. After the error is revealed, investors will adjust their investments, but, in this process, resources will be lost. Propositions 8 and 9 form the foundation of the Austrian theory of the business cycle. This explains how the government's expansionary monetary policy generates a malinvestment in the capital structure during the economic boom that must be corrected in the economic bust.

*Proposition 10: Social institutions are often the result of human action, but not of human design.* Many of the most important social institutions and social practices are not the result of direct human design but are the by-product of actions taken by individuals to achieve their goals. For instance, in the Midwest region of the United States, in the month of January, a student trying to get to class quickly in order to avoid the cold weather may take a shortcut across the quad rather than walk the long way around. Taking the shortcut across the quad in the snow leaves footprints. Other students, by following these footprints, turn the footprints into a path. Although the goal of each student is merely to get to class quickly in order to avoid the cold weather, as a by-product they create a path in the snow that helps other students who come later to achieve this goal more easily. This story can be used as a metaphor to illustrate that social institutions and social practices are the product of human action, but not of human design. The market economy and its price system have come about through a similar process. People do not intentionally create a market economy with its complex array of exchanges and price signals. However, people intentionally attempt to improve their own lot in life, and their behavior results in the market system. Other social phenomena—such as money, law, language, science, and so on—owe their origins not to human design, but to people who strove to achieve their own betterment and, in the process, produced an outcome that benefits the public. Not all spontaneously formed social institutions and social orders are beneficial, and, therefore, this proposition should not be regarded as an example of a Panglossian fallacy. Whether pursuing individual self-interest generates public benefits depends on the institutional context in which individuals pursue their self-interests. Individuals pursuing their self-interests can lead to the "invisible hand of market efficiency" or the "tragedy of the commons"; in one social setting, individuals generated social benefits, whereas in another social setting, individuals generated social losses. The "new institutional economics" focuses on the degree of the sensitivity of social outcomes to the institutional setting within which individuals interact. It is important to note that classical political economists and the early neoclassical economists were cognizant of this basic point of new institutional economists, and that it was only the mid-twentieth-century neoclassical fascination with formal proofs of general competitive equilibrium, on the one hand, and the Keynesian emphasis on aggregate variables, on the other, that tended to change the focus away from the institutional preconditions required for social cooperation.

These ten propositions have radical implications: (1) economic theory should be grounded in verbal logic; (2) empirical work should focus on historical narratives; and (3) public policy raises severe doubts about the ability of government officials to intervene optimally within the economic system, let alone to rationally manage the economy. The market economy develops based on individuals' natural inclination to improve their situation, which in turn leads them to discover the mutually beneficial exchanges that will accomplish that goal. Adam Smith first systematized this message, and the Austrian economists have been the proponents of this message.

## Post-Keynesian Economics

Post-Keynesian economics constitutes a new approach to the understanding of economic phenomena. Its major characteristics can be identified and analyzed. It consists of clearly identifiable themes. Its boundaries have not been precisely defined. This is partly because, in general, boundaries are almost impossible to be precisely defined. And it is partly because the development of post-Keynesianism, as a school of economic thought, is a relatively recent phenomenon, although the ideas associated with post-Keynesianism have a long history. The post-Keynesian approach has not yet managed to be persuasive enough because: (1) it cannot be represented with a single model, although the orthodox approaches cannot be represented with a single model either; (2) it concerns itself with economic issues that are controversial; (3) it involves substantially diverse theoretical premises; (4) it is the subject of ideological objections that emanate from the orthodox character of the economics profession; and (5) it tends to define its program as a reaction to neoclassical economics.[5]

Post-Keynesian economics is comprised of different "approaches," which are reflected in different methods and different features subsumed in its models.

This is as expected because in a relatively new approach there needs to exist divergences and disagreements within its ranks. Consequently, post-Keynesian methodology has been described as "horses for courses," and its mode of thought as "Babylonian," which together mean that post-Keynesianism is a holistic and non-dualistic approach, rather than a reductionist or an atomistic approach.

The post-Keynesian school of thought has its own methodology, ideology, and content. It is unified not just by its critical attitude toward neoclassical economics but, more importantly, by its attempt to provide an alternative approach to that of orthodox economics. This effort might seem to face difficulty when a synthesis is aimed at in order to ascertain whether a coherent post-Keynesian model can emerge. However, because there is no uniform way of dealing with all issues in economics, there is no need to synthesize various approaches in order to conclude coherence. More specifically, within post-Keynesian economics, there are various strands of thought that deal with different issues and with different levels of abstraction at the analytical level. Notwithstanding, coherence prevails within the strands identified as post-Keynesian. The prevalence of such coherence is founded on post-Keynesianism's vision and the framework, which embrace the diversity of methods. Post-Keynesians have endeavored to provide a coherent mode of thought. For instance, they have identified a post-Keynesian research program; they have offered a synthesis of post-Keynesianism and neo-Ricardianism to produce a post-classical modus operandi; and they have offered a synthesis of a number of strands within post-Keynesian economics that is amenable to both theoretical and empirical investigation.

Post-Keynesian economics mainly aims at completing the Keynesian revolution. It attempts at a generalization of the General Theory. It inherits the principle of effective demand as its backbone from Keynes's General Theory. This principle had been discovered well before Keynes by Michal Kalecki. Although there are differences in the two approaches, there are common elements between Kalecki's path-breaking work and the position adopted by post-Keynesian economics, which adheres to both Kalecki and Keynes.

In what follows, the main preoccupation will be with a post-Keynesian methodological and theoretical framework that incorporates the main elements of the fundamental themes within post-Keynesianism but does not encompass all the "approaches" that comprise the post-Keynesian school of thought. This approach stays consistent with the "horses for courses" and "Babylonian" approaches and goes beyond them to provide a coherent framework to explain the post-Keynesian economics. Perhaps this is consistent with the expected future developments within the post-Keynesian literature, that there would be a coherent core that will form the basis for theoretical and empirical explorations.

Post-Keynesians accept the following propositions: (1) the economy is a historical process; (2) in an uncertain world, expectations have a crucial impact on economic events; (3) institutions, both economic and political, significantly shape economic events; (4) realism plays an important role; and (5) capitalism is a class-divided society.

Post-Keynesians view economics as an integral part of society that is concerned with people who are organized in groups to satisfy their material needs. Their focus of analysis is on the behavior of these groups in historical time, such that the past is immutable, the future is uncertain and unknowable, and both past and future have a critical influence on the present. Consequently, it is paramount that the institutional framework within which the economic groups operate be considered clearly.

The most important institution is the large corporation or megacorp, which is organized oligopolistically and is the dominant institution in the technically more advanced sector of the economy. Megacorps set their prices in relation to their investment, such that prices provide sufficient retained earnings to enable megacorps to finance their planned investment. In the non-oligopolistic sector of the economy, there are small firms, but they do not behave as "perfectly competitive" firms in the neoclassical sense; instead, they behave in the way that Kalecki described as "pure imperfect competition." In any case, the production subsystem of the economy is essentially dominated by the megacorp.

On the other hand, there are the trade unions, whose members constitute a substantial proportion of workers. Trade unions enter into bargaining agreements with employers regarding conditions of employment in general and wages in particular. The interests of the trade unions and those of employers are in conflict, not harmony, such that the distribution between wages and profits is determined to a very large extent by the real wage demands of labor and the profit objectives of corporations. Actually, workers bargain over money wages, the acceptable level of which is determined by their target real wage rate, information on the immediate past inflation rate, and the expected future inflation rate. In this process, workers are at a disadvantage because the real wage rate that they will actually experience can be known only after the capitalists set their product prices. The resulting distribution between wages and profits is effectively determined by the capitalists' pricing decisions and not by the wage bargaining process, unless the degree of monopoly or megacorp power is somehow reduced in the meantime. This shows a decline in the role of the market as the mode of economic organization and the necessity to find out how the resulting economic performance should be made socially acceptable to as many people as possible.

The central government's actions influence the economic activities of corporations and workers. The central government is the institution that is vested with the power to pursue Keynesian contra-cyclical policies, that is, to reduce the amplitude of the cyclical behavior of capitalist economies. Central government, as an institution, can create money through the central bank as a lender of last resort, although most of the money in use in modern economies is credit money, which is created by the private banking system. Finally, there are international economic institutions that interact with national institutions.

The post-Keynesian paradigm partly owes its emergence to the development of the system or cybernetic framework. In this framework, the economy is considered as a group of dynamic subsystems, each of which interacts with all the other subsystems, that is, influencing them and being influenced by them. In this way, the economic system is only one of several societal systems, each of which has its own particular dynamics. Economics in this system is not regarded as the study of how scarce resources are allocated to meet finite needs. It is, instead, regarded as the study of how actual economic systems can expand their outputs over time through the production and distribution of the resulting social surplus. The expansion path of output is generally uneven and is likely to change the nature of economic systems in unexpected ways. In other words, post-Keynesian analysis views the economy as a continually evolving system whose path cannot be predicted, and it is not only without equilibrium but also erratic.

There are four more characteristics of the economic system that post-Keynesian analysis emphasizes. The first characteristic is the existence of uncertainty, in the sense that the future is unknown and unknowable, such that economic agents' expectations can easily prove to be wrong. Uncertainty is omnipresent in the real world and therefore constitutes one of the central elements of the post-Keynesian analysis. Uncertainty is in the structural nature of the market economy, as market forces cannot properly account for the unknowability and unpredictability of the future, and therefore disseminate incomplete, even misleading, information. The prices of goods and services today cannot properly inform buyers or sellers about what the consequences of their collective actions will be on prices tomorrow. Knowledge about the future can only be probabilistically formed based on past events. But the conditions under which such a probability can be ascertained are rarely met in everyday life, and therefore, such probabilities cannot be quantified. With the future being uncertain, the final stage of the uneven process of output expansion cannot be deduced; instead, the process of output expansion can be carefully and intelligently analyzed. The world is nonergodic: the observations of past events cannot produce knowledge about current and/or future events; in addition, the observations of current events provide no statistically reliable unbiased estimates about future time and/or space averages. In the presence of uncertainty, as distinct from risk, past and current events cannot be used to construct a statistical knowledge about future outcomes. The practical difference between risk and uncertainty is that in the case of risk, the probability distribution of the outcomes is known (either from a priori calculations or from the observations of past experiences), but in the case of uncertainty, this is not true, because any considered situation is to a high degree unique. While the future is uncertain, decisions about the future are made all the time. Consequently, such decisions will likely turn out to be not the right ones. As a result, continued adjustments must be made over time. In this process, equilibrium is neither achieved nor maintained. Thus, history matters.

The second characteristic of post-Keynesian economics is the existence of irreversible time, where economic agents enter into commitments well before outcomes can be predicted. During the lengthy process of production, companies pay in terms of money for their expenses—such as wages and other expenses of production—in the expectation of recouping such expenses by selling the products for money at a later date. Historical time is in sharp contrast to logical time, which is rejected in post-Keynesian economics. Logical time is closely related to rationality and logical calculus, which form two of the main characteristics of neoclassical economics. This mode of thought consequently assumes away problems associated with historical time. It reduces uncertainty to risk, which can be quantified through the calculus of probability, as a result of which history is turned into logical time. Then, the real economy tends toward a long-period "equilibrium" position, which is stable in the sense that there is no tendency to deviate away from it; and, indeed, if for any reason the system finds itself away from this "equilibrium" position, there will be forces that will take the system back to long-period "equilibrium." Post-Keynesian economists view this type of neoclassical steady state economics as having great intellectual complexity but also being so much out of time and out of history that they are practically futile and misleading. Therefore, these central concepts of neoclassical economics are completely inappropriate for an analysis that relies heavily on historical time.

The third characteristic of post-Keynesian economics is that economic agents sign contract agreements that are denominated in money. In this way, money and contracts are tightly related. This characteristic is pervasive because money comes into play along with debt contracts (which are contracts for deferred payment) and price lists (which are offers of contracts for sale or purchase). That is, money plays an important role as a link between the past and the present, as well as between the present and the future, where the past is given and unchangeable and the future is uncertain and unknowable. Indeed, it is the existence of uncertainty in the context of historical time that is both the necessary and the sufficient condition for the existence of money. There is no need for money in a stochastic, stationary, and ergodic world. The tight relationship between modern money and debt contracts underlies the proposition that money is credit-driven and demand-determined and that the supply of and demand for money are interdependent. This is because the supply of credit essentially depends on the demand for credit. That is, in a particular period of time, the determinants of the demand for credit influence the flow of supply of credit and thus the supply of money. Most of the demand for credit arises in relation to production. Production costs are paid before sales revenues are received. The need to bridge this gap—that is, the working capital requirement of the industrial and commercial companies—is met by borrowing from banks in addition to the companies' internally generated funds. The amount of borrowing from banks is dependent on the total wage bill, the raw material and tax payments bills, and other variables, such as unexpected changes in borrowing needs. In other words, industrial and commercial companies borrow to finance their current production and distribution costs in the expectation of future sales revenues. As long as these companies can provide sound and adequate collateral at the time of their credit application, commercial banks will supply the amount of credit requested by them. Bankers accommodate businessmen's demand for funds to invest in credit-worthy projects at interest rates based on markup over the central bank's supply price of reserves. This means that the endogenous nature of credit money allows investment expenditures to be carried out independently of the current saving flows. Investment determines savings, rather than the reverse. In this way, money in modern capitalist economies is credit-driven and demand-determined. Central banks do not have firm control over the amount of credit. They can only control the supply price of credit money via the discount rate, which is under their direct control.

The fourth characteristic of post-Keynesian economics is related to labor and labor markets. According to the post-Keynesian view, no labor market in the real world works in the way envisaged by neoclassical economics, where wages are determined, along with many other prices, by "market forces" in a general equilibrium framework. Instead, nominal wages are set through a bilateral administered pricing process between employers and employees. Such agreed-upon nominal labor contracts prevail over some future period. The process whereby these agreements are arrived at involves "conflict" of interests between employers and employees. Wage determination is influenced not only by economic factors but also many others, such as: political, historical, sociological, and psychological factors. After money wages are thus determined, prices adjust to money wages, not the other way round. Prices are set based on a markup over costs, and therefore, real wages are determined not just in labor markets but in product markets as well. It is, thus, possible to observe that higher wages are accompanied by additional demand for labor, not less. There is no functional relationship between wages and employment because the two variables are determined independently of each other.

Methodological premises of post-Keynesian economics are as follows. (1) A free-market economic process is inherently unstable. Post-Keynesian theory attempts to present reality, be context-specific, make repeated reappraisals of current developments, and build "realistic abstractions" rather than "imaginary models." (2) An emphasis on critical realism is required. In the realist view, the economy and society are an open system, whereas in the positivist view, it is closed. Positivists believe in the occurrence of constant conjunctions of actual events. Realists believe, in contrast, that the world in general is open, and constancy, or relative endurability, lies at the level of underlying causes. For realists, explanation rather than prediction is recognized as the relevant criterion for theory assessment. This has relevance to econometric modeling. Realists use stylized facts and econometrics as the starting point for their analysis of causal mechanisms. They do not aim to generalize, or render precise, any rough empirical pattern but to move toward an understanding of the underlying causal mechanisms that give rise to it. They regard "observations" as containing both objective and subjective elements. A certain degree of objectivity is involved when "facts" are observed, while the grouping of "facts" for purposes of theoretical analysis entails some degree of subjectivity. But even observation is selective and hence subjective.

(3) An organic, rather than atomistic, approach to economic processes is more relevant and appropriate. Post-Keynesians regard individuals as social rather than atomistic beings and therefore give considerable weight to social and economic institutions. (4) It is necessary to recognize the importance of "insufficient demand," rather than concentrating on "scarcity of resources," and to give central position to "effective demand." In exchange, an individual's choice is limited, because it is determined by income, class, and the technical conditions of production, rather than by relative prices. Income and not substitution effects, along with income distribution among social classes, should be the objects of analysis. (5) Monopolies and oligopolies have socio-political as well as economic power, based on which they administer product prices. This capacity, together with their power over input costs, especially wage costs, determines their gained surplus. This surplus, together with their expectations and effective demand, translates into investment, which is the engine for growth. (6) Individuals have limited capacity in acquiring and analyzing information. They suffer from "bounded rationality," that is, they cannot see problems in all their complexity. They rely on group behavior and conventions. They do not optimize. Procedures and rules are set by those individuals or groups who possess power, based on their place in the social or economic hierarchy, which allows them to impose their values upon the rest.

## Institutional Economics

The contribution of institutional economics to economic thought has distinguished institutionalism from traditional economics and melded it into a coherent body of thought. Although there is heterogeneity in institutional economics, such heterogeneity disappears as soon as institutional economics is compared with alternative economic methodological and philosophical persuasions. Despite such heterogeneity, a common thread in institutional economics is apparent that acts as an ideological nexus and binds institutionalism together to form a school.[6]

Institutional economics is distilled from the writings of major institutional economists. Its theoretical framework sets institutionalism apart from other schools of thought. More specifically, the methodologies of institutionalism and economic orthodoxy can be contrasted. The differences in their methodologies are based on differences in their epistemologies and theories of human nature, which are in turn the foundations of differences in their ethical viewpoints.

Institutionalism places emphasis on a specific area within the broad spectrum of economic thought. Economics can be divided into the study of: (1) resource allocation; (2) levels and rates of growth of employment, income, production, and prices; (3) income distribution; and (4) the structure of power. Whereas economic orthodoxy is concerned with the first three of these categories, institutionalism emphasizes the last one.

Institutionalists do not view the standard economic theory as entirely invalid or irrelevant. They do not totally discount the efficacy of market incentives. They, rather, see the primary weakness of economic orthodoxy in its self-limiting tendencies. They criticize economic orthodoxy not for its description of the mechanics of exchange but for its failure to account for the interaction of these processes with the economic superstructure, and for its application of the ceteris paribus assumption to the social, economic, and technological framework within which resource allocation and the level and distribution of income take place.

Institutionalists regard institutional economics as the general theory, of which economic orthodoxy is a special case. Institutionalists are concerned with the evolving framework within which economic activities occur, such as the evolution of the power structure, the rules of the game, the process of want creation, and conflict resolution. Standard economics, in contrast, describes the special case of exchange in a world with specific assumed characteristics, which do not mostly correspond to the world.

Institutional economics is evolutionary, collective, interdisciplinary, and non-predictive. It focuses on conflict rather than harmony, on waste rather than efficiency, and on uncertainty rather than perfect knowledge. It entirely rejects the orthodoxy's view of the market as an unbiased allocational and distributional mechanism, and consistently maintains a clear distinction between private and social costs and benefits. It is mainly concerned with the existence and abuse of power and privilege, rather than the orthodoxy's machinations of the atomistic individual.

Institutionalism distinguishes between "technological" and "institutional" patterns of behavior and modes of thought, which are present in varying degrees in all cultures. "Technological," or "instrumental," thought and action is based on reasoning from cause to effect. It is non-coercive, and it can be subjected to empirical verification by checking its ability in achieving its goal. "Institutional" or "ceremonial" behavior, in contrast, is based on considering rank and status. It is enforced by social pressure and verified through appeal to authority.

Instrumental activity, that is, the continuous advance in scientific understanding, is the driving force behind economic development. In contrast, institutions, that is, the habits of thought shared among people, are static. Institutions are entwined with the community's status system and are verified by such authority as custom, law, politics, religion, and morality. Thus, whereas instrumental behavior enhances development, ceremonial activity restricts or, at best, only permits change. Whereas technology involves people's creative tendencies, institutions involve people's predatory and exploitative propensities.

Technology is the state of the industrial arts and includes the existing level of understanding and technique as well as the tools and equipment that are available and utilized by a civilization. The technology of a society is a common stock, which is collectively held and advanced by a culture. Although the physical properties of available materials do not change over time, people's understanding of how to use them changes. Thus, it is the people's curiosity and intelligence that act as the driving force behind technological progress. People are active forces for, rather than passive accommodators of, change. Human beings apply their creative imagination and fashion, rather than merely adapt to, their environment. Technological progress enhances new methods of provisioning and changes in the quantity, quality, and composition of goods and services produced. Institutions, in response, adjust sluggishly and reluctantly. The existing institutions are not an immutable, natural condition of economic organization.

The orthodox economic literature stresses savings (a money fund) as the cause of capital formation and industrial progress. It defends income inequality as the source of savings. Institutionalists, in contrast, emphasize that the ability of an economy to produce more emanates from science, technology, invention, and innovation, and its source is not money but human creativity.

Institutionalists believe that all human activity takes place collectively. All transactions occur within institutions according to standards established by habits of thought. Individual tastes are shaped by emulation and social conditioning. The state of the industrial arts is a fact of group life, in the same way that mores and folkways are inherited from community. These are in contrast to the orthodoxy's concept of the hedonistic, atomistic individual.

Institutionalists believe that the transactions of individuals are limited and directed by standards of law and convention. They, in contrast to the orthodoxy, do not view the discipline of economics as a mechanistic "science of choice." This is because an individual's preference and selection are governed and restrained by law and custom; by information gaps and lags; by the coercion of the less powerful resulting from the more powerful; and by manipulated market forces based on the ability of those with market power who can interfere with it.

Institutionalists conceive of private ownership not as a "natural" condition but as having evolved through historical conditions and subject to human control. Property rights establish both power over use and power in exchange, especially as industrialization proceeds and transactions are increasingly taking place between competing collectivities. Property rights establish the right of superordinates to direct and control subordinates.

Conflicts of interest that result from scarcity are settled by goal-seeking individuals. People use their utmost power, whether granted or exacted, to achieve their goals, which are set in conjunction with their expectations about the future. Transactions may seem to be taking place between relative equals. But the existing working rules in society also sanction coercion, that is, the direction of some people by others. The result of the settlement of such conflicts is an indeterminate and imprecise compromise, rather than a unique, calculable, automatic solution. The compromise is based on the use of power within "reasonable" limits, as set by laws and customs, which have been and continue to be established on a case-by-case basis, especially when existing working rules no longer function satisfactorily. The outcome of all transactions is uncertain and transitory, and it is dependent on customary methods of procedure, varying expectations about the future, and relative power. The system is always in a state of flux, and it is never in the state of equilibrium imposed by outside forces.

Institutionalists, thus, do not envision the market as a neutral mechanism for allocational efficiency and distributional equity. They, rather, view the market as biased in many important respects. The prevailing structure of power is reflected in the existing operation of the market, such that not only does the market control, but also it is itself controlled. Terms of exchange is based on the existing power relations between negotiators. Institutionalists view the market as an institution that is constrained, which is in contrast to what the orthodoxy views as a "free market."

Institutionalists note that the economic system is often characterized by waste, rather than the orthodoxy's efficiency. They challenge the traditional economics' utility theory of value as well as the competitive model, which are based on the fundamental belief that all expenditures and productive effort are equally legitimate. They describe and explain the wasteful consumption practices of the monied classes. They explain that the demand for goods is often based not upon their utility, but upon the status that the possession confers upon the possessor. In other words, it is the show of expensiveness that is valued; it is accumulation for its own sake that is the goal; it is the medium that is the message.

Institutionalists call into question the concept of "consumer sovereignty" by reference to the manipulation of consumer wants by producers. When choices are subjected to manipulation, they are neither inherent nor informed. When demand is increased as much by manipulation as by intrinsic desires, then scarce resources are wasted in the production of goods of low social and individual serviceability, while public needs are ignored.

Institutionalists have also directed attention toward another form of waste: the underutilization of productive resources. They note the sabotage of industrial output by industrialists to create values. They identify the causal factors for the business cycle and its resultant unemployment. They emphasize the waste of resources as a result of unemployment and insist that while labor is a variable cost for business, it is a fixed cost for society. In the same way that a business suffers if it does not fully utilize its fixed plant and equipment, society suffers if it does not fully utilize its labor force.

Institutionalists portray an economic system that often involves inequity rather than justice. They observe the orthodoxy's notion that each factor of production receives the equivalent of its marginal product is incorrect. This is because no factor of production produces in isolation, but as part of an industrial system. Whereas the orthodoxy claims that the common practice is to reward those with scarce skills, institutionalists state that scarcity is often contrived.

Institutionalists distinguish private and social costs and benefits. They direct attention to externalities, and their concerns include and transcend the physical environment. They note that with industrialization, interdependencies multiply, and externalities proliferate. They also maintain that the existing social structure victimizes certain groups and that this victimization constitutes a social cost.

Institutionalists describe a perpetually evolving environment which is subject to human dominance, which is made possible through humans' continued development of methods of control. In the process of changing the environment, the human agent changes, which is the most profound development of all.

Institutionalists envision unceasing change, in which no pattern necessarily exists. Scientific understanding continuously expands, but its direction cannot be foretold, because it varies with the types of inquiries and the types of inquirers. Neither the growth of scientific understanding nor the development of an economy follows any law or principle.

Institutionalists view technology as a dynamic force in society. They, accordingly, regard human intelligence as the basic driving force. Their moral imperative is free inquiry, that is, freedom of thought and experimentation. Growth of understanding not only leads to an increase in productive potential, but also it facilitates an escape from tradition and authority as well as the creation of new working rules.

Institutionalists, thus, view economics as indeterminate and experimental. They conceive of economic knowledge not as the discovery of universal principles (as the orthodox does) but as the creation of tools of control in order to achieve a more reasonable society or an increased serviceability. This is to be achieved through trial and error in a search not for perfection (as in the orthodoxy) but for an improved accommodation.

Institutionalists, then, view the function of economists as not providing prediction (as in the orthodoxy) but performing critical inquiry and problem-solving. Traditional economists examine a specific institution, that is, the market, which has a moral beneficence or is neutral. Institutionalist economists, in contrast, search for the underlying bias of the current institutional structure and attempt to recognize how such institutions can be changed in order to disperse power and privilege with the aim of creating a more reasonable society.

Institutional and orthodox schools of economics are based on different methodologies, which are, in turn, based on different epistemologies and theories of human nature, which are, in turn, the bases of different ethical outlooks. Institutional economists have historically criticized orthodox theorists for their specific method of abstraction, their reliance on a priori reasoning, and their static, marginal approach.

Institutionalists criticize the orthodox method of abstraction not because of abstraction per se, but because of that from which the orthodox theory abstracts. Institutionalists well understand that in the method of abstraction, theory is based on certain selected variables while leaving other relevant factors out of consideration. The orthodox economics focuses on "rational economic men" whose goals are profit or utility maximization. Institutionalists criticize this hedonistic psychology of traditional theory. They conceive of people as active and sometimes irrational agents operating within an institutional framework that conditions and controls their behavior, while it is itself altered by the change in behavior.

Institutionalists call into question the explanatory and descriptive power of the orthodoxy's model, which posits the institutional and technological framework as exogenous, given, and fixed. Furthermore, without the ability to explain, the model cannot have the capacity to predict. Institutionalists view the environmental milieu as both controlled and controlling; that is, the environment is simultaneously a dependent and an independent variable. Individuals shape and are shaped by their environment. In other words, individuals create and are the creatures of their environment. The interface of individuals and their environment is one of continuous interaction and evolutionary change.

Institutionalists challenge both the models that traditional theorists construct based on disputable assumptions and the portrayal of these models as the goals of economic conduct and organization. They direct attention to the limited scope of admitted variables in the orthodox formulation. That is, the focus on the rational economic man whose transactions take place within a competitive market economy, the identification of the market with competition, and the equivalency of the model with the ideal. They contend that the orthodox theorists unrealistically portray the competitive market as the existing economic reality and as an ideal state toward which the economy would move in the absence of undesirable collusion or intervention.

Institutionalists also criticize orthodox theorists for their a priori methods. That is, orthodox theorists apply reasoning based on general principles but without regard to the facts of experience. Institutionalists believe that traditional economists rely on revelation, rather than observation, as the appropriate method of science. That is, orthodox theorists assume the existence of a set of natural laws and rights that are discoverable solely through the application of reason. Institutionalists also believe that conventional theorists attribute merit and truth to this set of natural laws and rights, and as a result the system becomes an apology for the existing institutional structure. Specific institutions, such as ownership and free contract, are regarded as "natural," rather than as human creations. These institutions, consequently, are taken as given and are considered beyond the scope of professional inquiry. The role of the economists reduces to the discovery and interpretation of universal principles. Theory, in orthodoxy's view, is strictly a logical construct with no need for reference to the facts.

## Social Economics

This section discusses the evolution and contribution of social economics to modern political economic analysis. Social economics is distinguished from classical political economy and contemporary neoclassical and mainstream economics—and, indeed, from most other political economic approaches—by its goal of explaining and premising the concept of "social" in economics. Its main organizing principle is that the economy is embedded in human society rather than vice versa.[7]

1. The Origins and Historical Development of Social Economics: Social economics as a distinct theoretical approach within political economy has two main connected histories. The first has its origins and initial development in eighteenth-century European "third way" cooperative movements—particularly in France, Belgium, the Netherlands, Germany, Italy, and Britain, where early modern capitalism was ascendant. The literature arising from these movements grappled with explaining non-market, local types of economic relationships in broad social system terms. The second, more recent history, involves the emergence and development of a professional academic social economics society and scholarly journals in the United States and Canada in the second half of the twentieth century through to the new millennium. The resulting literature focuses on confronting and resisting the market-centric economic analysis that has dominated economics since 1950 while advancing alternative foundations for a more humanistic economics. Post-millennium social economics thought has subsequently taken on new issues, normative concerns, and voices, including from outside Europe and North America, as capitalism has globalized.

The eighteenth- and nineteenth-century development of social economics in Europe emerged in connection with investigation of the "social economy" or what has come to be called the "third way" or "third sector" of modern capitalist market economies. These are understood primarily as associational and cooperative forms of community-based economic activities. The state and market had become the dominant forms of economic activity in emerging capitalist economies. Yet, distinct from and intermediate between these two forms, there also existed a wide variety of different kinds of local economic activity that operated neither in terms of market-driven self-interest nor state-based broad national goals, instead, focusing on advancing local concerns.

Social economics criticized, to various degrees, the development of classical political economy along the lines of a natural science following Smith, Ricardo, and others, with its "mechanical or mechanistic approach" that runs in terms of equilibria and gravitational movements. Social economics adopted, as a guiding principle, the idea that economic life is based on human relationships, that is, direct association and social interaction between people. Thus, contrary to political economy's epistemology, social values are deemed fundamental in economic life and economics—not only for explanations of local economic activity, but also for comprehending the economy as a whole.

Markets and the state give precedence to reciprocity, justice, and freedom because these values apply to people irrespective of who they are. Conversely, when communities emphasize social provisioning, mutuality, and dignity, it is because these values apply to people because of who they are. If thinking in terms of markets and the state means improving how markets work and compensating people when they fail, respectively, cooperative, community-based economic organizations concern themselves with local needs as determined by fraternal groups, family ties, churches, and craft affiliations.

After 1945, social economics acquired an additional mode of expression and development within a burgeoning US and Canadian academic economics that distanced itself from the newly dominant, market-centric neoclassical approach. Thus, whereas earlier social economists had seen themselves as offering an alternative to classical political economy, postwar social economists in the United States and Canada saw themselves as offering an alternative to US neoclassical economics.

In 1970, the Association for Social Economics (ASE) was formed to reflect its more diverse nature and actively opened its membership to heterodox economists. Feminist economists began to publish in the *Review of Social Economy* in the late 1980s and 1990s, which further extended the scope of association social values to include the rejection of patriarchy.

Broadly, then, social justice and human dignity became unifying social values for the diverse range of approaches within the association, such that social economics could be characterized as a "humanistic economics" or a "real-life" economics. Yet, at this stage, little significant attention was accorded to questions of race or the significant divide between rich and poor nations in the global economy.

However, in 1995, Routledge commenced publishing the journal and, consequently, promoted its international circulation. If submissions were still slow to come from the developing world, there was nonetheless increasing attention to international development and worldwide poverty. This gradually became a new dimension to social economics, whose origins and history had been framed by countries' domestic economies.

Broadly, three factors united most social economists in the second half of the twentieth century.

First, they accept Karl Polanyi's argument that the economy is embedded in human society rather than vice versa. Markets do not function independently of social relationships, and people are not simply self-interested economic agents. Instead, they are embedded in concrete, ongoing systems of social relations.

Second, social economists, thus, reject the strong version of Chicago School neoclassicism that explicitly reduces social relationships to market relationships and is built around extending the rational actor model. In contrast, social economists argue that economics needs to prioritize the human person. This implies that the utility maximization model of individuals as essentially self-interested should be abandoned, and a fuller conception of the person in economic life be developed in its place.

Third, social economists are also united in rejecting the increasingly strident positivism of postwar mainstream economics. For social economists, economics is inherently value-laden, because it is built around values regarding how economic life contributes to social life. Indeed, the mainstream market-centric view of the economy depends on emphasizing certain values and excluding others. Seeing the economy as embedded, thus, requires economic life to be explained in terms of the full range of values operating in society.

While social economics has historically explained economic relationships in terms of how communities organize economic life on a local level, the increasing integration of the world economy has meant that social economists have begun to operate with a more complex understanding of community. On this view, communities can extend across great distances, different cultures, and national boundaries when people see themselves sharing common experiences and circumstances. This has increased the importance of poverty and inequality, as well as sustainability and the environment, as important issues for social economists, because these issues particularly affect local communities throughout the world. Communities, then, are still local in regard to people's most immediate and familiar social relationships, but the well-being of people at this level around the world adds a second layer to how community is understood.

2. Social Economics versus Mainstream Economics: There are two primary, interconnected practical issues dividing social economics and most mainstream economics: what policies ought to exist toward markets, and what is the relationship between ethics and economics?

2.1. Policies toward Markets: For contrast, consider the standard neoclassical view of policies toward markets to which most mainstream economists adhere. If one believes that society is embedded in the economy and that one ought to model social relationships on economic relationships, then one is likely to understand policies toward markets solely in terms of what would make the latter operate efficiently. Further, if one believes that all social relationships are ultimately economic relationships, one may also hold that markets operate efficiently most of the time and that when they do not, it is only because an external factor (usually government) has interfered with their operation. Policies toward markets in mainstream economics, therefore, are essentially aimed at freeing markets from social interference. A more moderate mainstream position is that markets themselves sometimes fail on their own and that policies should additionally be designed to deal with market failure. Still, the goal is to make markets operate efficiently.

Conversely, the socio-economic view denies that all social relationships are ultimately economic relationships and should be modelled as such. Social economists do not favor the complete elimination of market relationships; instead, they posit that society should determine the extent and character of the market. On the one hand, where appropriate, this entails promotion and extension of the distinctive and valuable features of human life characterizing non-market social relationships. On the other hand, it means resisting and reversing the erosion of these relationships due to the augmentation of markets.

The socio-economic view of policies toward markets is, thus, concerned with setting boundaries on markets and influencing how they work. There are two primary ways in which this program has been pursued: (1) the "moral limits of markets" view and (2) the "taming the market" view. Both strategies utilize social values that go well beyond mainstream economics' utilitarian welfarist thinking and employ broader conceptions of human well-being.

The "*moral limits of markets*" view argues that normative principles cannot be modelled on the logic of market processes, that doing so is often "morally repugnant," and that markets often "crowd out" other normative principles. Thus, there are certain domains of social life that should simply be "off limits" to markets. In effect, some things in life are "priceless." The "*taming the market*" view focusses on how markets themselves work and how they ought to be transformed to be socially acceptable.

Two different strategies may be delineated here: one aims at intervening in how market outcomes are produced (a direct strategy), and the other seeks to change the underlying conditions affecting market outcomes (an indirect strategy). The former employs such interventions as price controls—for example, price floors in the case of minimum wages and price ceilings in the case of rent controls—and also quantity controls, such as when air and water quality is protected by capping industrial pollutants or when regulations in workplaces exist for worker safety. The indirect strategy aims to influence the underlying conditions in particular markets through such measures as taxes and subsidies, along with those conditions affecting markets generally, such as public expenditure and production of social goods. In effect, in the direct strategy markets are "tamed" from within, while the indirect strategy "tames" them from without. For most social economists, both strategies are motivated by the goals of improving social well-being; reducing the effects of social stratification; promoting equality, irrespective of race, gender, sexual orientation, age, and religion; and sustaining democracy.

2.2. Ethics and Economics: Regarding the status of ethics and economics, the postwar professionalization of science and academic research has sharpened and institutionalized differences between different disciplines. Working against this is the trend toward greater interconnectedness between different kinds of social scientific investigations, as well as between descriptive and normative economics. For social economics, this is important in that it may move economics toward a more serious appraisal of ethical concepts and normative reasoning, as well as a revaluation of the relationship between ethics and economics.

3. The Main Normative Goals and Social Values of Social Economics: Three primary areas of normative concern for social economists are: the nature of well-being, values in economic relationships, and the moral status of the person in economic life.

3.1. The Nature of Well-Being: On the Polanyian embeddedness view discussed above, economic life is a means to maintaining and improving people's well-being, not the purpose of life itself. From this perspective, the economy is a means of social provisioning—or a means of producing—not what people can afford, but what they need to live their lives both in and outside markets by drawing on the technologies and level of knowledge historically available at any given time. That is, the economy ought to promote not just better living standards and reduce poverty and inequality but also promote full human flourishing.

At first glance, this conception of social provisioning may appear no different from mainstream economics' concept of welfare. However, there is a fundamental difference. The latter concept is formulated as the satisfaction of individual preferences, which are defined as isolated individuals' private, subjective tastes. In contrast, the concept of social provisioning is based on comprehending people as social beings whose well-being transcends their private tastes and includes the nature of their social relationships, concern for others, and their existence in communities in which they live. By comparison, the mainstream welfare concept only calls for markets to work optimally as if people's lives were fully represented by their involvement in markets.

3.2. Values in Economic Relationships: In mainstream economics, the only values exhibited by social relationships are market values because the former are assumed to be ultimately reducible to their market form. For social economists, market relationships are only a subset of broader social relationships, which exhibit a much wider range of social values. For instance, if a key social value promoted by market relationships is economic freedom, freedom in a wider social sense also means being free from coercion and compulsion of all kinds and having the capacity to act freely regardless of one's circumstances. Similarly, while market relationships may promote justice in exchange, or commutative justice, social economics also posits the centrality of distributive and procedural justice—that is, whether resources, well-being, and opportunities in life are fairly and equitably distributed across people. Justice, in this latter sense, is indeed a precondition of commutative justice.

3.3. The Moral Status of the Person in Economic Life: Defenses of economic freedom are often coupled with defenses of the legal rights people need to participate effectively in markets. The wider sense of freedom defended by social economists entails a broader set of rights—human rights—that people need to secure their economic well-being in and beyond markets. Human rights accrue to people on the same basis that narrower legal rights do: that people are entitled to pursue their livelihoods as best they can while not causing harm to others. Human rights, in this sense, are preeminently individual rights, but social economists also defend community rights, since they see the inexorable interrelation between people's well-being as individuals and their lives in communities.

Defenses of human rights are motivated by a deep social value: namely, that people have inherent value and are entitled to respect simply by virtue of being human. Social economists make this the central, anchoring value of life—economic and otherwise—and refer to it as the dignity of the person. In Kantian philosophy, people are ends in themselves, have intrinsic worth, and ought never to be means to others' purposes. This means that ethics and economic policy ought always to be organized around reducing human vulnerability and promoting people's choices in life to the extent that this avoids causing harm to others.

Respect for others as human beings also means respecting others' choices in the expectation that people's choices and lives can be diverse. That is, the value of human dignity involves valuing human diversity and differences between people. This is a shared human value in that what people have in common is not some single characteristic, but that people are all uniquely different from one another. What people have in common, that is, is their diversity.

Overall, social economists' social values are a reflection of, and also a normative foundation for, their analysis of economic life lived in close interaction with others—whether in local or more far-reaching communities. Shared life with others, thus, not only invests all people with essential human dignity but also calls for an open, pluralist economic analysis. In this respect, social economics elevates and prioritizes the "social" in economic life and human life more broadly and, thereby, offers a humanistic, real-life alternative to mainstream economics.

## Radical Economics

The idea of socialism developed historically in opposition to capitalism. Accordingly, the basic goals of the socialist movement have been set in reaction to the inherent problems of capitalism. At its core, socialism has been committed to the following objectives:[8]

1. Equity: In capitalism, there are severe inequalities of income and wealth. In opposition, socialism aims at an egalitarian distribution of economic outcomes and opportunities by class race, gender, region, and so on.
2. Democracy: In capitalism, liberal democracy in the political sphere has characterized the most democratic societies. In opposition, socialism aims at economic democracy, which enables people to exercise control over their own economic fate.

3. Solidarity: In capitalism, it is the individual who is celebrated. In opposition, socialism aims at solidarity among the members of all communities covering small neighborhoods to the whole society, by encouraging people to develop themselves as social beings rather than individual beings.
4. Efficiency: In capitalism, inefficiency is endemic. In opposition, socialism aims at the wise and non-wasteful use of resources so that economic and social goals can be more successfully achieved.

In order to achieve these socialist goals, liberal-democratic socialists (radical economists) advocate market socialism, but communitarian socialists (Marxist economists) advocate participatory socialism.

Liberal-democratic socialists place emphasis on democracy, and they see liberal democracy—that is, a political system based on constitutionally protected civil rights and liberties, democratic elections, and so on—as a vital prerequisite for a socialist society. That is, socialist economic institutions that aim at achieving socialist goals, such as equity and solidarity, must be built upon a liberal-democratic political foundation. They do not regard the construction of socialist society as the replacement of "bourgeois democratic institutions" by a totally different and superior form of democracy but as deepening the democratic nature of such institutions and extending them from the political to the social and economic arenas. They never considered the political authoritarian character of Communist Party-directed societies as exemplars of socialism.

Liberal-democratic socialists favor democratic market socialism, which is a combination of: (1) liberal democracy; (2) an economic system mainly characterized by collective ownership of the means of production; and (3) the use of markets as the main means of resource allocation and distribution, but subject to some government planning, intervention, and regulation. Collective ownership of the means of production is intended to achieve equity and justice in both economic and political spheres; markets are expected to promote individual freedom of choice and efficient allocation of resources; and government regulation is enforced in order to ensure that general interest prevails over particular interests and to limit the development of substantial inequities.

The idea of a market-based form of socialism was seriously promoted in the 1920s by the social-democratic wing of Marxism as a desirable alternative to the market-less form of socialism, which was associated with Marx's vision of full communism as well as advocated by the Bolshevik wing of Marxism. The first systematic theoretical exposition of the functioning of a market-based socialist economy was made in the 1930s by Oskar Lange, who has since then been known as the pioneer of market socialism. Lange's original model consisted of: (1) actual markets (in consumer goods and labor), (2) simulated markets (in producer goods), and (3) a limited but important role for central planning (e.g., in controlling the rate of investment and the distribution of income). In this system, all enterprises are owned by the government but run by independent managers who follow profit-maximizing rules. Since the exposition of Lange's market socialism model, many economists—who have been either from or interested in the post-Second World War Eastern European countries—have done a great deal of work to improve upon Lange's model, especially in view of various problems raised by critics.

Although the continuing literature on the conceptualization of market socialism has resulted in a variety of different models, they all share the same set of goals. Market socialism seeks to attain the socialist goals of equity, democracy, and solidarity through retaining one major feature of capitalist economies—the market—but replacing another major feature of capitalism—private ownership of the means of production. Market socialism also involves some form of social ownership of enterprises for at least the major sectors and/or the most important enterprises in the economy.

"Ownership," as a complex concept, encompasses various rights, which can be assigned to various people. Market socialism identifies and distinguishes two such rights: (1) the right to enterprise control and (2) the right to enterprise income. The right to control involves the prerogatives and responsibilities of management. That is, those who control the enterprise (or their representatives) are entitled to make the decisions about: how the enterprise will be operated; who will work in it and under what conditions; if any aspects of the enterprise need to be expanded, contracted, sold, or liquidated; and so on. The right to income involves the claim to the monetary surplus generated by the enterprise. That is, it is the entitlement to claim the net (or residual) income after all fixed obligations have been paid.

In capitalism, an enterprise is owned by private individuals or shareholders, who appoint management and have (ultimate) control over management according to the nature and the number of their share ownership. It is possible for a small number of individuals or shareholders to have predominant control. In market socialism, enterprise control is not private but social. That is, the control of a market socialist enterprise is held by the people in the community.

Each member of the community—in principle—can equally influence the management of the enterprise. In practice, this (ultimate) control is usually exercised through the appointment of managerial staff. Depending on the nature of the community, the vested control rights can usually be exercised through one of the following two ways:

1. Public management: In this alternative, an enterprise is run by managers, whom are appointed by and are held accountable by an agency of the government—at the national, regional, or local level. The government agency represents the relevant politically constituted community of citizens.
2. Worker self-management: In this alternative, an enterprise is run by managers, whom are appointed by and are held accountable to those who work in the enterprise—or their elected representatives. The control rights ultimately rest with the community of enterprise workers, on a one-person one-vote basis.

In capitalism, ownership by private individuals or shareholders determines not only control rights but also income rights. The extent of these rights is determined according to the nature and the number of their share ownership. In market socialism, income rights are not held privately but socially. The monetary surplus of the market socialist enterprise belongs to the community of people, and is shared among them on a relatively egalitarian basis. Depending on the nature of the community, the income rights can usually be exercised in one of the following two ways:

1. Public surplus appropriation: In this alternative, the monetary surplus of the enterprise is distributed to an agency of government—at the national, regional or local level. The government agency represents the corresponding community of citizens.
2. Worker surplus appropriation: In this alternative, the monetary surplus of the enterprise is distributed to the enterprise workers.

In general, the two different ways of assigning control rights and the two different ways of assigning income rights can combine to generate a matrix of four different possible market socialist models. This can happen because there is no a priori reason for each set of rights to be assigned in the same way. However, most contemporary advocates of market socialism fall into one of the two schools of thought and favor one of the following two models: (1) one school favors what may be called the "public enterprise model," which is characterized by public management and public surplus appropriation; and (2) the other school favors what may be called the "worker enterprise model," which is characterized by worker self-management and worker surplus appropriation.

Although market socialism most clearly distinguishes itself from (market) capitalism by the replacement of social for private control and income rights at the enterprise level, market socialism also generally requires a greater degree of government intervention into markets than is the norm in capitalism. Such intervention is not primarily of the kind of quantitative controls, that is, not of the kind associated with the discredited system of centrally planned socialism. Instead, government intervention involves more government provision of public goods and services, public capital formation, regulation of enterprises, and use of taxes and subsidies to internalize external effects that would otherwise be ignored by individual consumers and producers in the market environment. The objective here is to use the market—rather than replace it—but shape the environment in which the market operates such that market price and cost valuations will approximate the social benefits and costs. With respect to government intervention, the difference between market socialism and (market) capitalism is one of degree rather than kind. In a market socialist system, the government intervenes in economic life slightly more than the governments in the more regulated (e.g., social-democratic) capitalist systems. The essential difference between market socialism and (market) capitalism is constituted by public control and income rights in enterprises.

Market socialism has been challenged on several grounds in regard to its ability to meet socialist goals with social ownership forms in the context of markets, that is, whether market socialism is socialist enough. The first challenge is the idea that the market system systematically undermines efforts to serve general public interests. That is, in the market environment, people are encouraged to better themselves at the expense of others—for example, through individual rent-seeking behavior, the formation of self-aggrandizing coalitions, and so on. As a result, markets appear to generate a systematic tendency for the general social interest to be undermined by the pursuit of particular private interests.

Although the idea of this challenge is theoretically plausible, it is not decisive. Rent-seeking behavior and self-aggrandizing coalitions can and will occur in any economic system that allows some people to live better than others. This is why every system requires institutions that limit antisocial behavior. That problem can be eradicated only by an economic system that controls the individual patterns of living to the extent that it can preclude any individual from enjoying the gains from self-interested behavior. This solution to the problem of such behavior, therefore, comes only at the expense of strict limits on privacy and freedom of choice. This is a high price that market socialists are unwilling to pay.

The second challenge to the market socialism model is the idea that market systems unfairly reward good luck. In market capitalist economies, owners of property are rewarded, in the form of capital income, for the productive contributions of their property. Such rewards to property ownership not only are the source of unequal distribution in society, but also, they are generally not necessary to assure deployment of the property in production. In market socialist economies, owners of labor power are rewarded, in the form of labor income, for the productive contributions of their labor. Yet market socialism, like capitalism, rewards people's natural abilities, even though such rewards may not be necessary to assure the deployment of those natural abilities in production. Moreover, worker self-management forms of market socialism are likely to reward those people who work in prosperous areas or enterprises despite the fact that they do not necessarily work harder or longer than other people who work in less prosperous areas or enterprises.

Although the idea of this challenge has some merits, it ignores the degree of difference between market socialism and (market) capitalism. In a more just economic system, people would be rewarded differently based on their different personal effort and personal sacrifice, not based on the luck of the genetic or economic draw. Although the market socialist system does not achieve this ideal, it gets substantially much closer to this ideal than the capitalist system does. Furthermore, in market socialism, the extent to which unwarranted returns to some people, due to their genetic or economic luck, result in differentials, a progressive system of income taxation is applied to diminish such differentials.

The third challenge to the market socialism model is the idea that any kind of market system leads to inequalities that contradict the socialist goals of equity and democracy. That is, market socialism generates a minority of elites of "coordinators"—for example, public investment bankers, public enterprise directors, self-managed firm managers, and government planners—who, over time, gain disproportionate economic and political power, similar to what capitalists do in a market capitalist system.

Although the idea of this challenge is meritorious, it ignores the degree of difference between the results of market socialism and (market) capitalism. There is no doubt that in market socialism, there are some people who occupy high positions and make key decisions, as well as have greater power and earn higher income than most of the population. That is, inequalities of income and power exist in market socialism, but they are much smaller than what they are in capitalism. This is because market socialism eliminates property ownership, and therefore, it eliminates returns to property ownership, which is the predominant source of inequalities under capitalism. In market socialism, there are inequalities that correspond to differential skills, talents, and responsibilities, but there are no inequalities that correspond to the propertied capitalist class in capitalism.

The fourth challenge to the market socialism model is the idea that markets undermine solidarity and community. This is because markets breed selfishness and competitiveness on the part of producers and consumers. As a consequence, markets divide people instead of uniting them, encourage indifference to other people instead of empathy for them, and therefore discourage the development of public-spirited community consciousness and solidarity.

Although the idea of this challenge is insightful, it overlooks the fact that the difference between the results of market socialism and (market) capitalism is a matter of degrees. There is no doubt that market transactions cause people to think in terms of their own individual (or family) welfare and set aside consideration for others. In addition, markets encourage anonymity, autonomy, and mobility rather than community, empathy, and solidarity. There is no doubt that market socialism, as a result, does not provide direct support for a culture of community, empathy, and solidarity. However, market socialism provides an environment that is less amenable to the development of such characteristics than (market) capitalism. Indeed, market socialism, by providing greater egalitarianism and stronger democracy, attenuates the consequences of unfettered markets and unrestricted private property ownership.

The fifth challenge to the market socialism model is whether market socialism is more successful than social-democratic variants of capitalism in achieving socialist goals. The market socialist approach is superior to the social-democratic approach in achieving socialist objectives, because it redefines and reassigns—to workers or communities—rights that form the point of departure for markets. In this way, market socialism intervenes in the market system before markets operate, which is in contrast to social democracy, that intervenes in the market system after markets operate. Consequently, social democracy can be weakened or disintegrated through political challenge, because tax-and-subsidy schemes and government regulation are much easier to reverse than property rights. Moreover, social democracy maintains properly owning capitalists who form a disproportionately powerful class with an interest in challenging social-democratic government policies. Although in market socialism there is a managerial class with disproportionate power, its power is less disproportionate because enterprise control rights and personal wealth are not as highly concentrated as in social-democratic capitalism.

## Marxist Economics

As noted in the radical humanist section, the idea of socialism developed historically in opposition to capitalism. Accordingly, the basic goals of the socialist movement have been set in reaction to the inherent problems of capitalism. At its core, socialism has been committed to the following objectives:[9]

1. Equity: In capitalism, there are severe inequalities of income and wealth. In opposition, socialism aims at an egalitarian distribution of economic outcomes and opportunities by class race, gender, region, and so on.
2. Democracy: In capitalism, liberal democracy in the political sphere has characterized the most democratic societies. In opposition, socialism aims at economic democracy, which enables people to exercise control over their own economic fate.
3. Solidarity: In capitalism, it is the individual who is celebrated. In opposition, socialism aims at solidarity among the members of all communities covering small neighborhoods to the whole society, by encouraging people to develop themselves as social beings rather than individual beings.
4. Efficiency: In capitalism, inefficiency is endemic. In opposition, socialism aims at the wise and non-wasteful use of resources so that economic and social goals can be more successfully achieved.

In order to achieve these socialist goals, liberal-democratic socialists (radical economists) advocate market socialism, but communitarian socialists (Marxist economists) advocate participatory socialism.

Communitarian socialists, similarly to liberal-democratic socialists, are committed to democracy, but the kind of democracy they advocate is a democracy of a less liberal and more participatory kind. In their vision, the socialist goal of solidarity receives the greatest emphasis. That is, people develop and sustain solidarity as active participating members of their communities, ranging from their neighborhood and their workplace to their society as a whole. In their view, the political and economic institutions of liberal-democratic capitalism need to be revolutionarily transformed into an egalitarian participatory society in which people jointly and directly control their own fate. Communitarian socialists reject the communist-party-directed socialism because it not only retains many of the individualistic patterns and hierarchical structures of capitalist societies, but also it betrays democratic ideals.

Communitarian socialists advocate a form of democratic participatory socialism in which not only there is collective social control of the means of production, but also there are decentralized participatory planning institutions, which replace markets as a mechanism for resource allocation and distribution. Thus, not only private property but also markets are abolished. Consequently, expressed in Marxist terms, both exploitation and alienation are overcome. Instead of acting as independent, self-interested individuals responding to market signals in the economic arena, people act as interdependent social beings, through communitarian participation, making consumption and production decisions.

Although, in recent years, market socialism has gained relative popularity on the Left, a much older socialist tradition has always rejected the idea of maintaining markets, except during a transitional phase after capitalism. Karl Marx wanted to rid humans not only of the inequalities through the abolition of private property but also of the alienation and commodity fetishism through the abolition of the market system. This was the Marxism of the Russian Bolshevik revolutionaries, and Soviet socialism maintained it as an important part of its ideology, though not its practice, for decades after the Revolution of 1917. Indeed, none of the communist-party-directed socialist economies of the USSR, Eastern Europe, China, Cuba, and so on, dispensed with markets, but they only limited the operation of markets in many ways.

Contemporary participatory socialists support the market-less Marxist ideal, but of a kind that is very different from that of the Bolshevik tradition. First of all, they insist on a democratic political framework, which is in sharp contrast to the authoritarian rule associated with the communist-party-directed socialist economies. Second, they insist on a process of decentralized planning based on the participation of all people as equals, which is in sharp contrast to the hierarchical central planning used as the main alternative to market exchange.

Similarly to market socialism, models of market-less participatory socialism have been developed in various ways. Although such models of participatory socialism differ in many respects, they all share the common goal of the replacement of market forces—which allocate resources based on individual economic agents who act in their own best interest and in response to market signals—by a system of decentralized and coordinated planning—which allocates resources based on negotiation among relevant groups of workers, consumers, community residents, and citizens in general.

The participatory system is typically constituted by two basic decision-making units: workplace workers' councils and neighborhood consumers' councils, in which workplace and neighborhood communities decide with respect to production and consumption. Of course, these basic decision-making units are embedded in a related larger network of politically constituted bodies whose concerns transcend the limited scope of individual workplaces and neighborhoods. Planning boards play a crucial role in the network of non-market decision-making institutions. The planning boards collect and disseminate information as well as coordinate the decisions of separate councils and entities such that decentralized production and consumption plans, which come from all the workplaces and neighborhoods, converge to a comprehensive overall plan of production and consumption. In their decision-making, they consider not only quantitative data about production and consumption processes but also qualitative ramifications of each production and consumption activity.

Advocates of participatory socialism believe that it can attain the socialist goals of egalitarianism, democracy, and solidarity far more successfully than market socialism—because there are no markets—and it can perform at least as efficiently as a market system—even though there are no markets. Advocates of market socialism, in contrast, find the omission of market forces highly impractical and problematic, and they find the feasibility, and at times even the desirability, of a participatory socialist system questionable.

Participatory socialism has been challenged on several grounds, of which the main ones are as follows. The first challenge is the idea that in a complex economy, the allocation of resources through participatory decision-making institutions places huge demands on information processing and disproportionate demands on people's time.

Advocates of the market system follow Adam Smith's original exposition of the "invisible hand" and emphasize the role of market prices in processing the enormous amount of information necessary for coordinated economic decision-making in a complex economy and in disseminating such information in a simple manner to individual economic actors, such that they have both the information and the incentive to act in an economically efficient manner. Some other economists believe that the only alternative method of resource allocation in a complex economy is through a centralized, hierarchical system of administrative commands, which has been discredited by the experience of the communist-party-directed socialist economies. Participatory socialists take up this challenge and develop a third method of resource allocation that avoids both the use of markets and the hierarchy of an administrative command system.

The participatory socialist model replaces the market without using administrative commands. This model requires a vast network of an enormous number of decision-making bodies on which individual members sit, process information, deliberate, and arrive at decisions. It requires these decision-making bodies to perform a detailed analysis of both the qualitative and the quantitative implications of alternative ways of resource allocation. This places on the system a staggering set of requirements: (1) to involve all members of society in group decision-making processes; (2) to compile an enormous amount of economic information and to make it available to individuals engaged in economic decision-making; (3) to develop a system of accounting for the measurement and comparison of the social value of different production and consumption activities so that individual decision-makers can gauge the overall social consequences of any given set of decisions; (4) to find a way for the individual members of any given decision-making body to decide in a harmonious and timely fashion; and (5) to develop a system to assure that the myriad separate micro decisions when aggregated form a consistent pattern of resource allocation for the economy as a whole.

There is doubt regarding how these requirements can possibly be functionally met. Even if computer technology can be used to process and disseminate the enormous amount of information needed to make the system work, people do not necessarily provide the needed information in an unbiased manner. And even if all the needed information can be accurately compiled, the participatory planning requires each individual to dedicate so much time, interest, and energy in decision-making meetings that most people feel overwhelmed.

The second challenge to participatory socialism is the idea that the process of democratic decision-making is so complex and problematic that it should be limited to a small range of critical decision-making areas.

Advocates of participatory socialism place great emphasis on democracy both as a desirable goal in itself and as the best means to arrive at decisions that truly reflect people's interests. However, they tend to ignore the many problems involved in establishing fair and efficient democratic decision-making processes, such as: (1) the complex and critical nature of choice among alternative voting conventions: simple majority, supermajority, and consensus; (2) the distinction between constitutionally protected rights and democratic voting; and (3) the weighing of various people's votes according to the extent to which they are affected by a pending decision.

Advocates of participatory socialism favor political forms of economic decision-making on the grounds that people take into account the larger social context and the interdependence of their decisions. However, the politicization of all decisions leads to excessive conflict, strife, and anger, as well as to the formation of political groups that reduce the diversity of individual views and preferences to the lowest common-denominator platforms and programs. Advocates of participatory socialism favor direct participatory democracy over indirect representative democracy on the grounds that people listen to and confront each other as directly as possible in arriving at decisions. However, the practice of participatory democracy is so difficult, time-consuming, and emotionally draining that it has to be limited to a relatively small range of decisions.

Advocates of participatory socialism favor decentralized and negotiated planning on the grounds that it assures egalitarianism in economic decision-making. However, in practice, it is possible for some people to exercise much greater influence over decisions than others. Although such disproportionate influence may not arise from disproportionate wealth or income, it is possible for it to arise from disproportionate interest in and aptitude for the relevant decision-making processes. Different people have different abilities in accessing and processing information, in negotiating with others, and in influencing group decision-making. As a result, political and economic inequalities can arise in market-less as well as in market societies.

The third challenge to participatory socialism is the idea that it is not efficient to allocate labor without using the market-determined incentive system that rewards individuals according to the value of their work contributions.

Advocates of participatory socialism argue that their model is more efficient (and equitable) than the market system because, in their model, people are rewarded for their work according to their effort rather than results. Their model links the individual's consumption opportunities to the individual's input into the production process, that is, the amount of personal effort made or personal sacrifice endured. They favor their model over the market system, in which individuals' rewards for work are linked to the market-determined value of their output, which depends on variables—such as natural talent, job location, and the vagaries of market demand—over which individuals have little or no control.

Participatory socialism model leads to greater equity in the reward for labor than the market-based alternative. Advocates of participatory socialism argue that their model provides the most efficient incentive, as people are rewarded according to their personal input that best motivates people to apply the one factor that is under their control. However, their claim of greater efficiency is misguided because their personal-input reward system is flawed on two counts:

First, there is immense difficulty in observing and measuring an individual's sacrifice or work effort and determining how much of the work result is due to such personal input rather than to other aspects of the work. Even if quantitative indices of personal input are developed, they tend to encourage the substitution of quantity for quality of effort. Moreover, people tend to associate good performance with their personal input and bad performance with bad luck.

Second, even if there are no measurement problems, an incentive structure that rewards individuals according to their personal input is inefficient. Although it can lead to greater work effort and sacrifice on the part of individuals, it cannot assure that such effort and sacrifice are expended in a desirable way. The social good is best served by undertaking those activities whose results are highly valued relative to the cost of undertaking those activities. In order to motivate people to direct their efforts to the most socially desirable goods, it is therefore necessary to reward their activities based on the value of work output rather than based on the quantity of work input. If market valuations of output do not properly reflect social interest, then those output valuations need to be modified.

The fourth challenge to participatory socialism is the idea that a participatory economic system requires that people's basic consciousness to have already been transformed from one that is individually oriented to one that is socially oriented.

Advocates of market socialism assume that individuals behave as homo economicus, who seek to maximize their individual rewards. Advocates of market socialism seek to achieve socialist goals through structuring the market environment such that self-interested individuals make decisions that have socially desirable consequences. In contrast, advocates of participatory socialism are highly critical of market-oriented motivational schemes and seek to diminish the role of incentives which are based on an individual's material self-interest. There are some possible alternative incentives. On the positive motivational side, people can derive satisfaction from: (1) the enjoyable parts of their work, (2) the social confirmation that they receive for a job well done, (3) the confirmation that they well performed their responsibilities to others in the society, and/or (4) the enjoyment by others from activities to which they contributed. On the negative motivational side, people can be discouraged from antisocial behavior by: (5) the watchfulness and peer pressure of others and/or (6) the inability to hide excessively high consumption or excessively low production behavior in a society that is committed to egalitarianism.

In order for such mechanisms to become a working system of motivation that can replace the incentive system of an individual's material self-interest, there needs to be a wholesale conversion of human behavior patterns from "homo economicus" to what may be called "homo socialis." That is, a wholesale conversion of an individual's consciousness from individually oriented to socially oriented. One of the fundamental premises of Marxism is that the behavior of people is strongly influenced by their socio-economic environment, that is, people's values and behavior change as historical and socio-economic conditions change. Accordingly, in a participatory economic environment, people might develop solidaristic and cooperative attitudes that reinforce the workings of a participatory socialist system. However, what is not clear is the process whereby the needed institutions, values, and behavior emerge.

## Conclusion

This chapter briefly discussed nine major extant schools of thought in economics, namely: neo-classical economics, new institutional economics, behavioral economics, Austrian economics, post-Keynesian economics, institutional economics, social economics, radical economics, and Marxist economics. It noted that any explanation of an economic phenomenon is based on a worldview. It reiterated the premise of this book—that is, that any worldview can be associated with one of the four broad paradigms: functionalist, interpretive, radical humanist, and radical structuralist—and located each of the schools of thought on the map of the four paradigms, as in Figure 7.1. It emphasizes that these schools of thought in economics are equally scientific and informative; they look at economic phenomena from their certain paradigmatic viewpoint, and together they provide a more balanced understanding of the economic phenomenon under consideration.

Each paradigm is logically coherent—in terms of its underlying assumptions—and conceptualizes and studies the phenomenon in a certain way and generates distinctive kinds of insight and understanding. Therefore, different paradigms in combination provide a broader understanding of the phenomenon under consideration. An understanding of different paradigms leads to a better understanding of the multifaceted nature of the phenomenon.

## Notes

1 For this literature, see Ansperger and Varoufakis (2006); Arrow and Debreu (1954); Blaug (1980); Boland (1991); Brown (1981); Davis (1989); Davis, Marciano, and Runde (2004); Dowling and Chin-Fang (2007); Dugger (1979); Emmet (2010); Friedman (1953); Fulton (1984); Gee (1991); Hahn (1981); Heijdra and Lowenberg (1988); Hetzel (2007); Mirowski (1987); Reder (1982); Robbins (1937); Sherman, Hunt, Nesiba, O'Hara, and Wiens-Tuers (2008); Stilwell (2012); Tollison (1989); Van Horn and Mirowski (2009); Van Overtveldt (2007); Walsh and Gram (1980); Weintraub (1985a, 1985b, 2002); and Wolff and Resnick (2012). This section is based on Lavoie (1992) and Ricketts (1988).

2 For this literature, see Acemoglu (2003); Alchian and Demsetz (1972); Alston, Libecap, and Schneider (1996); Brousseau and Glachant (2008); Coase (1937, 1960, 1988, 1998); Coeurderoy and Quelin (1997); Crocker and Masten (1996); Davis and North (1971); Drobak and Nye (1997); Dugger (1990); Forbes and Lederman (2009, 2010); Furubotn and Richter (1991a, 1991b, 1998, 2008); Geyskens, Steenkamp, and Kumar (2006); Gibbons (2010); Groenewegen, Spithoven, and Van Den Berg (2010); Hodgson (1989); Hutchinson (1984); Joskow (1988, 2008); Klein (1999); Libecap and Smith (1999); Macher and Richman (2008); Medema (1998); Menard and Shirley (2005); North (1986, 1990, 1991, 1994); Ostrom (2005); Pratten (2004); Richter (2005); Rutherford (1994); Rutherford (2001); Shelanski and Klein (1995); Vannoni (2002); Vromen (1995);

and Williamson (1975, 1985a, 1985b, 1996, 2000, 2010). This section is based on Furubotn and Richter (1991a).

3 For this literature, see Altman and Morris, (2006); Ariely (2008); Baddeley (2013); Baker and Nofsinger (2010); Barberis and Thaler (2003); Bardsley et al. (2010); Binmore (2008); Bruni and Sugden (2007); Camerer (2003, 2006); Camerer, Loewenstein, and Rabin (2004); Cartwright (2011); Cassar and Friedman (2004); Conlisk (1996); Della Vigna (2009); Diamond and Vartiainen (2007); Dowling and Chin-Fang (2007); Earl (1988); Earl (1990); Forbes (2009); Frey and Benz (2004); Fudenberg (2006); Gilad and Kaish (1986); Kahneman and Tversky (1979); List (2004); Maital (2007); Mullainathan and Thaler (2000); Pesendorfer (2006); Pompian (2012); Rabin (1998); Ricciardi and Simon (2000); Roth (1995); Schmidt, Starmer, and Sugden (2008); Sent (2004); Shefrin (2002); Shiller (2003); Shiv and Fedorikhin (1999); Simon (1955, 1998); Thaler (2005, 2008a, 2008b); Tomer (2007); Tversky and Kahneman (1974, 1981); Van Raaij (1991); and Velupillai and Chen (2012). This section is based on Camerer and Loewenstein (2004).

4 For this literature, see Backhaus (2005); Barry (1991); Boettke (1989, 1994, 1996); Boettke and Prychitko (1994); Dolan (1976); Gloria-Palermo (1999); Grassl and Smith (1986); Hall and Martin (2011); Kirzner (1981, 1992, 2000); Koppl (2008); Koppl, Horwitz, and Desrochers (2010); Lachmann (1998); Lewis (2004); Littlechild (1990); Loasby (1991); Meijer (1995); Mises (1962); Rima (2013); Menger (1981); Mises (1966); Samuels (1989); Shand (1984, 1990); and Vaughn (1994). This section is based on Boettke (2010).

5 For this literature, see Arestis (1990, 1996); Arestis, Dunn, and Sawyer (1999); Arestis and Skouras (1985); Bohm (1989); Brown (1981); Crotty (1980); Davidson (1981); Dow (1988, 1990, 1991, 1996); Eichner (1979); Eichner and Kregel (1975); Hamouda and Harcourt (1988); Harcourt (1987, 2006); Hodgson (1989); Holt (2007); Holt and Pressman (2001, 2007); King (2003); Kregel (1975); Lavoie (1992a, 1992b); Lawson (1994, 1999); Lee (2002, 2009); Lee and Lavoie (2012); McKenna and Zannoni (1993); Palley (1996); Papadimitriou and Wray (2010); Pheby (1989); Rothem (1999); Sawyer (1988); Sawyer (1991); and Walters and Young (1997, 1999). This section is based on Arestis (1992).

6 For this literature, see Ayers (1951); Boettke (1989); Bowles (1998); Commons (1931, 1934, 1936); Dugger (1990); Dugger and Sherman (1994); Gruchy (1957, 1969, 1972, 1987); Hodgson (1988, 1989a, 1989b, 1998, 2000, 2002, 2003, 2004a, 2004b); Hodgson, Samuels, and Tool (1994); Hutchinson (1984); Kapp (1968, 1976, 2011); Lawson (2005); Miller (1978); Milonakis and Fine (2008); Mirowski (1987); Myrdal (1978); Nelson and Sampat (2001); O'Hara (2007); Peterson (1987); Rima (2013); Rutherford (1994); Rutherford (2001); Sackrey, Schneider, and Knoedler (2008); Samuels (1988, 1989); Schlicht (1998); Stanfield (1999);

Stilwell (2012); Tool (1981, 1988a, 1988b); Tool and Bush (2003); Wilber and Harrison (1978); Whalen (1996); and Witte (1954). This section is based on Miller (1978).

7 For this literature, see Boulding (1969); Cedrini and Marchionatti (2017); Clary (2008); Crespo (2013); Danner (2002); Davis (2003, 2006, 2008, 2009, 2015, 2019, 2022); Davis and Dolfsma (2015); Davis and McMaster (2017); DeMartino (1999, 2019); Dolfsma et al. (2016); Dow (1997); Dugger and Peach (2009); Dugger and Waller (1996); Ekins and Max-Neef (1992); Elliott (1979); Elliott and Davis (1989); Figart (2007); Finn (2006); Granovetter (1985); Henderson (1993); Lutz (1990, 1999); Lutz and Lux (1988); Mueller (1977); Mulcahy (1952); Myrdal (1958); Nitsch (1987, 1990); Nussbaum (2000); O'Boyle (1998, 2005); Peach and Dugger (2006); Polanyi (1944); Putnam (2002); Putnam and Garrett (2020); Roth (2007); Rutherford (2011); Sandel (2012); Sen (1987, 2005); Shower (1974); Stanfield (1989); van Staveren (2001); Waters (1979, 1984, 1990, 1993); and White (2011, 2018). This section is based on Davis (2022).

8 For this literature, see Albert et al. (1986); Amariglio et al. (1996); Amariglio, Resnik, and Wolff (1993); Amariglio and Ruccio (1994); Arestis and Sawyer (1994); Baiman, Boushey, and Saunders (2000); Bowles and Edwards (1990); Cullenberg (1994); Dugger and Sherman (1994); Edwards and MacEwan (1970); Hahnel (2002); Kotz, McDonough, and Reich (1994); Lippit (1996); Milberg (1991); Nell (1981); O'Connor (1984); O'Connor (1994); Palermo (2007); Panitch and Leys (1999); Prychitko (1998); Resnick and Wolff (1987); Roberts and Feiner (1992); Sawyer (1989); Scott (1991); Sherman (1987); Ward (1977); and Wolff and Resnick (2012). This section is based on Wiesskopf (1992).

9 For this literature, see Amin (1974, 1988), Baran and Sweezy (1966), Brewer (2001), Desai (1979), Fine (1980), Foster and McChesney (2004), Howard and King (1975, 1992), King (1990), Kotz (1991), Mandel (1968), McLellan (2000), Mermelstein (1970), Panitch and Leys (1999), Scott (1991), Singer (1999), Stilwell (2012), Sweezy (1942), Sweezy and Magdoff (1972), Wallerstein (1974), and Warren (1980). This section is based on Wiesskopf (1992).

## References

Acemoglu, D. (2003), "Root Causes: A Historical Approach to Assessing the Role of Institutions in Economic Development," *Finance and Development*, 40:2, 27–30.

Albert, Michael, Cagan, Leslie, Chomsky, Noam, Hahnel, Robin, King, Mel, Sargent, Lydia, and Sklar, Holly (1986), *Liberating Theory*, New York, NY: South End Press.

Alchian, Armen and Demsetz, H. (1972), "Production, Information Costs, and Economic Organization," *American Economic Review*, 62, December, 777–95.

Alston, L.J., Libecap, G.D., and Schneider, R. (1996), "The Determinants and Impact of Property Rights: Land Titles on the Brazilian Frontier," *Journal of Law, Economics and Organization*, 12, 25–61.

Altman, Morris (2006), *Handbook of Contemporary Behavioral Economics: Foundations and Developments*, Armonk, NY: M.E. Sharpe.

Amariglio, Jack, Callari, Antonio, Resnick, Stephen, Ruccio, David, and Wolff, Richard D. (1996), "Nondeterminist Marxism: The Birth of a Postmodern Tradition in Economics," in Foldvary, Fred E. (ed.), *Beyond Neoclassical Economics: Heterodox Approaches to Economic Theory*, Cheltenham: Edward Elgar, Chapter 8, pp. 134–47.

Amariglio, Jack, Resnik, Stephen, and Wolff, Richard D. (1993), "Division and Difference in the 'Discipline' of Economics," *Critical Inquiry*, 17, Autumn, 108–37. Reprinted in Messer-Davidow, E, Shumway, D.R., and Sylvan, D.J., eds. (1994), *Knowledges: Historical and Critical Studies in Disciplinarity*, Charlottsville, VA: University of Virginia Press, pp. 150–84.

Amariglio, Jack and Ruccio, David F. (1994), "Postmodernism, Marxism, and the Critique of Modern Economic Thought," *Rethinking Marxism*, 7:3, Fall, 7–35.

Amin, Samir (1974), *Accumulation on a World Scale: A Critique of the Theory of Underdevelopment*, New York, NY: Monthly Review Press.

Amin, Samir (1988), "Accumulation on a World Scale: Thirty Years Later," *Rethinking Marxism*, 1:2, Summer, 54–75.

Ansperger, Christian and Varoufakis, Yanis (2006), "What is Neoclassical Economics," *Post-Autistic Review*, 38:1, July, 2–13.

Arestis, Philip (1990), "Post-Keynesianism: A New Approach to Economics," *Review of Social Economy*, 48:3, Fall, 222–46.

Arestis, Philip (1992), *The Post-Keynesian Approach to Economics: An Alternative Analysis of Economic Theory and Policy*, Aldershot: Edward Elgar Publishing Company.

Arestis, Philip (1996), "Post-Keynesian Economics: Towards Coherence," *Cambridge Journal of Economics*, 20, 111–35.

Arestis, Philip, Dunn, Stephen P., and Sawyer, Malcolm (1999), "Post Keynesian Economics and Its Critics," *Journal of Post Keynesian Economics*, 21:4, Summer, 527–49.

Arestis, Philip and Sawyer, Malcolm, eds. (1994), *The Elgar Companion to Radical Political Economy*, Aldershot, Hants: Edward Elgar Publishing Company.

Arestis, Philip and Skouras, Thanos, eds. (1985), *Post Keynesian Economic Theory: A Challenge to Neo-Classical Economics*, Brighton: Wheatsheaf Books Ltd.

Ariely, D. (2008), *Predictably Irrational: The Hidden Forces that Shape Our Decisions*, New York, NY: Harper Collins.

Arrow, K.J. and Debreu, G. (1954), "Existence of an Equilibrium for a Competitive Economy," *Econometrica*, 22:3, 265–90.

Ayers, Clarence E. (1951), "The Co-Ordinates of Institutionalism," *American Economic Review*, 41, May, 47–55.

Backhaus, Jurgen G., ed. (2005), *Modern Applications of Austrian Thought*, New York, NY: Routledge.

Baddeley, Michelle (2013), *Behavioral Economics and Finance*, New York, NY: Routledge.

Baiman, Ron, Boushey, Heather, and Saunders, Dawn, eds. (2000), *Political Economy and Contemporary Capitalism: Radical Perspectives on Economic Theory and Policy*, Armonk, NY: M.E. Sharpe.

Baker, H. Kent and Nofsinger, John R., eds. (2010), *Behavioral Finance: Investors, Corporations, and Markets*, Hoboken, NJ: Wiley.

Baran, Paul and Sweezy, Paul (1966), *Monopoly Capital*, London: Penguin Books.

Barberis, Nicholas and Thaler, Richard (2003), "A Survey of Behavioral Finance," in Constantinides, G.M., Harris, M., and Stulz, R. (eds.), *Handbook of the Economics of Finance*, The Netherlands: Elsevier Science B.V, 1053–123.

Bardsley, N., Cubitt, R., Loomes, G., Moffat, P., Starmer, C., and Sugden, R. (2010), *Experimental Economics: Rethinking the Rules*, Princeton, NJ: Princeton University Press.

Barry, Norman P. (1991), "Austrian Economics: A Dissent from Orthodoxy," in Greenaway, David, Bleaney, Michael, and Stewart, Ian (eds.), *Companion to Contemporary Economic Thought*, London: Routledge, Chapter 5, pp. 68–87.

Binmore, Ken (2008), "Review of Behavioral Economics and Its Applications," *Economic Journal*, 118:529, June, 248–51.

Blaug, Mark (1980), "Economic Methodology in One Easy Lesson," *British Review of Economic Issues*, 2:5, 1–16.

Boettke, Peter J. (1989), "Evolution and Economics: Austrian as Institutionalists," *Research in the History of Thought and Methodology*, 6, 73–91.

Boettke, Peter J., ed. (1994), *The Elgar Companion to Austrian Economics*, Cheltenham: Edward Elgar Publishing Limited.

Boettke, Peter J. (1996), "What Is Wrong with Neoclassical Economics (and What Is Still Wrong with Austrian Economics)?," in Foldvary, Fred E. (ed.), *Beyond Neoclassical Economics: Heterodox Approaches to Economic Theory*, Cheltenham: Edward Elgar, Chapter 2, pp. 22–40.

Boettke, Peter J. (2010), *Handbook on Contemporary Austrian Economics*, Northampton, MA: Edward Elgar.

Boettke, Peter J. and Prychitko, David L., eds. (1994), *The Market Process: Essays in Contemporary Austrian Economics*, Brookfield, Vermont: Edward Elgar Publishing Company.

Bohm, Stephan (1989), "Subjectivism and Post-Keynesianism: Towards a Better Understanding," in Pheby, John (ed.), *New Directions in Post-Keynesian Economics*, Aldershot, Hants: Edward Elgar Publishing Limited, Chapter 4, pp. 59–93.

Boland, Lawrence A. (1991), "Current Views on Economic Positivism," in Greenaway, David, Bleaney, Michael, and Stewart, Ian (eds.), *Companion to Contemporary Economic Thought*, London: Routledge, Chapter 6, pp. 88–104.

Boulding, Kenneth (1969), "Economics as a Moral Science," *American Economic Review*, 59:1, 1–12.

Bowles, Samuel (1998), "Endogenous Preferences: The Cultural Consequences of Markets and other Economic Institutions," *Journal of Economic Literature*, 36:1, March, 75–111.

Bowles, Samuel and Edwards, Richard, eds. (1990), *Radical Political Economy, Volumes I and II*, Aldershot, Hants: Edward Elgar Publishing Limited.

Brewer, Anthony (2001), *Marxist Theories of Imperialism: A Critical Survey*, London: Routledge and Kegan Paul.

Brousseau, Eric and Glachant, Jean-Michel, eds. (2008), *New Institutional Economics: A Guidebook*, Cambridge: Cambridge University Press.

Brown, Elba K. (1981), "The Neoclassical and Post-Keynesian Research Programs: The Methodological Issues," *Review of Social Economy*, 39:2, October, 111–32.

Bruni, L. and Sugden, R. (2007), "The Road Not Taken: How Psychology Was Removed from Economics, and How It Might Be Brought Back," *Economic Journal*, 117, 146–73.

Camerer, Colin F. (2003), *Behavioral Game Theory: Experiments in Strategic Interaction*, Princeton, NJ: Princeton University Press.

Camerer, Colin F. (2006), "Behavioral Economics," in Blundell, Richard, Newey, Whitney K., and Persson, Rorsten (eds.), *Advances in Economics and Econometrics: Theory and Applications, Ninth World Congress, Volume II*, Cambridge: Cambridge University Press, pp. 181–214.

Camerer, Colin F., Loewenstein, George, and Rabin, Matthew, eds. (2004), *Advances in Bahavioral Economics*, Princeton, NJ: Princeton University Press.

Cartwright, Edward (2011), *Behavioral Economics*, New York, NY: Routledge.

Cassar, A. and Friedman, D. (2004), *Economics Lab: An Introduction to Experimental Economics*, London: Routledge.

Cedrini, Mario and Marchionatti, Roberto (2017), "Theoretical and Practical Relevance of the Concept of the Gift to the Development of a Non-Imperialist Economics," *Review of Radical Political Economics*, 49:4, 633–49.

Clary, Betsy Jane (2008), "The Evolution of the Allied Social Science Associations," *American Journal of Economics and Sociology*, 67:5, 985–1005.

Coase, Ronald H. (1937), "The Nature of the Firm," *Economica*, 386–405. Reprinted in Coase, Ronald H. (1988), *The Firm, the Market and the Law*, Chicago, IL: University of Chicago Press, pp. 55–75.

Coase, Ronald H. (1960), "The Problem of Social Cost," *Journal of Law and Economics*, 3:1, 1–44.

Coase, Ronald H. (1988), *The Firm, the Market, and the Law*, Chicago, IL: University of Chicago Press.

Coase, Ronald H. (1998), "The New Institutional Economics," *American Economic Review Papers and Proceedings*, 88:2, May, 72–4.

Coeurderoy, R. and Quelin, B. (1997), "Transaction Cost Theory: A Survey of Empirical Studies on Vertical Integration," *Review of Economic Policy*, 107:2, 145–81.

Commons, John R. (1931), "Institutional Economics," *American Economic Review*, 21:4, December, 648–57.

Commons, John R. (1934), *Institutional Economics*, London: Macmillan.

Commons, John R. (1936), "Institutional Economics," *American Economic Review*, 26:1, March, 237–49.

Conlisk, J. (1996) "Why Bounded Rationality," *Journal of Economic Literature*, 34, 669–700.

Crespo, Ricardo (2013), *Philosophy of the Economy: An Aristotelian Approach*, Cham: Springer.

Crocker, K.J. and Masten, S.E. (1996), "Regulation and Administered Contracts Revisited: Lesson from Transaction-Cost Economics for Public Utility Regulation," *Journal of Regulation Economics*, 9, 5–40.

Crotty, James R. (1980), "Post-Keynesian Economic Theory: An Overview and Evaluation," *American Economic Review*, 70:2, May, 20–5.

Cullenberg, Stephen (1994), *The Falling Rate of Profit: Recasting the Marxian Debate*, Boulder, CO: Pluto Press.

Danner, Peter (2002), *The Economic Person: Acting and Analyzing*, Lanham, MD: Rowman and Littlefield.

Davidson, Paul (1981), "Post Keynesian Economics: Solving the Crisis in Economic Theory," in Bell, Daniel and Kristol, Irving (eds.), *The Crisis in Economic Theory*, New York, New York: Basic Books, Inc., Chapter 10, pp. 151–73.

Davis, John B. (1989), "Axiomatic General Equilibrium Theory and Referentiality," *Journal of Post Keynesian Economics*, 11:3, Spring, 424–38.

Davis, John B. (2003), *The Theory of the Individual in Economics*, London: Routledge.

Davis, John B. (2006), "The Turn in Economics: Neoclassical Dominance to Mainstream Pluralism?" *Journal of Institutional Economics*, 2:1, 1–20.

Davis, John B. (2008), "The Turn in Recent Economics and Return of Orthodoxy," *Cambridge Journal of Economics*, 32:3, 349–66.

Davis, John B. (2009), *Global Social Economy: Development, Work and Policy*, London: Routledge.

Davis, John B. (2015), "Economists' Odd Stand on the Positive-Normative Distinction: A Behavioral Economics View," in DeMartino, G. and McCloskey, D. (eds.),

*Oxford University Press Handbook on Professional Economic Ethics: Views from the Economics Profession and Beyond*, Oxford: Oxford University Press, pp. 200–15.
Davis, John B. (2019), "Ethics and Economics: A Complex Systems Approach," in White, Mark (ed.), *Oxford Handbook on Ethics and Economics*, Oxford: Oxford University Press: pp. 208–28.
Davis, John B (2022), "Social Economics," in Stilwell, Frank, Primrose, David, and Thornton, Tim B. (eds.), *Elgar Handbook of Alternative Theories of Political Economy*, Cheltenham: Edward Elgar, Chapter 20, pp. 286–300.
Davis, John B. and Dolfsma, Wilfred, eds. (2015), *The Elgar Companion to Social Economics*, Second Edition, Cheltenham: Edward Elgar Publishing.
Davis, John B., Marciano, Alain, and Runde, Jochen, eds. (2004), *The Elgar Companion to Economics and Philosophy*, Cheltenham: Edward Elgar.
Davis, John B. and McMaster, Rober, (2017), *Health Care Economics*, London: Routledge.
Davis, Lance E. and North, Douglass C. (1971), *Institutional Change and American Economic Growth*, New York, NY: Cambridge University Press.
Della Vigna, Stefano (2009), "Psychology and Economics: Evidence from the Field," *Journal of Economic Literature*, 47:2, 315–72.
DeMartino, George (1999), *Global Economy, Global Justice: Theoretical Objections and Policy Alternatives to Neoliberalism*, London: Routledge.
DeMartino, George (2019), "Econogenic Harm and the Case for 'Economy Harm Profile' Analysis," *New Political Economy*, 24:6, 798–815.
Desai, Meghnad (1979), *Marxian Economics*, Oxford: Basil Blackwell.
Diamond, Peter and Vartiainen, Hannu (2007), *Behavioral Economics and Its Applications*, Princeton, NJ: Princeton University Press.
Dolan, Edwin G., ed. (1976), *The Foundations of Modern Austrian Economics*, Kansas City: Sheed and Ward, Inc.
Dolfsma, Wilfred, Figart, Deborah, McMaster, Robert, Mutari, Ellen, and White, Mark, eds. (2016), *Social Economics*, Critical Concepts in Economics Series, London: Routledge.
Dow, Sheila C. (1988), "Post Keynesian Economics: Conceptual Underpinnings," *British Review of Economic Issues*, 10:23, Autumn, 1–18.
Dow, Sheila C. (1990), "Post Keynesianism as Political Economy: A Methodological Discussion," *Review of Political Economy*, 2:3, 345–58.
Dow, Sheila C. (1991), "The Post-Keynesian School," in Mair, Douglas and Miller, Anne G. (eds.), *A Modern Guide to Economic Thought: An Introduction to Comparative Schools of Thought in Economics*, Aldershot, Hants: Edward Elgar, Chapter 7, pp. 176–206.
Dow, Sheila C. (1996), *The Methodology of Macroeconomics Thought: A Conceptual Analysis of Schools of Thought in Economics*, Cheltenham: Edward Elgar.

Dow, Sheila C. (1997), "Methodological Pluralism and Pluralism of Method," in Salanti, Andrea and Screpanti, Ernesto (eds.), *Pluralism in Economics: Theory, History and Methodology*, Cheltenham: Edward Elgar, pp. 89–99.

Dowling, John Malcolm and Chin-Fang, Yap (2007), *Modern Developments in Behavioral Economics: Social Science Perspectives on Choice and Decision Making*, London: World Scientific Publishing Co. Pte. Ltd.

Drobak, John N. and Nye, John V.C. (eds.), (1997), *The Frontiers of the New Institutional Economics*, New York, NY: Academic Press.

Dugger, William M. (1979), "Methodological Differences Between Institutional and Neoclassical Economics," *Journal of Economic Issues*, 13:4, December, 899–909. Reprinted in Samuels, Warren J., ed. (1988), *Institutional Economics, Volumes I, II, and III*, Aldershot, Hants: Edward Elgar, Chapter 5, pp. 84–94.

Dugger, William M. (1990), "The New Institutionalism: New But Not Institutionalist," *Journal of Economic Issues*, 24:2, June, 423–31.

Dugger, William M. and Peach, James (2009), *Economic Abundance: An Introduction*, London: Routledge.

Dugger, William M. and Sherman, Howard J. (1994), "Comparisons of Marxism and Institutionalism," *Journal of Economic Issues*, 28:1, March, 101–27. Reprinted in Prychitko, David L., ed. (1998), *Why Economists Disagree: An Introduction to the Alternative Schools of Thought*, Albany, New York: State University of New York Press, Chapter 9, pp. 211–36.

Dugger, William M. and Waller, William (1996), "Radical Institutionalism: From Technological to Democratic Instrumentalism," *Review of Social Economy*, 54:2, 169–90.

Earl, Peter E., ed. (1988), *Behavioral Economics, Vols I and II*, Aldershot: Edward Elgar Publishing Limited.

Earl, Peter E. (1990), "Economics and Psychology: A Survey," *Economic Journal*, 100, 718–55.

Edwards, Richard and MacEwan, Arthur (1970), "A Radical Approach to Economics: Basis for a New Curriculum," *American Economic Review*, 60:2, May, 352–63.

Eichner, Alfred S. ed. (1979), *A Guide to Post-Keynesian Economics*, While Plains, NY: M.E. Sharpe, Inc.

Eichner, Alfred S. and Kregel, J.A. (1975), "An Essay on Post-Keynesian Theory: A New Paradigm in Economics," *Journal of Economic Literature*, 13:4, December, 1293–314. Reprinted in Prychitko, David L., ed. (1998), *Why Economists Disagree: An Introduction to the Alternative Schools of Thought*, Albany, NY: State University of New York Press, Chapter 5, pp. 83–114.

Ekins, Paul and Max-Neef, Manfred, eds. (1992), *Real-Life Economics: Understanding Wealth Creation*, London: Routledge.

Elliott, John E. (1979), "Social and Institutional Dimensions of Marx's Theory of Capitalism," *Review of Social Economy*, 37:3, 261–74.

Elliott, John E. and Davis, John, eds. (1989), "Issues in Contemporary Marxism," *Review of Social Economy*, 47:4, 338–436.

Emmet, Ross B., ed. (2010), *The Elgar Companion to the Chicago School of Economics*, Cheltenham: Edward Elgar.

Figart, Deborah (2007), "Social Responsibility for Living Standards," *Review of Social Economy*, 65:4, 391–405.

Fine, Ben(1980), *Economic Theory and Ideology*, London: Edward Arnold Publishers Ltd.

Finn, Daniel (2006), *The Moral Ecology of Markets: Assessing Claims about Markets and Justice*, Cambridge: Cambridge University Press.

Forbes, Silke Januszewski and Lederman, Mara (2009), "Adaptation and Vertical Integration in the Airline Industry," *American Economic Review*, 99:5, 1831–49.

Forbes, Silke Januszewski and Lederman, Mara (2010), "Does Vertical Integration Affect Firm Performance? Evidence from the Airline Industry," *Rand Journal of Economics*, 41:4, 765–90.

Forbes, W. (2009), *Behavioral Finance*, Chichester: John Wiley.

Foster, John Bellamy and McChesney, Robert W. (2004), *Pox Americana: Exposing the American Empire*, New York, NY: Monthly Review Press.

Frey, Bruno S. and Benz, Matthias (2004), "From Imperialism to Inspiration: A Survey of Economics and Psychology," in Davis, John B., Marciano, Alain, and Runde, Jochen (eds.), *The Elgar Companion to Economics and Philosophy*, Cheltenham: Edward Elgar, Chapter 4, pp. 61–83.

Friedman, Milton (1953), *Essays in Positive Economics*, Chicago, IL: University of Chicago Press.

Fudenberg, Drew (2006), "Advancing Beyond Advances in Behavioral Economics," *Journal of Economic Literature*, 44:3, September, 694–711.

Fulton, G. (1984), "Research Programs in Economics," *History of Political Economy*, 16:2, Summer, 187–205.

Furubotn, Eirik G. and Richter, Rudolf (1991a), "The New Institutional Economics: An Assessment," in Furubotn, Eirik G. and Richter, Rudolf (eds.), *The New Institutional Economics: A Collection of Articles from the Journal of Institutional and Theoretical Economics*, College Station, Texas: Texas A&M University Press, pp. 1–32.

Furubotn, Eirik G. and Richter, Rudolf, eds. (1991b), *The New Institutional Economics: A Collection of Articles from the Journal of Institutional and Theoretical Economics*, College Station, TX: Texas A&M University Press.

Furubotn, Eirik G. and Richter, Rudolf (1998), *Institutions and Economic Theory: The Contribution of the New Institutional Economics*, Second Edition, Ann Arbor, MI: University of Michigan Press.

Furubotn, Eirik G. and Richter, Rudolf (2008), "The New Institutional Economics: A Different Approach to Economic Analysis," *Economic Affairs*, 28:3, September, 15–23.

Gee, J.M. Alec (1991), "The Neoclassical School," in Mair, Douglas and Miller, Anne G. (eds.), *A Modern Guide to Economic Thought: An Introduction to Comparative Schools of Thought in Economics*, Aldershot, Hants: Edward Elgar, Chapter 4, pp. 71–108.

Geyskens, Inge, Steenkamp, Jan-Benedict E.M., and Kumar, Nirmalya (2006), "Make, Buy, or Ally: A Meta-Analysis of Transaction Cost Theory," *Academy of Management Journal*, 49:3, 519–43.

Gibbons, Robert S. (2010), "Transaction-Cost Economics: Past, Present, and Future?" *Scandinavian Journal of Economics*, 112:2, June, 263–88.

Gilad, Benjamin and Kaish, Stanley, eds. (1986), *Handbook of Behavioral Economics, Volumes A and B*, Greenwich, CT: JAI Press Inc.

Gloria-Palermo, Sandye (1999), *The Evolution of Austrian Economics: From Menger to Lachmann*, New York, NY: Routledge.

Granovetter, Mark (1985), "Economic Action and Social Structure: The Problem of Embeddedness," *American Journal of Sociology*, 91:3, 481–510.

Grassl, Wolfgang and Smith, Barry, eds. (1986), *Austrian Economics: Historical and Philosophical Background*, New York, NY: New York University Press.

Groenewegen, John, Spithoven, Antoon, and Van Den Berg, Annette (2010), *Institutional Economics: An Introduction*, New York, NY: Palgrave Macmillan.

Gruchy, Allan Garfield (1957), "Institutional Economics, A New Look at Institutionalism: Discussion," *American Economic Review, Supplement*, 47:2, May, 13–27.

Gruchy, Allan Garfield (1969), "Neoinstitutionalism and the Economics of Dissent," *Journal of Economic Issues*, 3, March, 3–17.

Gruchy, Allan Garfield (1972), *Contemporary Economic Thought: The Contribution of Neo-Institutional Economics*, Clifton, NJ: Augustus Kelley Publishers.

Gruchy, Allan Garfield (1987), *The Reconstruction of Economics: An Analysis of the Fundamentals of Institutional Economics*, Westport, CT: Greenwood Press.

Hahn, Frank (1981), "General Equilibrium Theory," in Bell, Daniel and Kristol, Irving (eds.), *The Crisis in Economic Theory*, New York, NY: Basic Books, Inc., Chapter 8, pp. 123–38.

Hahnel, Robin (2002), *The ABCs of Political Economy: A Modern Approach*, London: Pluto Press.

Hall, Joshua C. and Martin, Adam (2011), "Austrian Economics: Methodology, Concepts, and Implications for Economic Education," *Journal of Economics and Finance Education*, Special Issue on Austrian Economics, 10:2, Fall, pp. 1–15.

Hamouda, O.F. and Harcourt, G.C. (1988), "Post Keynesianism: From Criticism to Coherence?" *Bulletin of Economic Research*, 40:1, January, 1–33. Reprinted in Pheby, J., ed. (1989), *New Directions in Post-Keynesian Economics*, Aldershot, Hants: Edward Elgar Publishing Limited, pp. 1–34.

Harcourt, G.C. (1987), "Post-Keynesian Economics," in Eatwell, John, Milgate, Murray, and Newman, Peter (eds.), *The New Palgrave: A Dictionary of Economics, Volume 3*, London: Macmillan, pp. 924–28.

Harcourt, G.C. (2006), *The Structure of Post-Keynesian Economics: The Core Contributions of the Pioneers*, Cambridge: Cambridge University Press.

Heijdra, Ben J. and Lowenberg, Anthon D. (1988), "The Neoclassical Economic Research Program: Some Lakatosian and other Considerations," *Australian Economic Papers*, December, 27:1, December, 272–84.

Henderson, James, ed. (1993), "Challenges Facing Social Economists in the Twenty-First Century," *Review of Social Economy*, 51:4, 412–525.

Hetzel, Robert L. (2007), "The Contributions of Milton Friedman to Economics," *Economic Quarterly*, 93:1, Winter, 1–30.

Hodgson, Geoffrey Martin (1988), *Economics and Institutions: A Manifesto for a Modern Institutional Economics*, Philadelphia, PA: University of Pennsylvania Press.

Hodgson, Geoffrey Martin (1989a), "Institutional Economic Theory: The Old versus the New," *Review of Political Economy*, 1:3, November, 249–70. Reprinted in Prychitko, David L., ed. (1998), *Why Economists Disagree: An Introduction to the Alternative Schools of Thought*, Albany, NY: State University of New York Press, Chapter 7, pp. 155–78.

Hodgson, Geoffrey Martin (1989b), "Post-Keynesianism and Institutionalism: The Missing Link," in Pheby, John, ed. *New Directions in Post-Keynesian Economics*, Aldershot, Hants: Edward Elgar Publishing Limited, Chapter 5, pp. 94–123.

Hodgson, Geoffrey Martin (1998), "The Approach of Institutional Economics," *Journal of Economic Literature*, 36:1, March, 166–92.

Hodgson, Geoffrey Martin (2000), "What Is the Essence of Institutional Economics," *Journal of Economic Issues*, 34:2, June, 317–29.

Hodgson, Geoffrey Martin, ed. (2002), *A Modern Reader in Institutional and Evolutionary Economics: Key Concepts*, Cheltenham: Edward Elgar.

Hodgson, Geoffrey Martin, ed. (2003), *Recent Developments in Institutional Economics*, Cheltenham: Edward Elgar.

Hodgson, Geoffrey Martin (2004a), *The Evolution of Institutional Economics: Agency, Structure and Darwinism in American Institutionalism*, London: Routledge.

Hodgson, Geoffrey Martin (2004b), "Institutional Economics: From Menger and Veblen to Coase and North," in Davis, John B., Marciano, Alain, and Runde, Jochen (eds.), *The Elgar Companion to Economics and Philosophy*, Cheltenham: Edward Elgar, Chapter 5, pp. 84–101.

Hodgson, Geoffrey Martin, Samuels, Warren J., and Tool, Marc R., eds. (1994), *The Elgar Companion to Institutional and Evolutionary Economics*, Aldershot: Edward Elgar.

Holt, Richard P.F. (2007), "What is Post Keynesian Economics," in Forstater, Mathew, Mongiovi, Gary, and Pressman, Steven (eds.), *Post-Keynesian Macroeconomics: Essays in Honor of Ingrid Rima*, London: Routledge, Chapter 6, pp. 89–107.

Holt, Richard P.F. and Pressman, Steven, eds. (2001), *A New Guide to Post Keynesian Economics*, London: Routledge.

Holt, Richard P.F. and Pressman, Steven, eds. (2007), *Empirical Post Keynesian Economics: Looking at the Real World*, Armonk, NY: M.E. Sharpe.

Howard, M.C. and King, J.E. (1975), *The Political Economy of Marx*, Harlow, Essex: Longman Group Limited.

Howard, M.C. and King, J.E. (1992), *A History of Marxian Economics*, Princeton, NJ: Princeton University Press.

Hutchinson, Terence W. (1984), "Institutional Economics Old and New," *Journal of Institutional and Theoretical Economics*, 140, 20–9. Reprinted in Furubotn, Eirik G. and Richter, Rudolf, eds. (1991), *The New Institutional Economics: A Collection of Articles from the Journal of Institutional and Theoretical Economics*, College Station, Texas: Texas A&M University Press, pp. 35–44.

Joskow, Paul L. (1988), "Asset Specifity and the Structure of Vertical Relationships: Empirical Evidence," *Journal of Law, Economics and Organization*, 4, 95–117.

Joskow, Paul L. (2008), "Introduction to New Institutional Economics: A Report Card," in Brousseau, Eric and Glachant, Jean-Michel (eds.), *New Institutional Economics: A Guidebook*, Cambridge: Cambridge University Press, pp. 1–19.

Kahneman, Daniel and Tversky, Amos (1979), "Prospect Theory: An Analysis of Decision under Risk," *Econometrica*, 47:2, March, 263–91.

Kapp, K. William (1968), "In Defense of Institutional Economics," *Swedish Journal of Economics*, 70, March, 1–18.

Kapp, K. William (1976), "The Nature and Significance of Institutional Economics," *Kyklos*, 29:2, June, 209–32.

Kapp, Karl William (2011), *The Foundations of Institutional Economics*, New York, NY: Routledge.

King, John E., ed. (1990), *Marxian Economics, Volumes I, II, and III*, Hants: Edward Elgar Publishing Limited.

King, John E., ed. (2003), *The Elgar Companion to Post Keynesian Economics*, Cheltenham: Edward Elgar.

Kirzner, Israel M. (1981), "The 'Austrian' Perspective," in Bell, Daniel and Kristol, Irving (eds.), *The Crisis in Economic Theory*, New York, NY: Basic Books, Inc., Publishers, Chapter 7, pp. 111–22.

Kirzner, Israel M. (1992), *The Meaning of Market Process: Essays in the Development of Modern Austrian Economics*, New York, NY: Routledge.

Kirzner, Israel M. (2000), *Driving Force of the Market: Essays in Austrian Economics*, New York, NY: Routledge.

Klein, P. (1999), "New Institutional Economics," in Bouckaert, B. and De Geest, G. (eds.), *Encyclopedia of Law and Economics, Volume 1*, Cheltenham: Edward Elgar, pp. 456–89.

Koppl, Roger, ed. (2008), *Explorations in Austrian Economics*, Bingley: JAI Press.

Koppl, Roger, Horwitz, Steven, and Desrochers, Pierre, eds. (2010), *Advances in Austrian Economics: What Is So Austrian about Austrian Economics?*, Bingley: Emerald.

Kotz, David M. (1991), "Accumulation, Money, and Credit in the Circuit of Capital," *Rethinking Marxism*, 4:2, 119–33.

Kotz, David M., McDonough, Terrence, and Reich, Michael, eds. (1994), *Social Structures of Accumulation: The Political Economy of Growth and Crisis*, Cambridge: Cambridge University Press.

Kregel, J.A. (1975), *The Reconstruction of Political Economy: An Introduction to Post-Keynesian Economics*, London: Macmillan.

Lachmann, Ludwig M. (1998), "From Mises to Shackle: An Essay on Austrian Economics and the Kaleidic Society," in Prychitko, David L. (ed.), *Why Economists Disagree: An Introduction to the Alternative Schools of Thought*, Albany, NY: State University of New York Press, Chapter 3, pp. 53–66.

Lavoie, Marc (1992a), *Foundations of Post-Keynesian Economic Analysis*, Cheltenham: Edward Elgar.

Lavoie, Marc (1992b), "Toward a New Research Program for Post-Keynesianism and Neo-Ricardianism," *Review of Political Economy*, 4:1, January, 37–78.

Lawson, Tony (1994), "The Nature of Post Keynesianism and Its Links to other Traditions: A Realist Perspective," *Journal of Post Keynesian Economics*, 16:4, summer, 503–38. Reprinted in Prychitko, David L., ed. (1998), *Why Economists Disagree: An Introduction to the Contemporary Schools of Thought*, New York, NY: State University of New York Press, Chapter 6, pp. 115–54.

Lawson, Tony (1999), "Connections and Distinctions: Post Keynesianism and Critical Realism," *Journal of Post Keynesian Economics*, 22:1, Fall, 3–14.

Lawson, Tony (2005), "The Nature of Institutional Economics," *Evolutionary and Institutional Economics Review*, 2:1, 7–20.

Lee, Frederic S. (2002), "Theory Foundation and Methodological Foundations of Post Keynesian Economics," *Cambridge Journal of Economics*, 26:4, 789–804, reprinted *in* Downward, Paul, ed. (2003), *Applied Economics and the Critical Realist Critique*, New York, NY: Routledge, pp. 170–93.

Lee, Frederic S. (2009), "The History of Post Keynesian Economics in America, 1971–95," in Lee, Frederic S. *A History of Heterodox Economics: Challenging the Mainstream in the Twentieth Century*, New York, NY: Routledge, Chapter 5, pp. 78–96.

Lee, Frederic S. and Lavoie, Marc (2012), *In Defense of Post-Keynesian and Heterodox Economics: Responses to Their Critics*, New York, NY: Routledge.

Lewis, Paul A. (2004), "Structure and Agency in Economic Analysis: The Case of Austrian Economics and the Material Embeddedness of Socio-Economic Life," in Davis, John B. and List, John (2004), "Neoclassical Theory versus Prospect Theory: Evidence from the Marketplace," *Econometrica*, 72:2, 615–25.

Libecap, G.D. and Smith, J.L. (1999), "The Self-Enforcing Provisions of Oil and Gas Unit Operating Agreements: Theory and Evidence," *Journal of Law, Economics and Organization*, 15:2, 526–48.

Lippit, Victor D., ed. (1996), *Radical Political Economy: Explorations in Alternative Economic Analysis*, Armonk, NY: M.E. Sharpe.

List, John, (2004) "Neoclassical Theory versus Prospect Theory: Evidence from the Marketplace," *Econometrica*, 72:2, 615–25.

Littlechild, Stephen, ed. (1990), *Austrian Economics, Volumes I, II, III*, Aldershot: Edward Elgar Publishing.

Loasby, Brian J. (1991), "The Austrian School," in Mair, D. and Miller, A.G. (eds.), *A Modern Guide to Economic Thought: An Introduction to Comparative Schools of Thought in Economics*, Aldershot, Hants: Edward Elgar, Chapter 3, pp. 40–70.

Lutz, Mark (1990), "Emphasizing the Social: Social Economics and Socio-Economics," *Review of Social Economy*, 48:3, 303–20.

Lutz, Mark (1999), *Economics for the Common Good: Two Centuries of Social Economic Thought in the Humanistic Tradition*, London: Routledge.

Lutz, Mark and Lux, Kenneth (1988), *Humanistic Economics: The New Challenge*, New York, NY: Bootstrap Press.

Macher, J.T. and Richman, B.D. (2008), "Transaction Cost Economics: An Assessment of Empirical Research in the Social Sciences," *Business and Politics*, 10:1, 1–63.

Maital, Shlomo, ed. (2007), *Recent Developments in Behavioral Economics*, Cheltenham: Edward Elgar Publishing Limited.

Mandel, Ernest (1968), *Marxist Economic Theory*, New York, NY: Monthly Review Press.

Marciano, Alain, and Runde, Jochen, eds. *The Elgar Companion to Economics and Philosophy*, Cheltenham: Edward Elgar, Chapter 18, pp. 364–85.

McKenna, Edward J. and Zannoni, Diane C. (1993), "Philosophical Foundations of Post Keynesian Economics," *Journal of Post Keynesian Economics*, 15:3, Spring, 395–407.

McLellan, David, ed. (2000), *Karl Marx: Selected Writings*, Oxford: Oxford University Press.

Medema, Steven, ed. (1998), *Coasian Economics: Law and Economics and the New Institutional Economics*, Boston, MA: Kluwer Academic Publishing.

Meijer, Gerrit, ed. (1995), *New Perspectives on Austrian Economics*, New York, NY: Routledge.

Menard, Claude and Shirley, Mary M., eds. (2005), *Handbook of New Institutional Economics*, Dordrecht: Springer.

Menger, Carl (1981), *Principles of Economics*, New York, NY: New York University Press.

Mermelstein, David, ed. (1970), *Economics: Mainstream Readings and Radical Critiques*, New York, NY: Random House.

Milberg, William (1991), "Marxism, Poststructuralism, and the Discourse of Economics," *Rethinking Marxism*, 4:2, 92–104.

Miller, Edythes S. (1978), "Institutional Economics: Philosophy, Methodology and Theory," *Social Science Journal*, 15:1, January, 13–25. Reprinted in Samuels, Warren J., ed. (1988), *Institutional Economics, Volume II*, Aldershot, Hants: Edward Elgar Publishing, Chapter 3, pp. 50–62.

Milonakis, Dimitris and Fine, Ben (2008), *From Political Economy to Economics: Method, the Social and the Historical in the Evolution of Economic Theory*, New York, NY: Routledge.

Mirowski, Philip (1987), "The Philosophical Bases of Institutionalist Economics," *Journal of Economic Issues*, 21:3, September, 1001–38.

Mises, Ludwig von (1962), *The Ultimate Foundation of Economic Science: An Essay on Method*, Princeton, NJ: D. Van Nostrand Company.

Mises, Ludwig von (1966), *Human Action: A Treaties on Economics*, Chicago, IL: Henry Regnery.

Mueller, Franz (1977), "Social Economics: The Perspective of Pesch and Solidarism," *Review of Social Economy*, 35:3, 293–7.

Mulcahy, Richard (1952), *The Economics of Heinrich Pesch*, New York, NY: Henry Holt.

Mullainathan, Sendhil and Thaler, Richard (2000), "Behavioral Economics," in *International Encyclopedia of the Social and Behavioral Sciences*, Cambridge, MA: MIT Press, pp. 1094–100.

Myrdal, Gunnar (1958), *Value in Social Theory*, London: Routledge.

Myrdal, Gunnar (1978), "Institutional Economics," *Journal of Economic Issues*, 12:4, December, 771–83.

Nell, Edward J. (1981), "Value and Capital in Marxian Economics," in Bell, Daniel and Kristol, Irving (eds.), *The Crisis in Economic Theory*, New York, NY: Basic Books, Inc., Chapter 11, pp. 174–200.

Nelson, Richard R. and Sampat, Bhaven N. (2001), "Making Sense of Institutions as a Factor Shaping Economic Performance," *Journal of Economic Behavior and Organization*, 44:1, 31–54.

Nitsch, Thomas (1987), "Social Economics: From Search for Identity to Quest for Roots," *International Journal of Social Economics*, 14:3/4/5, 70–90.

Nitsch, Thomas (1990), "Social Economics: The First 200 Years," in Lutz, M. (ed.), *Social Economics: Retrospect and Prospect*, London: Kluwer, pp. 5–90.

North, Douglass C. (1986), "The New Institutional Economics," *Journal of Institutional and Theoretical Economics*, 142, 230–7.

North, Douglass C. (1990), *Institutions, Institutional Change and Economic Performance*, Cambridge: Cambridge University Press.

North, Douglass C. (1991), "Institutions," *Journal of Economic Perspectives*, 5:1, Winter, 97–112.

North, Douglass C. (1994), "Economic Performance through Time," *American Economic Review*, 84:3, 359–68.

Nussbaum, Martha (2000), *Women and Human Development: The Capabilities Approach*, Cambridge: Cambridge University Press.

O'Boyle, Edward J. (1998), *Personalist Economics: Moral Convictions, Economic Realities, and Social Action*, Cham, Switzerland: Springer.

O'Boyle, Edward J., ed. (2005), "The Best of the *Review of Social Economy*," *Review of Social Economy*, 63:3, 317–536.

O'Connor, James (1984), *Accumulation Crisis*, New York, NY: Basil Blackwell.

O'Connor, Martin, ed. (1994), *Is Capitalism Sustainable?: Political Economy and the Politics of Ecology*, New York, NY: Guildford Press.

O'Hara, Phillip Anthony (2007), "Principles of Institutional-Evolutionary Political Economy: Converging Themes from the Schools of Heterodoxy," *Journal of Economic Issues*, 41:1, March, 1–42.

Ostrom, Elinor (2005), "Doing Institutional Analysis: Digging Deeper than Markets and Hierarchies," in Menard, Claude and Shirley, Mary M. (eds.), *Handbook of New Institutional Economics*, Dordrecht: Springer, Chapter 30, pp. 819–48.

Palermo, Giulio (2007), "The Ontology of Economic Power in Capitalism: Mainstream Economics and Marx," *Cambridge Journal of Economics*, 31:4, 539–61.

Palley, Thomas I. (1996), *Post Keynesian Economics: Debt, Distribution and the Macro Economy*, New York, NY: St. Matin's Press.

Papadimitriou, Dimitri B. and Wray, L. Randall, eds. (2010), *The Elgar Companion to Hyman Minsky*, Cheltenham: Edward Elgar.

Panitch, Leo and Leys, Colin, eds. (1999), *Global Capitalism versus Democracy: Socialist Register 1999*, New York, NY: Monthly Review Press.

Peach, Jim and Dugger, William (2006), "An Intellectual History of Abundance," *Journal of Economic Issues*, 40:3, 693–706.

Pesendorfer, Wolfgang (2006), "Behavioral Economics Comes of Age: A Review Essay on Advances in Behavioral Economics," *Journal of Economic Literature*, 44:3, September, 712–21.

Peterson, Wallace C. (1987), "Macroeconomic Theory and Policy in an Institutionalist Perspective," *Journal of Economic Issues*, 21:4, December, 1587–622.

Pheby, John, ed. (1989), *New Directions in Post-Keynesian Economics*, Aldershot, Hants: Edward Elgar Publishing Limited.

Polanyi, Karl (1944), *The Great Transformation*, Boston, MA: Beacon Press.

Pompian, Michael M. (2012), *Behavioral Finance and Wealth Management: How to Build Investment Strategies that Account for Investor Biases*, Hoboken, NJ: Wiley.

Pratten, Stephen (2004), "The Conflict Between Formalism and Realisticness in Modern Economics: The Case of the New Institutional Economics," in Davis, John

B., Marciano, Alain, and Runde, Jochen (eds.), *The Elgar Companion to Economics and Philosophy*, Cheltenham: Edward Elgar, Chapter 17, pp. 339–63.

Prychitko, David L., ed. (1998), *Why Economists Disagree: An Introduction to the Alternative Schools of Thought*, Albany, NY: State University of New York Press.

Putnam, Hilary (2002), *The Collapse of the Fact/Value Dichotomy and Other Essays*, Cambridge, MA: Harvard University Press.

Putnam, Robert and Garrett, Shaylyn (2020), *The Upswing: How America Came Together a Century Ago and How We can Do It Again*, New York, NY: Simon Schuster.

Rabin, Matthew (1998), "Psychology and Economics," *Journal of Economic Literature*, 36:1, March, 11–46.

Reder, Melvin W. (1982), "Chicago Economics: Permanence and Change," *Journal of Economic Literature*, 20:1, March, 1–38.

Resnick, Stephen A. and Wolff, Richard D. (1987), *Knowledge and Class: A Marxian Critique of Political Economy*, Chicago, IL: University of Chicago Press.

Ricciardi, Victor and Simon, Helen K. (2000), "What Is Behavioral Finance?," *Business, Education and Technology Journal*, Fall, 2:2, 1–9.

Richter, R. (2005), "The New Institutional Economics: Its Start, Its Meaning, Its Prospects," *European Business Organization Law Review*, 6, 161–200.

Ricketts, Martin, ed. (1988), *Neoclassical Microeconomics, Volumes I, II*, Aldershot: Edward Elgar Publishing.

Rima, Ingrid (2013), "German-Austrian Economics," in Rima, Ingrid, *A Primer on Heterodox Economics*, New York, NY: Routledge, Chapter 8, pp. 179–92.

Rima, Ingrid (2013), *A Primer on Heterodox Economics*, New York, NY: Routledge.

Robbins, Lionell (1937), *An Essay on the Nature and Significance of Economic Science*, London: Macmillan.

Roberts, Bruce and Feiner, Susan, eds. (1992), *Radical Economics*, Boston, MA: Kluwer Academic Publishers.

Roth, Alvin E. (1995), "Introduction to Experimental Economics," in Kagel, J. and Roth, A. (eds.), *Handbook of Experimental Economics*, Princeton, NJ: Princeton University Press, pp. 3–109.

Roth, Alvin E. (2007), "Repugnance as a Constraint on Markets," *Journal of Economic Perspectives*, 21:3, 37–58.

Rothem, Roy J. (1999), "Post Keynesian Economics and Realist Philosophy," *Journal of Post Keynesian Economics*, 22:1, Fall, 71–103.

Rutherford, Malcolm (1994), *Institutions in Economics: The Old and the New Institutionalism*, Cambridge: Cambridge University Press.

Rutherford, Malcolm (2001), "Institutional Economics: Then and Now," *Journal of Economic Perspectives*, 15:3, Summer, 173–94.

Rutherford, Malcolm (2011), *The Institutionalist Movement in American Economics, 1918–1947: Science and Social Control*, Cambridge: Cambridge University Press.

Sackrey, Charles, Schneider, Geoffrey, and Knoedler, Janet (2008), *Introduction to Political Economy*, New York, NY: Dollars and Sense.

Samuels, Warren J., ed. (1988), *Institutional Economics, Vols I, II, and III*, Aldershot, Hants: Edward Elgar.

Samuels, Warren J. (1989), "Austrian and Institutional Economics: Some Common Elements," *Research in the History of Economic Thought and Methodology*, 6, 53–72.

Sandel, Michael (2012), *What Money Can't Buy: The Moral Limits of Markets*, New York, NY: Farrar, Straus, and Giroux.

Sawyer, Malcolm C., ed. (1988), *Post-Keynesian Economics*, Aldershot: Edward Elgar.

Sawyer, Malcolm C. (1989), *The Challenge of Radical Political Economy: An Introduction to the Alternatives to Neoclassical Economics*, Savage, MD: Barnes and Noble Books.

Sawyer, Malcolm C. (1991), "Post-Keynesian Macroeconomics," in Greenaway, David, Bleaney, Michael, and Stewart, Ian (eds.), *Companion to Contemporary Economic Thought*, London: Routledge, Chapter 11, pp. 184–206.

Schlicht, Ekkehart (1998), "The Texture of Customs," in *On Custom in the Economy*, Oxford: Claredon Press, Chapter 15, pp. 269–75.

Schmidt, U., Starmer, C., and Sugden, R. (2008), "Third Generation Prospect Theory," *Journal of Risk and Uncertainty*, 36, 203–23.

Scott, Andrew (1991), "Marxian and Radical Economics," in Mair, Douglas and Miller, Anne G. (eds.), *A Modern Guide to Economic Thought: An Introduction to Comparative Schools of Thought in Economics*, Aldershot, Hants: Edward Elgar, Chapter 9, pp. 233–62.

Sen, Amartya (1987), *On Ethics and Economics*, Oxford: Basil Blackwell.

Sen, Amartya (2005), "Human Rights and Capabilities," *Journal of Human Development*, 6:2, 151–66.

Sent, E.M. (2004), "Behavioral Economics: How Psychology Made Its (Limited) Way Back into Economics," *History of Political Economy*, 36, 735–60.

Shand, Alexander H. (1984), *The Capitalist Alternative: An Introduction to Neo-Austrian Economics*, New York, NY: New York University Press.

Shand, Alexander H. (1990), *Free Market Morality: The Political Economy of the Austrian School*, London: Routledge.

Shefrin, Hersh (2002), *Beyond Greed and Fear: Understanding Behavioral Finance and the Psychology of Investing*, Oxford: Oxford University Press.

Shelanski, Howard A. and Klein, Peter G. (1995), "Empirical Research in Transaction Cost Economics: A Review and Assessment," *Journal of Law, Economics, and Organization*, 11:2, October, 335–61.

Sherman, Howard J. (1987), *Foundations of Radical Political Economy*, Armonk, NY: M.E. Sharpe.

Sherman, Howard J., Hunt, E.K., Nesiba, Reynold F., O'Hara, Philip A., and Wiens-Tuers, Barbara (2008), *Economics: An Introduction to Traditional and Progressive Views*, Armonk, NY: M.E. Sharpe.

Shiller, R.J. (2003), "From Efficient Markets Theory to Behavioral Finance," *Journal of Economic Perspectives*, 17, 83–104.

Shiv, B. and Fedorikhin, A. (1999), "Heart and Mind in Conflict: The Interplay of Affect and Cognition in Consumer Decision Making," *Journal of Consumer Research*, 26, 278–92.

Shower, Brian (1974), "Social Economics: A Branch or New Roots?" *International Journal of Social Economics*, 1:1, 4–12.

Simon, Herbert A. (1955), "A Behavioral Model of Rational Choice," *Quarterly Journal of Economics*, 69, 99–118.

Simon, Herbert A. (1998), "Behavioral Economics," in Eatwell, J., Milgate, M., and Newman, P. (eds.), *The New Palgrave Dictionary of Economics, Vol 1*, London: Macmillan, pp. 221–25.

Singer, Daniel (1999), *Whose Millennium? Theirs or Ours?* New York, NY: Monthly Review Press.

Stanfield, James Ronald (1989), "Karl Polanyi and Contemporary Economic Thought," *Review of Social Economy*, 47:3, 266–92.

Stanfield, James Ronald (1999), "The Scope, Method, and Significance of Original Institutional Economics," *Journal of Economic Issues*, 33:2, June, 231–55.

Stilwell, Frank (2012), *Political Economy: The Contest of Economic Ideas*, Oxford: Oxford University Press.

Sweezy, Paul M. (1942), *The Theory of Capitalist Development: Principles of Marxian Political Economy*, New York, NY: Monthly Review Press.

Sweezy, Paul M. and Magdoff, Harry (1972), *The Dynamics of U.S. Capitalism: Corporate Structure, Inflation, Credit, Gold, and the Dollar*, New York, NY: Monthly Review Press.

Thaler, R.H., ed. (2005), *Advances in Behavioral Finance*, New York, NY: Russell Sage Foundations.

Thaler, R.H. (2008a), "Mental Accounting and Consumer Choice: Anatomy of a Failure," *Marketing Science*, 27, 1–14.

Thaler, R.H. (2008b), "Mental Accounting and Consumer Choice," *Marketing Science*, 27, 15–25.

Tollison, Robert D. (1989), "Chicago Political Economy," *Public Choice*, 63:3, December, 293–8.

Tomer, John F. (2007), "What Is Behavioral Economics?" *Journal of Socio-Economics*, 36:3, June, 463–79.

Tool, Marc R. (1981), "The Compulsive Shift to Institutional Analysis," *Journal of Economic Issues*, 15:3, September, 569–92.

Tool, Marc R. (1988a), *Evolutionary Economics, Volume I: Foundations of Institutional Thought*, Armonk, NY: M.E. Shape.

Tool, Marc R. (1988b), *Evolutionary Economics, Volume II: Institutional Theory and Policy*, Armonk, NY: M.E. Shape.

Tool, Marc R. and Bush, Paul Dale, eds. (2003), *Institutional Analysis and Economic Policy*, Boston, MA: Kluwer Academic Publishers.

Tversky, A. and Kahneman, D. (1974), "Judgment under Uncertainty: Heuristics and Biases," *Science*, 185, 1124–31.

Tversky, A. and Kahneman, D. (1981), "The Framing of Decisions and the Psychology of Choice," *Science*, 211, 453–8.

Van Horn, Robert and Mirowski, Philip (2009), "The Rise of Chicago School of Economics and the Birth of Neoliberalism," in Mirowski, P. and Plehwe, D. (eds.), *The Road from Mont Pelerin: The Making of the Neoliberal Thought Collective*, Cambridge, MA: Harvard University Press, pp. 149–63.

Vannoni, D. (2002), "Empirical Studies of Vertical Integration: The Transaction Cost Orthodoxy," *International Review of Economics and Business*, 49, 113–41.

Van Overtveldt, Johan (2007), *The Chicago School: How the University of Chicago Assembled the Thinkers Who Revolutionized Economics and Business*, Chicago, IL: Agate.

Van Raaij, W. Fred (1991), "Economics and Psychology," in Greenaway, David, Bleaney, Michael, and Stewart, Ian (eds.), *Companion to Contemporary Economic Thought*, London: Routledge, Chapter 40, pp. 797–811.

van Staveren, Irene (2001), *The Values of Economics: An Aristotelian Perspective*, London: Routledge.

Vaughn, Karen I. (1994), *Austrian Economics in America: The Migration of a Tradition*, New York, NY: Cambridge University Press.

Velupillai, Kumaraswamy and Chen, Shu-Heng, eds. (2012), *Behavioral Economics*, New York, NY: Routledge.

Vromen, Jack J. (1995), *Economic Evolution: An Inquiry into the Foundations of New Institutional Economics*, London: Routledge.

Wallerstein, Immanuel (1974), *The Modern World-System*, San Diego, CA: Academic Press.

Walsh, Vivian and Gram, Harvey (1980), *Classical and Neoclassical Theories of General Equilibrium: Historical Origins and Mathematical Structure*, Oxford: Oxford University Press.

Walters, Bernard and Young, David (1997), "On the Coherence of Post-Keynesian Economics," 44:3, August, 329–49.

Walters, Bernard and Young, David (1999), "Is Critical Realism the Appropriate Basis for Post Keynesianism?," *Journal of Post Keynesian Economics*, 22:1, Fall, 105–23.

Ward, Dwayne (1977), *Toward a Critical Political Economics: A Critique of Liberal and Radical Economic Thought*, Santa Monica, CA: Goodyear Publishing Company.

Warren, Bill (1980), *Imperialism: Pioneer of Capitalism*, London: Verso.

Waters, William, ed. (1979), "Karl Marx, Social Economist," *Review of Social Economy*, 37:3, 261–387.

Waters, William, ed. (1984), "Community Dimensions of Economic Enterprise," *Review of Social Economy*, 42:3, 219–438.

Waters, William (1990), "Evolution of Social Economics in America," in Lutz, M. (ed.), *Social Economics: Retrospect and Prospect*, London: Kluwer, pp. 91–117.

Waters, William (1993), "A Review of the Troops: Social Economics in the Twentieth Century," *Review of Social Economy*, 51:3, 262–86.

Weintraub, E. Roy (1985a), *General Equilibrium Analysis: Studies in Appraisal*, Cambridge: Cambridge University Press.

Weintraub, E. Roy (1985b), "Appraising General Equilibrium Analysis," *Economics and Philosophy*, 1:1, 23–37.

Weintraub, E. Roy (2002), *How Economics Became a Mathematical Science*, Durham, North Carolina: Duke University Press.

Whalen, Charles J. (1996), "The Institutional Approach to Political Economy," in Foldvary, Fred E. (ed.), *Beyond Neoclassical Economics: Heterodox Approaches to Economic Theory*, Cheltenham: Edward Elgar, Chapter 5, pp. 83–99.

White, Mark (2011), *Kantian Ethics and Economics: Autonomy, Dignity, and Character*, Stanford, CA: Stanford University Press.

White, Mark (2018), "On the Relationship between Economics and Ethics", *Annals of the Fondazione Luigi Einaudi*, 52:1, 47–57.

Wiesskopf, Thomas E. (1992), "Toward a Socialism for the Future in the Wake of the Demise of the Socialism of the Past," *Review of Radical Political Economics*, 24:3/4, Fall/Winter. Reprinted in Prychitko, David L., ed. (1998), *Why Economists Disagree: An Introduction to the Alternative Schools of Thought*, Albany, NY: State University of New York Press, Chapter 11, pp. 275–306.

Wilber, Charles K. and Harrison, Robert S. (1978), "The Methodological Basis of Institutional Economics: Pattern Model, Story Telling, and Holism," *Journal of Economic Issues*, 12:1, March, 61–89.

Williamson, Oliver E. (1975), *Markets and Hierarchies: Analysis and Antitrust Implications*, New York, NY: Free Press.

Williamson, Oliver E. (1985a), *The Economic Institutions of Capitalism: Firms, Markets and Relational Contracting*, New York, NY: Free Press.

Williamson, Oliver E. (1985b), "Reflections on the New Institutional Economics," *Journal of Institutional and Theoretical Economics*, 141, 187–95.

Williamson, Oliver E. (1996), *The Mechanisms of Governance*, New York, NY: Oxford University Press.

Williamson, Oliver E. (2000), "The New Institutional Economics: Taking Stock, Looking Ahead," *Journal of Economic Literature*, 38:3, September, 595–613.

Williamson, Oliver E. (2010), "Transaction Cost Economics: The Natural Progression," *American Economic Review*, 100:3, 673–90.

Witte, Edwin E. (1954), "Institutional Economics as Seen by an Institutional Economist," *Southern Economic Journal*, 21:2, October, 131–40.

Wolff, Richard D. and Resnick, Stephen A. (2012), *Contending Economic Theories: Neoclassical, Keynesian, and Marxian*, Cambridge, MA: MIT Press.

# Conclusion

Social theory can usefully be conceived in terms of four key paradigms: functionalist, interpretive, radical humanist, and radical structuralist. The four paradigms are founded upon different assumptions about the nature of social science and the nature of society. Each generates theories, concepts, and analytical tools that are different from those of other paradigms.

All theories are based on a philosophy of science and a theory of society. Many theorists appear to be unaware of, or ignore, the assumptions underlying these philosophies. They emphasize only some aspects of the phenomenon and ignore others. Unless they bring out the basic philosophical assumptions of the theories, their analysis can be misleading; by emphasizing differences between theories, they imply diversity in approach. While there appear to be different kinds of theory, they are founded on a certain philosophy, worldview, or paradigm. This becomes evident when these theories are related to the wider background of social theory.

The functionalist paradigm has provided the framework for the current mainstream in academic research and accounts for the largest proportion of theory and research in academic fields.

In order to understand a new paradigm, theorists should be fully aware of the assumptions upon which their own paradigm is based. Moreover, to understand a new paradigm, one has to explore it from within, since the concepts in one paradigm cannot easily be interpreted in terms of those of another. No attempt should be made to criticize or evaluate a paradigm from the outside. This is self-defeating since it is based on a separate paradigm. All four paradigms can be easily criticized and ruined in this way.

These four paradigms are of paramount importance to any scientist, because the process of learning about a favored paradigm is also the process of learning what that paradigm is not. The knowledge of paradigms makes scientists aware of the boundaries within which they approach their subject. Each of the four paradigms implies a different way of social theorizing.

Scientists often approach their subject from a frame of reference based upon assumptions that are taken for granted. Since these assumptions are continually affirmed and reinforced, they remain not only unquestioned, but also beyond conscious awareness. In this way, most researchers tend to favor the functionalist paradigm.

The partial nature of this view only becomes apparent when the researcher exposes basic assumptions to the challenge of alternative ways of seeing and starts to appreciate these alternatives in their own terms. To do this, one has to explore other paradigms from within, since the concepts in one paradigm cannot easily be interpreted in terms of those of another.

The diversity of research possibilities referred to in this book is vast. While each paradigm advocates a research strategy that is logically coherent, in terms of underlying assumptions, these vary from paradigm to paradigm. The phenomenon to be researched can be conceptualized and studied in many different ways, each generating distinctive kinds of insight and understanding. There are many different ways of studying the same social phenomenon, and given that the insights generated by any one approach are at best partial and incomplete, the social researcher can gain much by reflecting on the nature and merits of different approaches. It is clear that social scientists, like other generators of knowledge, deal with the realization of possible types of knowledge, which are connected with the particular paradigm adopted.

Mainstream academic research is based upon the functionalist paradigm, and for the most part, theorists are not always entirely aware of the traditions to which they belong. This book recommends serious conscious thinking about the social philosophy upon which social research is based and the alternative avenues for development.

Academic research can gain much by exploiting the new perspectives coming from other paradigms. An understanding of different paradigms leads to a better understanding of the multifaceted nature of social phenomena. Although a researcher may decide to conduct research from the point of view of a certain paradigm, an understanding of the nature of other paradigms leads to a better understanding of what one is doing.

Paradigm diversity is based on the idea that more than one theoretical construction can be placed upon a given collection of data. In other words, any single theory, research method, or particular empirical study is incapable of explaining the nature of reality in all its complexities.

It is possible to establish exact solutions to problems if one defines the boundary and domain of reality. Functionalist research, through its research approach, defines an area in which objectivity and truth can be found. Any change in the research approach, or any change in the area of applicability, would tend to result in the breakdown of such objectivity and truth.

The knowledge generated through functionalist research relates to certain aspects of the phenomenon under consideration. Recognition of the existence of the phenomenon beyond that dictated by the research approach results in the recognition of the limitations of the knowledge generated within the confines of that approach.

It is almost impossible to find a foundational solution to the problem of creating a specific kind of knowledge. Researchers are encouraged to explore what is possible by identifying untapped possibilities. By comparing a favored research approach in relation to others, the nature, strengths, and limitations of the favored approach become evident. By understanding what others do, researchers are able to understand what they are not doing. This leads to the development and refinement of the favored research approach. The concern is not about deciding which research approach is best or substituting one for another. The concern is about the merits of diversity, which seeks to enrich research rather than constrain it, through a search for an optimum way of doing diverse research.

There is no unique evaluative perspective for assessing knowledge generated by different research approaches. Therefore, it becomes necessary to get beyond the idea that knowledge is foundational and can be evaluated in an absolute way.

Different research approaches provide different interpretations of a phenomenon and understand the phenomenon in a particular way. Some may support a traditional view, while others say something new. In this way, knowledge is treated as being tentative rather than absolute.

All research approaches have something to contribute. The interaction among them may lead to synthesis, compromise, consensus, transformation, polarization, or simply clarification and an improved understanding of differences. Such interaction, which is based on differences of viewpoints, is not concerned with reaching a consensus or an end point that establishes a foundational truth. On the contrary, it is concerned with learning from the process itself and encouraging the interaction to continue as long as disagreement lasts. Likewise, it is not concerned with producing uniformity but promoting improved diversity.

Paradigm diversity is based on the idea that research is a creative process and that there are many ways of doing research. This approach leads to the development of knowledge in many different, and sometimes contradictory, directions such that new ways of knowing will emerge. There can be no objective criteria for choosing between alternative perspectives. The number of ways of generating new knowledge is bounded only by the ingenuity of researchers in inventing new approaches.

The functionalist paradigm regards research as a technical activity and depersonalizes the research process. It removes responsibility from the researcher and reduces him or her to an agent engaged in what the institutionalized research demands.

Paradigm diversity reorients the role of researchers and places responsibility for the conduct and consequences of research directly with them. Researchers examine the nature of their activity to choose an appropriate approach, develop a capacity to observe and question what they are doing, and take responsibility for making intelligent choices, which are open to realizing the many potential types of knowledge.

To implement paradigm diversity, some fundamental changes need to be directed to the way research is presently managed in academic fields. In other words, paradigm diversity implies and requires changes. The most fundamental change is to understand the multifaceted nature of social phenomena.

An understanding of paradigms provides a valuable means for exploring the nature of the phenomenon being investigated. Furthermore, an understanding of other paradigms provides an invaluable basis for recognizing what one is doing.

It is interesting to note that this recommendation is consistent with the four paradigms:

1. It increases efficiency in research: This is because diversity in the research approach prevents or delays reaching the point of diminishing marginal return. Therefore, the recommendation is consistent with the functionalist paradigm, which emphasizes purposive rationality and the benefit of diversification.
2. It advocates diversity in research approach: This is consistent with the interpretive paradigm, which emphasizes shared multiple realities.
3. It leads to the realization of researchers' full potentials: This is consistent with the radical humanist paradigm, which emphasizes human beings'

emancipation from the structures which limit their potential for development.

4. It enhances class awareness: This is consistent with the radical structuralist paradigm, which emphasizes class struggle.

Knowledge is ultimately a product of the researcher's paradigmatic approach to the multifaceted social phenomenon. Viewed from this angle, the pursuit of knowledge is seen as much an ethical, moral, ideological, and political activity as a technical one. Mainstream academic research can gain much from the contributions of other paradigms.

# Index

# About the Author

**Kavous Ardalan** is a professor of finance at Marist University, Poughkeepsie, New York. He holds PhDs in both economics and finance. His research interests are in the theoretical, practical, educational, social, and philosophical aspects of economics and finance. He has written eleven books and more than ninety journal articles. Some of his research papers have received awards at international conferences; have been regarded very highly by publishers; have been referenced in the *Handbook of Finance*, journal articles, and books; and have been used as course reading materials at top universities worldwide. He teaches finance in both undergraduate and graduate programs.

Made in the USA
Las Vegas, NV
19 September 2026

b4e09877-9a28-4eaf-8068-bf726dfc0040R01